DISABLING INTERPRETATIONS

DISABLING INTERPRETATIONS

The Americans with Disabilities Act | *in Federal Court*

Susan Gluck Mezey

UNIVERSITY OF PITTSBURGH PRESS

Published by the University of Pittsburgh Press,
Pittsburgh, Pa., 15260
Manufactured in the United States of America
Printed on acid-free paper
10 9 8 7 6 5 4 3 2 1

Library of Congress Cataloging-in-Publication Data
Mezey, Susan Gluck, 1944–
  Disabling interpretations: the Americans with Disabilities Act
in federal court / Susan Gluck Mezey.
    p. cm.
  Includes bibliographical references and index.
  ISBN 0-8229-5879-1 (pb: alk. paper)
  1. United States. Americans with Disabilities Act of 1990—
Cases. 2. People with disabilities—Legal status, laws, etc. —
United States—Cases. I. Title.
  KF480.M49 2005
  342.7308'7—dc22

Chapter 4 appeared in an earlier version as "The Americans with
Disabilities Act in Federal Court: Litigating against Public Entities" by Susan Gluck Mezey et al., *Disability & Society* 17, no. 1
(2002): 49–64. Copyright 2002 by Taylor & Francis Ltd. Reprinted
with permission. An earlier version of chapter 5 appeared as "The
Federal Courts and Disability Rights" by Susan Gluck Mezey, *Journal of Disability Policy Studies* 15, no. 3 (2004): 147–58. Copyright
2004 by PRO-ED, Inc. Reprinted with permission.

For Paula Musen Gluck

CONTENTS

ACKNOWLEDGMENTS

As I learned more about the disability rights movement, my esteem for the individuals in it grew. Some became involved in the cause of disability rights because of the discrimination they or a family member faced; some became advocates because they believed in disability rights as a civil right. Whatever their motivation and whatever role they played, I found much to admire in their efforts to alter society's perceptions and treatment of people with disabilities. In part, this book is dedicated to them.

Judicial implementation of disability rights policy primarily arises out of rulings in lawsuits brought to enforce the Americans with Disabilities Act. Understanding disability rights litigation requires reading hundreds of cases brought by, or on behalf of, people demanding that the courts effectuate society's commitment to end discrimination on the basis of disability.

The primary research for this book was drawn from these legal actions. In this effort, I was ably assisted by several of Loyola's graduate students: Kris Beeler, Catherine Carabetta, Douglas Davis, Nathaniel Gest, Mary Hakken, Will Jordan, Megan Sholar, and Patrick Van Inwegen; they helped me find, sort out, and analyze the large number of cases involved in this study. I also want to thank a special undergraduate, Ashley Burden, who proved that he was more than ready for the law school career he was about to begin. Janne Varghese also merits thanks for her efficiency, competence, and willingness to help with the innumerable tasks involved in preparing the manuscript. I was benefited by a summer research award from Loyola as well.

I want to express my appreciation to Niels Aaboe, no longer at University of Pittsburgh Press, who was enthusiastic about this project from the beginning. Thanks also go to Sara Lickey, Nathan MacBrien, Cynthia Miller, Ann Walston, and their colleagues at the press as well as Kathleen Meyer, a great copy editor. The publishers of *Disability and Society* and the *Journal of Disability Policy Studies* graciously gave me permission to reprint work that appeared there first.

On a personal note, I am grateful for the support and encouragement I always receive from my husband, Michael, as well as my children. And I dedicate this book to my mother, Paula Gluck, a survivor, who, by overcoming numerous daunting challenges in her own life, gave me the strength to succeed in mine.

ABBREVIATIONS

AAPD	American Association of People with Disabilities
ABA	American Bar Association
ACAA	Air Carrier Access Act
ACIR	Advisory Commission on Intergovernmental Relations
ADA	Americans with Disabilities Act
ADAAG	Americans with Disabilities Act Accessibility Guidelines for Buildings and Facilities
ADAPT	Americans Disabled for Accessible Public Transportation
ADEA	Age Discrimination in Employment Act
CBO	Congressional Budget Office
CCD	Consortium of Citizens with Disabilities
DDA	Developmental Disabilities Assistance and Bill of Rights Act
DOJ	Department of Justice
DOT	Department of Transportation
DREDF	Disability Rights Education and Defense Fund, Inc.
EAHCA	Education of All Handicapped Children Act
EEOC	Equal Employment Opportunity Commission
ESEA	Elementary and Secondary Education Act
FHA	Fair Housing Act
FHAA	Fair Housing Act Amendments
FLSA	Fair Labor Standards Act

FMLA   Family and Medical Leave Act
HEW   Department of Health, Education, and Welfare
HHS   Department of Health and Human Services
IDEA   Individuals with Disabilities Education Act
LCCR   Leadership Conference on Civil Rights
MHPA   Mental Health Parity Act
NAPAS   National Association of Protection and Advocacy Systems
NCD   National Council on Disability
NCH   National Council on the Handicapped
NFI   New Freedom Initiative
NFIB   National Federation of Independent Businesses
NOD   National Organization on Disability
OCR   Office of Civil Rights
OSHA   Occupational Safety and Health Act
RFRA   Religious Freedom Restoration Act
SSDI   Social Security Disability Insurance
UFAS   Uniform Federal Accessibility Standards
UMRA   Unfunded Mandates Reform Act

1 Introduction

This book examines judicial implementation of the 1990 Americans with Disabilities Act (ADA), the nation's newest civil rights law and its most far-reaching attempt to combat discrimination on the basis of disabilities. Centering on the role of the federal courts in disability rights policymaking in the United States, it also assesses the interaction among the courts, Congress, and subnational governments in the enforcement of civil rights guarantees for people with disabilities.

The ADA has been extolled as "a milestone on the path to a more decent, tolerant, progressive society" (*Board of Trustees of the University of Alabama v. Garrett* 2001, 375).[1] Also described as "the most progressive and aggressive piece of legislation passed since the Civil Rights Act of 1964" (Bauer 1993, 10), it was estimated that it affected the lives of 43 million persons at the time of its passage. Less than a decade later, it was reported that there were 49.7 million people aged five and over with a disability, nearly one in five residents (U.S. Bureau of the Census 2000, table 1).[2]

The rhetoric soared when public officials spoke about the ADA and its aims of eliminating discrimination against people with disabilities. In remarks in a ceremony attended by more than two thousand people on the White House lawn on July 26, 1990, President George H. W. Bush compared the event to the tearing down of the Berlin Wall, declaring that "every man, woman, and child with a disability can now pass through once closed doors into a bright new era of equality, independence, and freedom" (Bush 1990a).

A similar theme was struck by President Bill Clinton in remarks made at the Franklin D. Roosevelt Memorial while signing the Ticket to Work and

Work Incentives Improvement Act of 1999, the first major disability rights law enacted since the ADA. Stressing the symbolism of his presence there, Clinton proclaimed that the new law would remove the necessity of having to choose between health care coverage and work. He emphasized that it "was fundamentally about the dignity of each human being, about the realization of a quality of opportunity, about recognizing that work is at the heart of the American dream" (Clinton 1999).

Shortly after his inauguration on February 1, 2001, President George W. Bush (2001) announced a set of proposals called the "New Freedom Initiative" (NFI), the heart of which was to increase access to assistive technologies and foster work opportunities for people with disabilities. Bush described the purpose of NFI as allowing people with disabilities to participate more fully in society. He affirmed that "whenever any barrier stands between you and the full rights and dignity of citizenship, we must work to remove it, in the name of simple decency and simple justice."

The Intent of the ADA

Following the model of earlier civil rights statutes, the ADA was based on Congress's authority under the Fourteenth Amendment and the Interstate Commerce Clause.[3] Congress broadly stated that the purpose of the act was to establish a "national mandate" to end discrimination against people with disabilities and to guarantee that the federal government would play a key role in enforcing the law. To place it within the context of civil rights laws, a house committee report analogized the experiences of people with disabilities to those of African Americans. Quoting from *Brown v. Board of Education* (1954, 494), it said, "segregation for persons with disabilities 'may affect their hearts and minds in a way unlikely ever to be undone'" (U.S. House Committee on Education and Labor 1990, 26).

In enacting the ADA, Congress guaranteed civil rights protection to persons with disabilities in employment (Title I), in the delivery of state and local government services, including public transportation (Title II), in public accommodations (Title III), and in telecommunications (Title IV). Although Congress had enacted laws to protect the rights of disabled persons in the past—the Architectural Barriers Act of 1968; the Urban Mass Transportation Act of 1970; the Rehabilitation Act of 1973; the Education of All Handicapped Children Act of 1975, later amended and renamed the Individuals with Disabilities Education Act; the Air Carrier Access Act of 1986; and the Fair Housing Act Amendments of 1988—it was not until the ADA was passed that the nation adopted a comprehensive approach to combating discrimination on the basis of disabilities, producing a law that drew in large part on well-established principles of civil rights guarantees. And consistent with earlier civil rights laws, Congress established the federal courts as "the gatekeepers of the ADA" (O'Brien 2001, 161).

Despite the good intentions that accompanied the passage of the law, "somewhere between Capitol Hill and the federal courthouse, however, the joyous noise of the ADA's adoption turned into a wail of frustration" (Befort and Thomas 1999, 29). As this study will show, the frustration arose from the disability rights community's disappointment with the results of federal court litigation, largely—although not entirely—as a result of the constricted interpretation of the law by the federal judiciary. Given the key role disability advocates played in drafting the law, they believed that its language and legislative history clearly manifested Congress's intent that the statute be broadly applied to eradicate discrimination in society against people with disabilities.

Disability Rights Groups

The disability rights community consists of a loosely organized coalition of groups—some disability-specific, some cross-disability— that worked to achieve passage of the ADA. Today, in various combinations, they work for equal opportunities for people with disabilities through direct services, public education, grass roots organizing, litigation, and lobbying. The community consists of national and local groups such as the Disability Rights Education and Defense Fund, the David Bazelon Center for Mental Health Law, Paralyzed Veterans of America, Easter Seals, the Chicago based Council for Disability Rights, the American Association of People with Disabilities, the Association for Retarded Citizens, and numerous others. One group, Justice for All, founded in 1995 and largely based in cyberspace, provides information about disability rights issues through the Internet and e-mail alerts.

A few eschew litigation entirely, others include it as part of the range of activities that promote civil rights for people with disabilities; others devote most of their attention to litigation or at least include attorneys on their staff to monitor lawsuits in which they might have an interest and produce amicus briefs or other forms of legal assistance. The National Association of Protection and Advocacy Systems serves as an umbrella organization for state agencies that have litigated a number of important disability rights cases throughout the nation.[4]

The groups came together in the late 1980s to organize lobbying activities and public education for the ADA. They worked with congressional staffers from the offices of Senators Ted Kennedy, Massachusetts Democrat; Tom Harkin, Democrat from Iowa; and Lowell Weicker, Connecticut Republican; as well as Representatives Tony Coelho, Democrat from California; Steny Hoyer, Maryland Democrat; and Augustus Hawkins, California Democrat. Encouraged by members of the White House staff, such as C. Boyden Gray, they persuaded Congress to enact the most important civil rights law in nearly thirty years.

Today, many of these organizations have diverged from each other, divided by type of disability, clientele, and services. Many have become disappointed in the enforcement process, convinced that the courts, the principal enforcement authority, have flouted congressional intent by narrowly construing the law. Members of the disability community recognize that the ADA has changed public attitudes and created greater acceptance of the need for accessibility and inclusion, but a large number still believe that the ADA has not fully lived up to its expectations.[5]

Disability Rights and the Federal Courts

"Despite its initial glamour and fanfare, the ADA has proven to be only a modest protector of the disabled" (Ziegler 2002, 842). Although many disability rights advocates believe that the ADA has produced a sea change in the nation's landscape with respect to integrating people with disabilities into society, there is also a widespread belief among them that discrimination on the basis of disability—both intentional and unintentional— remains a fact of life in the United States. Tucker (2001, 338), for example, believes that "the ADA has not yet succeeded in requiring many people and entities to do what they do not wish to do—for one primary reason: many, perhaps most, courts are not enforcing the law, but instead are finding incredibly inventive means of interpreting the ADA to achieve the opposite result that the Act was intended to achieve." Another critic sharply noted that "the [Supreme] Court has turned an important civil rights statute into an unseemly hash" (Soifer 2003, 1287). Disability rights advocates are also alarmed at the Supreme Court's "new federalism" jurisprudence, in which the Court has shielded states from damage liability under the ADA by expanding the scope of their sovereign immunity under the Eleventh Amendment.

An Empirical Study of ADA Litigation

"Laden with ambiguous new legal terms, the ADA has become a rich source of litigation in its short history" (Stowe 2000, 300). With more than 90 percent of ADA trial court cases litigated in the federal courts (Colker 1999, 109n45), judicial interpretation of the law plays a key role in implementing disability rights. Many members of the disability rights community are convinced that the act has not lived up to its potential as a civil rights law because of the federal judiciary's narrow interpretation in adjudicating ADA claims, particularly in employment discrimination actions.

Despite the ADA's importance for disability policymaking, however, in part because of difficulty in gathering data on lower court cases, there are few empirical investigations of ADA litigation in the lower federal courts, especially outside the employment arena. This book assesses the degree to which the federal courts have effectuated the remedial purposes of the ADA by advancing Congress's stated aim of guaranteeing the civil rights of people with disabilities. Bridging the gap between law and public policy, the book examines judicial interpretation of the ADA by the federal courts and assesses the effectiveness of litigation in furthering disability rights guarantees.

This study is based on an analysis of the outcome of reported federal court cases, including the Supreme Court, in disability rights litigation over the last decade—since the enactment of the law. In addition to traditional sources of legal information, such as case law, litigants' briefs, congressional documents, government reports, and scholarly literature, this book draws on information gathered from personal interviews with over fifty individuals involved in the disability rights movement in the United States, focusing on those engaged in the litigation process. The interviews elicited responses to a series of open-ended questions; ranging from thirty-five minutes to two hours, most sessions lasted about an hour. The interview net was widely cast to include leading figures in the disability rights movement, many of whom played an instrumental role in drafting the legislation and securing its passage.

Ranging from Washington DC, Chicago, Boston, and Berkeley, most of the respondents are attorneys involved in ADA litigation; others are members of disability rights groups, former congressional staffers, public relations personnel, and national and local government officials. Today, depending upon their positions and the nature of their organizations, they are involved in litigation, teaching, lobbying, political mobilization, public education, organizing grass roots activity, technical assistance, government contracting, and direct services. They are the leaders of the multifaceted disability rights movement. Some of their groups focus more narrowly on mental or physical disabilities; others deal with a range of disabilities. Some serve specific clientele, such as veterans, children, or senior citizens; others serve diverse populations. And some litigate particular types of claims, such as voting, transportation, or education.

The respondents, many of whom were instrumental in putting disability rights on the public policy agenda and engineering the passage of the law, represent the leaders of today's disability rights movement. The interview questions were far-reaching, resulting in a mixture of fact and opinion. Among other things, respondents were asked about their role in the passage of the ADA as well as their current work as disability rights advocates or public officials. They were asked their views on the extent of compliance with the act, the effectiveness of litigation as an enforcement measure, the role of the judiciary in disability rights policymaking, and the comparison between the ADA and the traditional civil rights laws of the 1960s and 1970s.

The litigation that resulted from the passage of the ADA, especially when measured by the outcome of reported decisions, represents a snapshot of disability rights enforcement and is only one indicator of the effectiveness of this civil rights law. Other indicators include greater societal awareness of disability rights, voluntary compliance, the knowledge of people with disabilities that the law is on their side, the complaints not filed, and the complaints filed and settled. Some of these indicators are quantifiable, many are not. In assessing federal court enforcement of the law, this study is consistent with the view held by many that the federal judiciary is the most important, though not the sole, influence on disability rights policy in the nation today.

2 Disability Rights

as Civil Rights

Applying the civil rights model to people with disabilities, Congress instituted a system of judicial review that placed the courts at the center of the implementation process, establishing the judiciary as the final arbiter of rights and responsibilities under the ADA.[1] Although Congress also assigned enforcement authority to the Equal Employment Opportunity Commission (EEOC) and the Department of Justice (DOJ), advocates view litigation as "a primary tool" with which to secure disability rights (Switzer 2003, 131). Moreover, as Burris and Moss note (2000, 33–34), although only a proportion of potential ADA disputes are litigated to a final judicial resolution, litigation includes a range of behaviors, including conciliation and pretrial settlement. And because it is always an available option, disability rights advocates believe litigation sets the tone for compliance and enforcement of disability rights. Thus, despite the fact that litigation represents only a snapshot image of the implementation process, it occupies a central role in the struggle for disability rights.

Following the example of traditional civil rights groups, disability rights advocates turned to the federal courts to further their legislative victories, urging the judiciary to follow the well-established principle of statutory construction and effectuate the remedial purpose of the law.[2] They bolstered their claims by citing the legislative history and intent of the framers of the ADA, as expressed in floor debates and committee reports, as well as administrative regulations and interpretative guidelines.[3]

Because disability rights advocates believe the legislative history and intent clearly favor their position, their litigation aims have been thwarted in large part by the high court's adoption of the "textualist" approach advocated by Justice Antonin Scalia, among others. Following the precepts of "textualism," the Court's interpretative methodology has been altered, and "the search for a more elusive statutory 'purpose' or 'intent' has given way to a new emphasis on text . . . [an emphasis] that has changed the rules of the game" (Gregory 2002, 453; see Eskridge 1990). In assigning this priority to the text of the statute, the Court has turned away from the teachings of Justices Oliver Wendell Holmes and Benjamin Cardozo, who were more inclined to adopt a broader view of the statutory purpose in interpreting a law (see Levi 1963; Popkin 1999).[4] Noting that Scalia's desire to abandon consideration of the statute's legislative history, purpose, and intent has not caused the Court to eschew its traditional approach to statutory interpretation entirely, Eskridge (1990, 656) nevertheless concludes that the justice has had a significant impact on "the Court's practice" with respect to "the statutory text."

This method of analysis has led to constrained interpretations of rights and obligations in remedial laws, especially in the newly enacted civil rights statutes such as the ADA.[5] Attempting to discern the "plain meaning" of the law, the Court seeks guidance from the statute as a whole, as well as interpretative aids such as grammar books and dictionaries, often slighting evidence of legislative intent and purpose (Parmet 2003, 134). Critical of this approach, Justice John Paul Stevens wrote in dissent in *Sutton v. United Air Lines* (1999, 504) that "it has long been a 'familiar canon of statutory construction that remedial legislation should be construed broadly to effectuate its purposes'" (quoting *Tcherepnin v. Knight* 1967, 336). However, according to the majority, after determining that the text of the statute contradicted the plaintiffs' argument, there was "no reason to consider the ADA's legislative history" (*Sutton v. United Air Lines* 1999, 482). Justice Clarence Thomas's dissent in *Olmstead v. L.C.* (1999), in which he cited the *Random House Dictionary* and *Webster's Third New International Dictionary,* exemplifies how an appeal to the dictionary plays an instrumental role in rejecting a plaintiffs' claim of discrimination. In sum, in employing the methodology of textual analysis, the Court has disappointed the disability community—many of whom played a significant role in drafting the legislation—which had looked to the courts to advance the civil rights aims of the law.

Disability Rights Litigation

The genesis of disability rights litigation can be traced back to the 1950s and 1960s when African Americans and women, two historically oppressed groups in the United States, became increasingly insistent on their right to be fully included within the Constitution's civil rights guarantees. Although the exact nature of the rights and the venue in which the claims were advanced varied, their demands shared a common theme of equality (Watson 1993; Pfeiffer 1993). When their demands were transformed into legislation, such as the historic 1964 Civil Rights Act and the 1965 Voting Rights Act, the focus of attention of the civil rights community turned to the judicial and executive branches to implement the laws in conformity with the intent of Congress. Legislative intent becomes difficult to discern, however, when, as is frequently the case with civil rights statutes, the legislation reflects the compromises necessary to garner enough support to secure the bill's passage. As Bullock and Lamb's (1984) classic study of civil rights policies in such areas as equal employment opportunity, fair housing, and school desegregation demonstrates, implementation of civil rights policy depends in part on the nature of the policy and the available enforcement mechanisms (see also Stein 2000a).

During the late 1960s and 1970s, disability rights advocates added their voices to those in the civil rights community, demanding that government take a stand against discrimination on the basis of disability. And as with the earlier civil rights movement, with the legislative guarantees in place, the courts assumed a crucial role in disability policymaking by determining the parameters of disability rights (Berkowitz 1987). Indeed, as the earlier battles for equality of race and sex illustrate, the nature of a civil rights struggle places the courts in a central role by "enforcing [and articulating] the norms that are established" (Diller 2000, 35).

Percy's (1989) book on policy implementation, published before the enactment of the ADA, also cites the growing importance of the courts as an arena for implementing disability policy.[6] Moreover, since passage of the ADA, the judiciary has assumed even greater significance in disability policymaking. In his recent analysis of ADA litigation, Burke (2002, 92) emphasizes the judiciary's role, stating that "implementation of the ADA is ultimately in the hands of the judges." Thus, although Congress and the executive branch are key actors in the disability policymaking process (see Percy 2000), the courts have the primary responsibility for implementing disability rights policies.

Bishop and Jones (1993, 122) perceived the passage of the ADA as an opportunity to construct a model of prospective implementation, arguing that it is beneficial for public policy analysts to evaluate the implementation process at its onset, that is, before the law takes effect. Adapting Bullock and Lamb's (1984) model of civil rights policy implementation, they isolated five variables that would lead to successful implementation of the ADA: "(1) the organized support of beneficiaries, (2) clearly articulated compliance standards, (3) identification of implementing agencies, (4) specification of enforcement procedures, and (5) clarity of policy goals." After assessing the status of the five variables at the start of the implementation process, they concluded that the prospects for successful implementation of the ADA were good, assuming that government officials and advocates continued to advance the goals throughout the process. However, they cautioned, the implementation process would flounder if certain conditions arose: two related to problems within enforcement agencies and the third revolved around judicial interpretation of the law. Underscoring the importance of litigation in the implementation process, they warned that "if opponents of the ADA succeed in using the courts to cast doubt as to the proper interpretation of the law and regulations, confusion and delay may mute the enforcement of the act" (Bishop and Jones 1993, 127).

The Origins of Disability Rights Policies

Disability policymaking can be traced back to the post–World War I era with the passage of the Smith-Fess Act in 1920. For more than four decades, disability policies emphasized vocational rehabilitation rather than rights. The aim was to transform people with disabilities rather than to transform society by ending social and economic discrimination against them (O'Brien 2001). The empowerment of people with disabilities and the recognition of disability rights as civil rights did not come about until much later—in the late 1960s.

As with other civil rights activists, disability activists demanded an end to discrimination as a matter of right, arguing that disability should be viewed through a sociopolitical rather than a medical lens and that attempting to rehabilitate people with disabilities was equivalent to attempting to rehabilitate women or African Americans to end the discrimination against them. As Arlene Mayerson (2001), directing attorney at the Disability Rights Education and Defense Fund, Inc. (DREDF), explains, disability rights activists believe the focus should be on the interaction between society and the individual, which is a social construct rather than a medical one. In rejecting the medical model, which regards the person with a disability as a patient, the new approach to disability studies "views the disabled person as the primary actor and the focus of the research," encompassing a wide range of policy areas such as health, housing, transportation, and education, to name just a few (Pfeiffer 1993, 730; see Krieger 2000; Scotch 2001; Tucker 2001).[7]

The struggle of the individuals who formed the disability rights movement has been eloquently told by many (see, for example, Percy 1989; Shapiro 1994; see also Pfeiffer 1993). Influenced in part by the activism of women's groups and racial minority groups, people with disabilities became aware that theirs must be the predominant voices in the public policy debates circulating within the new movement. They realized that one of the first steps was to wrest power from the old guard of disability advocates—frequently people without disabilities who often perceived people with disabilities as pitiable and objects of charity—and build a movement that cut across disabilities as well as race, class, and sex boundaries (see Shapiro 1994; Burke 2002). The passage of the 1968 Architectural Barriers Act —mandating that buildings and transportation facilities constructed, altered, or financed with federal funds after 1969 comply with federal accessibility standards for people with mobility, visual, and auditory disabilities—was the first legislative success of the nascent movement. It "signal[ed] a new awareness of mainstream society of the needs and frustration of disabled persons" (Percy 1989, 52; see Scotch 2001).

The Rehabilitation Act of 1973

Throughout the 1970s, it became more commonplace to link disability rights with civil rights, as evidenced in the debate over the passage of the 1973 Rehabilitation Act.[8] The heart of this measure was section 504, at the time a little-debated and little-noticed provision, modeled after Title VI of the Civil Rights Act of 1964 and Title IX of the Education Amendments of 1972, which prohibit discrimination in federally assisted programs on the basis of race and sex, respectively.

The genesis of section 504 lay in the actions of two members of Congress. The first was Representative Charles Vanik, Democrat of Ohio, who introduced legislation in December 1971 to amend Title VI of the 1964 Civil Rights Act to ban discrimination on the basis of disability in federally assisted programs. Vanik decried the treatment of people with disabilities as one of the nation's "shameful oversights," the product of indifference and lack of concern (quoted in Burgdorf 1997, 417). He also attempted to amend Title

VII, the employment discrimination provision of the Civil Rights Act, to prohibit discrimination on the basis of disability. The second was Senator Hubert Humphrey, Democrat from Minnesota, who introduced a companion bill in the Senate in early 1972 urging Congress to guarantee "the civil rights of 40 million Americans" (quoted in Burgdorf 1997, 418).

Although the bills had numerous cosponsors, they died in committee before hearings were held, in part, according to O'Brien (2001, 114),because the traditional civil rights community did not want to tamper with the 1964 Civil Rights Act. Marca Bristo, chair of the National Council on Disability (NCD) in 1994, and currently the president of Access Living in Chicago, says that although she initially believed it more advisable to amend the 1964 Civil Rights Act to guarantee disability rights, she changed her views for a number of reasons. First, the traditional civil rights community was concerned about opening the 1964 act to new amendments; second, she came to realize that a disability rights law would not fit easily within the framework of traditional civil rights laws because of its unique requirement of a reasonable accommodations provision (Bristo 2002; Young 1997, 19).

In 1972, when the Vocational Rehabilitation Act came up for reauthorization, once again an antidiscrimination provision was introduced in the amended version of the bill, now called the Rehabilitation Act; the name change was intended to signify a new approach to disability. Most of Congress's attention during debate over the law focused on the cost of the rehabilitation programs. Equating discrimination on the basis of disability with discrimination on the basis of sex or race, it proposed to bring a new type of civil rights guarantee into effect, including within its reach government entities such as public schools, hospitals, transportation systems, and private federal contractors. Despite support in Congress, however, the bill was twice vetoed by President Richard Nixon, who feared its constraints on federal authority and its impact on the budget.

In May 1973, another version of the Rehabilitation Act passed. Although primarily intended to fund vocational rehabilitational programs, the nucleus of the 1973 act was section 504, which stated that "no otherwise qualified handicapped individual in the United States . . . shall, solely by reason of his handicap, be excluded from participation in, be denied the benefits of, or be subjected to discrimination under any program or activity receiving Federal financial assistance."[9] Despite the impact section 504 would have on disability rights, there was virtually no discussion of it in committee hearings. Inserted by congressional staffers who borrowed the language of Title VI, "the rights provision, section 504, was an unanticipated consequence" of the disability policymaking process (O'Brien 2001, 5).

Bristo (2002) characterizes section 504 as "an anomaly of history," enacted with little or no participation by the disability community; it was a "law [that] preceded the movement." Burgdorf (1997, 419) describes the drafting of section 504 as "shrouded in mystery" and Young (1997, 20) calls it a "stealth measure [enacted] in the midst of a backlash against civil rights." In discussing the origins of the ADA, a number of respondents expressed disappointment at the ineffectiveness of section 504, attributing it to lax enforcement.

The implications of section 504 were not debated during its passage, and no member of Congress even mentioned it during floor debate (Young 1997, 21). Indeed, as Scotch (2001, 4) points out, neither the Senate nor House committee reports contained cost estimates for section 504, indicating, in his view, that members of Congress likely believed it would not require an allocation of federal funds.

Other provisions of the 1973 act required federal agencies to develop affirmative action plans for hiring people with disabilities (section 501); created an Architectural and Transportation Barriers Compliance Board to develop guidelines and accessibility standards and monitor compliance with the Architectural Barriers Act (section 502);[10] and mandated that federal contractors adopt affirmative action plans to employ people with disabilities (section 503). A year later, the Rehabilitation Act Amendments of 1974 broadened the definition of disability, defining a "handicapped individual" as a person with "(1) a physical or mental impairment which substantially limits one or more of such person's major life activities, (ii) has a record of such an impairment, or (iii) is regarded as having such an impairment."[11] This language would be replicated in the ADA sixteen years later. Then in 1978 Congress added a new section, section 505, specifying that section 504 litigants were entitled to the "same remedies, procedures, and rights," including attorneys' fees for prevailing plaintiffs, as Title VI (of the 1964 Civil Rights Act) litigants.[12] In 1998 Congress again amended the 1973 act to add section 508, a provision requiring all federal agencies to comply with accessibility standards administered by the Architectural and Transportation Barriers Compliance Board to ensure that people with disabilities have access to electronic and information technology.[13]

Implementation of a law typically begins with the promulgation of administrative regulations. In this case, although the statute did not mandate it, the Department of Health, Education, and Welfare (HEW) prepared the implementing regulations.[14] During the summer of 1975, HEW's Office of Civil Rights (OCR), under the direction of John Wodatch, completed its final draft of the section 504 regulations.[15] The OCR, staffed by lawyers largely sympathetic to the goals of the disability rights activists, believed in committing federal authority to impose a high bar of accessibility on federal aid recipients. Their emerging ties to leaders of the disability community strengthened their resolve to produce strong regulations (Scotch 2001, 143–45). Under HEW procedure, the secretary was required to sign off on proposed regulations before they were sent to the Federal Register to initiate the public comment period. In part because HEW was concerned about the cost of compliance with section 504, the regulatory process was delayed, first by Caspar Weinberger, Gerald Ford's secretary at HEW, and later by his replacement, David Mathews, who refused to approve the regulations despite congressional urging and an eventual court order (Shapiro 1994, chap. 2; Scotch 2001, chap. 5).[16]

Disability rights activists were initially relieved when the Nixon-Ford administration was replaced by the Carter White House in 1977. But although Carter had criticized the Ford administration for refusing to promulgate the disability regulations during the presidential campaign (Scotch 2001, 104), his HEW secretary, Joseph Califano, also delayed implementation of the regulations, saying he needed additional time for review. Disability activists were especially concerned about Califano's failure to sign because it soon became clear that his delay was partially attributable to an attempt to rewrite the regulations to introduce cost as a defense for noncompliance (O'Brien 2001, 127).[17] Finally, in April 1977, in response to his continued refusal to release the regulations, disability activists in Washington DC demonstrated at Califano's house and, two days later, conducted sit-ins in the DC HEW office and at the ten regional offices around the country. The demonstration attracting the most attention was in Washington DC, with Califano taking a hard line by refusing to allow anyone to enter or leave the building and preventing food from being brought in as well as cutting off telephone communication.

With the exception of the demonstrators at the San Francisco federal building, most of the protestors were soon routed. Led by Judy Heumann, deputy director of Berkeley's Center for Independent Living, and consisting of people with mental and physical disabilities, the sit-in persisted for almost a month in HEW's San Francisco office.[18] Shapiro (1994, 68) asserts that "the San Francisco sit-in marked the political coming of age of the disability rights movement." Fleischer and Zames (1998, 52) describe the San Francisco protest as "the first major political action by people with different disabilities themselves that had an impact on the consciousness and the lives of the general disability population as well as the wider society."

With rising public support, the demonstrators demanded that Califano sign the regulations, equating inaccessible buildings with the segregated facilities that kept African Americans apart from white society. The parallels between the civil rights sit-ins of the early 1960s and the disability sit-ins of the late 1970s are obvious. Burke (2002, 69) compares the mobilization over section 504 to the Montgomery bus boycott that had energized the nascent African American civil rights struggle, translating barriers to societal integration as an act of discrimination. Finally, on April 28, 1977, Califano announced he would sign the rules, almost three years after the law was enacted. According to Chai Feldblum (2000b)—a Georgetown law professor who chaired the legal task force of the Consortium of Citizens with Disabilities from 1988 to 1989—1977 marked the onset of section 504 enforcement.

Like its predecessors, Titles VI and Title IX, litigation became the primary enforcement mechanism for section 504, with implementation largely in the hands of the federal courts because Congress had not committed enforcement authority to an executive branch agency like the EEOC. The problem with this solution, however, according to O'Brien (2001, 109), was that "the federal courts could not be described as strong proponents of promoting disability rights, particularly not in the workplace."

The Education of All Handicapped Children Act

Shortly after the passage of the Rehabilitation Act in 1973, Congress enacted the Education of All Handicapped Children Act (EAHCA) in 1975; in 1990, during reauthorization, it was renamed the Individuals with Disabilities Education Act (IDEA). The House Education and Labor Committee report (1975, 3–4) accompanying the bill pointed to two lower federal court rulings decided in the early 1970s that had spurred Congress to action. These two cases, *Pennsylvania Association for Retarded Children (PARC) v. Pennsylvania* (1971) and *Mills v. Board of Education* (1972), played a pivotal role in the effort to equalize educational opportunities for children with disabilities, in part by mobilizing disability activists who, in turn, influenced Congress (Jeon and Haider-Markel 2001).

A class action suit, *PARC* was brought by plaintiffs on constitutional grounds, citing due process and equal protection violations. The case ended in a consent decree in which the state agreed to abandon its policy of excluding "uneducable" and "untrainable" children with mental retardation (or children with a mental age less than five) from the public school system.[19] The lengthy consent agreement concluded by stating that "every retarded person between the ages of six and twenty-one years shall be provided access to a free public program of education and training appropriate to his capacities as soon as possible" (*PARC* 1971, 1266).

Mills, also a class action suit, was brought by plaintiffs who charged the District of Columbia public schools with failing to provide free education and training for mentally and physically disabled (that is, "exceptional") children and with establishing disciplinary policies that violated due process by denying them hearings and timely reviews of their status. There were estimates that perhaps as many as 18,000 of the approximately 22,000 "exceptional" children in the district were not being properly educated. Following the school district's failure to comply with the consent agreement it entered into as well as its failure to obey a court order to file a proposed plan of implementation, the court finally ruled. Citing violations of the equal protection and due process clauses, as well as District of Columbia law, the court ordered the district to provide "to each child of school age a free and suitable publicly-supported education regardless of the degree of the child's mental, physical or emotional disability or impairment" (*Mills* 1972, 878).

In 1966, Congress amended the 1965 Elementary and Secondary Education Act (ESEA) by adding a new section, Title VI, which established a grant program to assist states in educating children with disabilities. In 1970, under pressure from interest groups, Congress repealed that program and substituted the Education of the Handicapped Act for Title VI. It authorized a higher level of funding, some earmarked for grant programs designed to encourage states to develop educational programs and train personnel (Salomone 1986, chap. 5).

The precursor to the EAHCA, the 1974 Education of the Handicapped Act Amendments, embodied a number of the principles of the *PARC* and *Mills* decisions. Advocates for children with disabilities lobbied for increasing federal aid as well as federal mandates on state and local governments to establish special education programs to serve children with disabilities, primarily mental disabilities (Percy 1989, chap. 3). According to estimates provided by HEW, there were at least eight million children needing special educational services (Hill 1986, 136).

Prior to passage of the EAHCA, the major unresolved issue was whether the states or the federal government should undertake primary responsibility for educating children with disabilities. In 1975, Congress settled the matter by mandating that public school systems provide a "free, appropriate education," regardless of disability, "in the least restrictive environment." Congress believed such a law was necessary because children with disabilities "were either totally excluded from schools or [were] sitting idly in regular classrooms awaiting the time when they were old enough to 'drop out'" (U.S. House Education and Labor Committee 1975, 2).

In addition to allocating federal dollars to the states, the law imposed numerous mandates and restrictions on them. The heart of the bill was a grants-in-aid program requiring significant state expenditures for educating children with disabilities. States only had to comply with the provisions of the law if they wanted federal funding; they could avoid the requirements of the act by refusing the federal funds. Over the next decade, however, although the state's responsibility for educating children with disabilities expanded, the federal contribution did not grow proportionately, greatly adding to the states' burdens, especially in hard economic times (Salomone 1986, 146–47). Subsequent amendments to the EAHCA expanded the state's responsibility to children from birth to twenty-one, guaranteed a wide range of educational and support services, and specified that all children were covered, whether they lived at home or in a foster care or institutional setting.

The ban on discrimination in section 504 and the EAHCA's guarantee of free and appropriate education together provided a panoply of rights and remedies to children with disabilities.[20] They fit together well because the EAHCA is "narrow and specific," while section 504 is "broad and general in coverage" (Guernsey 1989, 566). In large part, because of the specificity of its provisions, the EAHCA became the primary vehicle under which litigants sued for relief for violation of the rights guaranteed to children with disabilities (Wegner 1988, 387). Indeed, in *Smith v. Robinson* (1984), the Supreme Court held that Congress had intended the EAHCA to be the exclusive vehicle for children claiming a "free appropriate education" in a public school setting.

During the 1980s and 1990s, Congress continued to enact laws affecting the rights of people with disabilities, although none were as sweeping as the 1973 Rehabilitation Act and the EAHCA, and ultimately, the ADA. Among other things, the Civil Rights of Institutionalized Persons Act, enacted in 1980, authorizes the U.S. attorney general to file civil actions in cases where persons in state institutions such as prisons, residential mental health care facilities, or pretrial juvenile detention facilities are deprived of their constitutional or statutory rights.

Two other laws revolved around voting. The 1984 Voting Accessibility for the Elderly and Handicapped Act required federal polling places to be physically accessible and mandated that states make registration and voting aids available to elderly people and people with disabilities. The National Voter Registration Act of 1993 (the "Motor Voter" Act) mandated that states facilitate voting registration by persons with disabilities, among others, by providing enhanced voter registration services in drivers' license and state-funded disability agencies. Section 255 of the Telecommunications Act of 1996 amended the Communications Act of 1934 to require manufacturers of telecommunications equipment and service providers to address the needs of persons with disabilities in designing and producing accessible equipment.

Perhaps the most comprehensive legislation predating the ADA was the Fair Housing Act Amendments (FHAA) of 1988, which amended the 1968 Fair Housing Act (FHA). The 1968 FHA prohibited discrimination in the sale and rental of public and private housing on the basis of race, religion, and national origin. The 1988 FHAA extended the law to include discrimination based on disability in selling, renting, financing, zoning, new construction design, and advertising. And in 1999, President Clinton signed the Ticket to Work and Work Incentives Improvement Act, which expanded the Medicaid and Medicare programs to allow people with disabilities to retain medical coverage after returning to work. These laws are evidence of the power of the disability rights movement to affect public policy through lobbying, media attention, litigation, and political mobilization (Jeon and Haider-Markel 2001).

Disability Rights in the Supreme Court

Supreme Court rulings in the decade following passage of section 504 and the EAHCA show that the Court's interpretation of disability rights was constrained and, although there were exceptions, for the most part the Court narrowed the parameters of the nation's disability rights laws.[21]

Surveying about ten years of the Supreme Court's section 504 rulings, Percy (1989, 96) describes them as "generally conservative and restrictive." Similarly, Wegner (1988, 388) contends that the "Supreme Court has significantly limited the substantive rights and remedies once believed to be available under the EAHCA." More generally, Katzman (1986, 14), depicts the Court's record on disability rights litigation as "an account of judicial contraction."

The Supreme Court's first section 504 ruling, *Southeastern Community*

College v. Davis (1979), exemplified the Court's approach to disability rights claims. The plaintiff, Frances Davis, who had a severe hearing impairment, sought an associate nursing degree as a pathway to becoming a registered nurse. She filed suit after she was denied admission to the program, claiming that the school, a recipient of federal funds, violated section 504. The school argued that her hearing disability was an insurmountable obstacle to her participation in its clinical program as well as her ability to practice as a nurse.[22]

The appellate court had ruled that she must be evaluated on her qualifications without regard to her disability and that section 504 imposed an obligation on the school to accommodate her disability without regard to cost (*Davis v. Southeastern Community College* 1978). The Supreme Court reversed the appellate court ruling in her favor, holding that neither the law nor the regulations forbade an educational institution from imposing reasonable physical requirements on an applicant. The Court ruled that to be "otherwise qualified," one must be able to perform a task "in spite" of a disability (*Southeastern Community College v. Davis* 1979, 406). The school did not have to accommodate her disability by waiving the course requirements and providing special attention from the nursing faculty because that would create a "fundamental alteration in the nature of the program," far exceeding what the regulations required (*Southeastern Community College v. Davis* 1979, 410). Acknowledging that the line between discrimination and a refusal to accommodate a disability is not always evident, the Court concluded by noting that the law was not intended to create "undue financial and administrative burdens" for a state (*Southeastern Community College v. Davis* 1979, 412).[23] *Davis* "dealt a severe blow" to disability rights advocates and their supporters, "for whom section 504 was a central part of their policy aspirations" (Katzman 1986, 166).[24] Mayerson (1993, 20) charged that *Davis* "revealed what was at best a lack of understanding and at worst a hostility toward even applying the concept of discrimination to exclusion based on disability."

Shortly after *Davis* was decided, the Court was asked to rule on whether the 1975 Developmental Disabilities Assistance and Bill of Rights Act (DDA) contained an implied cause of action that permitted plaintiffs to sue states for failing to provide "appropriate treatment" in the "least restrictive environment" to people with mental retardation (*Pennhurst State School and Hospital v. Halderman* 1981, 18). Enacted under pressure from the Consortium of Citizens with Disabilities (CCD), the DDA, like the EAHCA, was a federal grants-in-aid program to assist states in creating developmental disability councils for planning and advocacy.[25]

The lower courts ruled for the plaintiffs, but the Supreme Court reversed, holding that the statute was merely a funding statute and Congress had not explicitly conditioned the receipt of federal funds on the state's compliance with the law as it was required to do. Despite the language of the Bill of Rights provision stating that developmentally disabled individuals are entitled to "appropriate treatment" in "the setting that is least restrictive" (42 U.S.C. §6009(2)), the Court held that Congress had not "intended to require States to assume the high cost of providing 'appropriate treatment' in the 'least restrictive environment' to their mentally retarded citizens" (*Pennhurst* 1981, 18). The provision did not create any judicially enforceable substantive rights; rather, the Court said, it merely stated Congress's preference for certain policy goals.

In *Board of Education of the Henrik Hudson Central School District v. Rowley* (1982), the Supreme Court's first EAHCA case, it was asked to determine if the law required a child's school to provide her with a sign language interpreter. The case arose when the school denied Amy Rowley's parents' request for the services of an interpreter "because 'Amy was achieving educationally, academically, and socially without such assistance'" (*Rowley* 1982, 185). The district court found that although she was making excellent progress in school, she was not fulfilling her potential because of her hearing impairment. The court of appeals affirmed.

Although both lower courts had held that Congress had not provided adequate guidance for the meaning of the term, "free appropriate education," the high court disagreed, ruling that Congress had only intended to guarantee that children with disabilities "benefit" from the educational services provided; there was no indication that it meant that schools must "maximize the[ir] potential" (188–89). As long as a school provided the personalized instruction and support services that enabled a child to achieve passing marks and advance to a higher grade, it satisfied the requirements of the act.

The Court also cited *Pennhurst,* reiterating that legislation enacted under Congress's spending clause authority must unambiguously indicate the conditions for receiving federal funds. Therefore, even if Congress had intended to impose a higher standard of education services on the states as a condition of federal funding, it had not expressly stated its intention to do so. Finally, responding to the lower courts' understanding that the judiciary was supposed to define the meaning of "appropriate education," the Court indicated that the primary responsibility for determining suitable educational services resided with the school in cooperation with the parents.

Warning against judicial activism, the high court ordered the lower courts to refrain from engaging in educational policymaking and to limit themselves to ascertaining if the state was complying with the procedures of the act. If the procedural requirements were met, the courts' only task was to decide if the education provided was reasonably likely to allow the child to benefit from the services.

Scholars almost uniformly criticized *Rowley,* accusing the Court of undermining congressional intent by requiring only minimal benefits for children with disabilities. They charged that the Court's primary motivation was to avoid the ensuing litigation that would have followed a contrary ruling. As it turned out, most lower courts have either distinguished *Rowley* or simply have failed to apply the law as narrowly as the high court instructed (Weber 1990, 374–76).

Two years after *Rowley,* in *Irving Independent School District v. Tatro* (1984), the Court expanded the reach of the EAHCA by holding that "clean intermittent catheterization" (CIC), was a "related service" within the meaning of the act, and the school's refusal to provide it during school hours violated both the EAHCA and section 504. The Court found that CIC was a "supportive service," without which the child could not benefit from her education, and did not fall into the category of a "medical service" that could only be provided by a licensed physician.[26]

In *Smith v. Robinson* (1984), however, the Court dealt another blow to disability rights litigants when it ruled that attorneys' fees were not available in actions brought to vindicate rights under the EAHCA.[27] Congress reversed by passing the Handicapped Children's Protection Act in 1986 to amend the EAHCA to authorize attorneys' fees to parents who prevail in judicial or administrative hearings under the EAHCA and allow education suits under section 504 (Guernsey 1989, 567–69). Although not directly related to disability rights, the Supreme Court's decision in *Grove City College v. Bell* (1984) was a significant setback for members of the civil rights community, including disability rights groups. The Court held that Congress intended the "program or activity" language of Title IX of the Education Amendments to be narrowly interpreted; thus, the federal loans and grants to its students only bound the college's financial aid office to the nondiscrimination requirements of the act. A year later, *City of Cleburne v. Cleburne Living Center* (1985) established the boundaries of the equal protection guarantee of the Fourteenth Amendment for people with disabilities. Although the plaintiffs prevailed in their challenge to a zoning regulation, the Court ruled that mental retardation was not a suspect (or quasi-suspect) classification so that laws based on disability were not subject to the heightened scrutiny applied to classifications based on race and sex.

Grove City had been greeted with dismay by members of the civil rights community, who feared its effect on other civil rights statutes such as Title VI of the 1964 Civil Rights Act, section 504 of the 1973 Rehabilitation Act, and the 1975 Age Discrimination Act, all of which had the same "program" or "activity" language as Title IX. They believed that the Court's insistence on erecting walls around individual programs within institutions threatened the major civil rights advances of the 1960s and 1970s. Their fears seemed justified when the Supreme Court held in *Department of Transportation v. Paralyzed Veterans of America* (1986) that federal aid to airports and the air traffic control system did not bring commercial airlines within the reach of the 1973 Rehabilitation Act because they were not direct recipients of federal funding. To counter the Court's ruling in *Paralyzed Veterans,* Congress enacted the Air Carrier Access Act (ACAA) in 1986, prohibiting domestic and foreign airlines from discriminating against people with mental or physical disabilities.

In 1988, after repeated attempts to enact legislation to reverse *Grove City,* Congress succeeded in overriding Reagan's veto and passed the Civil Rights Restoration Act, extending coverage of civil rights laws to the entire institution or system, not simply the unit receiving the federal aid. With this action, the Court's narrow interpretation of the program-specific language of the nation's federal civil rights laws was reversed and, according to its congressional sponsors, Congress had ensured that these laws would be interpreted according to their original intent.

Although the struggle to reverse *Grove City* lasted more than three years, it provided an opportunity for disability rights groups to work with traditional civil rights groups to secure a common goal. According to Arlene Mayerson and Ralph Neas, head of the Leadership Conference on Civil Rights (LCCR), the collaboration benefited both sides, developing trust and respect among all parties involved (Young 1997, 40).

The ADA Evolves

During the 1970s, there had been a good deal of support for ending discrimination against people with disabilities, in part fueled by the disability community's association with the ideology and rhetoric of the civil rights movement, including their facility with protest activity and mobilization of public opinion (Jeon and Haider-Markel 2001, 215–31). Throughout the

1980s, the grass roots movement of disability rights groups expanded rapidly, epitomized by such organizations as Americans Disabled for Accessible Public Transportation (ADAPT). It consisted of both cross-disability and disability-specific groups, which were becoming increasingly adept at political organization, mobilization, and action (Young 1997, 43–46). The demand for equality for people with disabilities was consistent with the earlier struggle for civil rights as disability rights activists gave convincing accounts of discrimination against people with disabilities that were reminiscent of the experiences of African Americans whose battle for equal rights had led to the passage of the 1964 Civil Rights Act and the 1965 Voting Rights Act.

However, by 1980 the sentiment for people with disabilities among members of Congress "had begun to erode . . . and the blank check of civil rights entitlement had finally come up against serious political and financial constraints" (Scotch 2001, 136). Signs of the backlash against disability rights loomed large in the Reagan administration, epitomized by the government's efforts to trim administrative regulations under the auspices of Vice President George Bush's Task Force for Regulatory Relief (Milani 2000). One of this office's first tasks was to put section 504, the EAHCA, and the Architectural and Transportation Barriers Compliance Board regulations under the microscope. Because of an immediate and forceful reaction to these measures, Bush agreed to meet with representatives of disability advocacy groups. This led to his introduction to Evan Kemp Jr., who was to play an important role in disability rights advocacy.[28]

In early 1983, Bush announced that the section 504 and EAHCA regulations would remain intact. Despite their victory over the task force, however, the civil rights community remained concerned that civil rights enforcement, including disability rights, might still be subjected to "rollback" (Percy 1989, 104–5).

The task force's decision to refrain from cutting back on section 504 regulations was greatly facilitated by conversations between Kemp and Bush in which Kemp appealed to the antiwelfare ideology of the Republican Party, stressing independence for people with disabilities rather than government support or welfare. Kemp, who was also a personal friend of Bush's chief counsel, is widely regarded as the person who sparked the Bush administration's support for the ADA and had the honor of introducing Bush at the ADA signing ceremony on July 26, 1990.[29]

An unanticipated consequence of the Bush task force was the arrival of Patrisha Wright in Washington DC in 1980 to open a lobbying office for DREDF. Spurred by the possibility that section 504 would be eviscerated,

Wright's initial work in DC involved lobbying the task force to keep it from weakening the section 504 regulations. Founded in 1979, DREDF was a successor to the Disability Law Resource Center, which arose out of the Berkeley Center for Independent Living.[30] The Disability Rights Education and Defense Fund was formed because there was a need for a national law and policy organization to advance civil rights for people with disabilities; it was modeled after the NAACP Legal Defense and Educational Fund, Inc. An important voice in the disability rights movement, DREDF arose out of a civil rights model. Its leadership worked to persuade leaders of the civil rights community to join with them, and Wright subsequently became a member of the national LCCR (Wright 2000; Breslin 2001).

During the decade of the 1980s, with section 504 and the 1964 Civil Rights Act providing the legal foundation for the ADA, members of the "disability community attained a new sophistication in legal expertise, developed a political presence in the White House and on Capitol Hill, and established credibility with the broader civil rights community" (Young 1997, 27). By the late 1980s, disability advocates had become convinced that section 504 was inadequate to achieve their goal of removing barriers to their full participation in society, in part, according to Mary Lou Breslin (2001), one of the co-founders of DREDF and now a senior policy advisor, because there was never a real commitment to enforce it and because it only applied to recipients of federal funds. Mayerson (2001) characterizes section 504 "as almost like a hidden law," saying "it never got the publicity, it was never part of the national agenda, the national debate."

The idea of a successor to section 504 was supported by Justin Dart Jr., vice chair of the National Council on the Handicapped (NCH) from 1982 to 1985.[31] Dart (2001), who describes himself "as a voice in the wilderness in the early 1980s," headed the Task Force on the Rights and Empowerment of Americans with Disabilities from 1987 to 1989. In May 1988, the chair of the House Subcommittee on Select Education directed the task force to compile national data on discrimination against people with disabilities. Under Dart's direction, it conducted sixty-three open forums in all fifty states, gathering testimony from a broad range of people with disabilities about discrimination in a variety of settings (Dart 2001; see also Dart 1993). Evoking the rhetoric of the civil rights movement, members of the task force were repeatedly reminded that people with disabilities were entitled to equal rights as citizens (Dart 2001).[32] Most members of the NCH were Reagan appointees who supported the idea of the civil rights model and disability rights legislation in part because it would reduce dependency among people with disabilities as well as lower welfare costs (Burke 1997).

In 1986, the NCH—renamed the National Council on Disability (NCD) in 1988—was charged with advising the president and Congress on public policies related to people with disabilities. Its first report, *Toward Independence* (1986), was a pathbreaking document.[33] The council recommended that Congress enact "a comprehensive law requiring equal opportunity for individuals with disabilities . . . perhaps under such a title as 'The Americans with Disabilities Act of 1986'" (NCH 1986, 18). The document, drafted by Robert L. Burgdorf Jr., included a broad array of entities subject to the nondiscrimination provisions of the envisioned act; it applied to the federal government, recipients of federal funds, federal contractors, employers, transportation and insurance industries, and state and local governments. It would have demanded full accessibility in two to five years for almost all entities (Young 1997, 59). Over the next two years, Burgdorf's ideas were transformed into the law that would eventually become the 1990 ADA (Shapiro 1994, chap. 5). With Dart's encouragement as well as the NCD's, Burgdorf, who had long advocated a stand-alone civil rights law prohibiting discrimination on the basis of disabilities, produced the bill. In part because of his belief as well as Dart's that section 504 lacked teeth and was limited in scope by the federal funding requirement, his disability rights law, termed an "equal opportunity law," was modeled after the 1964 Civil Rights Act.[34]

The NCD recruited Lowell Weicker and Tony Coelho to introduce the law in the 100th Congress. In 1988, on April 28 and 29, respectively, they introduced the ADA in the Senate and House. They did not anticipate that it would pass that year, but saw it as an opportunity to draw attention to the nation's discrimination against people with disabilities.[35] Moreover, they planned to capitalize on the presidential election "to publicize the ADA and gain a foothold as a top priority for the next session of Congress" (Young 1997, 9). The bill received little attention at the time; many who were aware of it considered it too radical and believed it lacked any chance of passage (*Congressional Record* 1988, S5106–18; *Congressional Record* 1988, E1308–10). Although it passed the Senate, it died in the House.

Disability rights remained on the public agenda, with Bush's endorsement at the Republican National Convention. His promise, "I'm going to do whatever it takes to make sure the disabled are included in the mainstream," helped him secure votes from the disability community in the 1988 presidential election (Shapiro 1994, 124). Analyzing Bush's percent margin of victory over Dukakis, Pfeiffer (1993, 28) believes that from 1 to 3 percent of Bush's 7 percent lead was attributable to voters in the disability community.

At the outset of the Bush administration in 1989, according to Dart (1993), the disability community consulted with a wide range of groups in the business community, as well as members of Congress and the administration. Wright and her allies brilliantly forged a coalition of disability rights groups, including the CCD and the LCCR, cutting across class, race, and sex boundaries, and, most important, representing a broad range of mental and physical disabilities; almost two hundred national organizations threw their support behind the ADA (Shapiro 1994, 127). Ultimately, representatives from all the disability rights organizations in the country became involved in the movement (Switzer 2001, 629). Additionally, there was broad support from the traditional civil rights community; Ralph Neas, who made disability rights part of his group's agenda as early as 1980, played a leading role. He had been present at the meeting in San Francisco held under the auspices of DREDF in the fall of 1980, a meeting that was aimed at helping it to establish ties with members of traditional civil rights groups. His support for the ADA provided a critical link between disability rights advocates and traditional civil rights leaders (Young 1997, 34). Katy Beh Neas (2002), assistant vice president for government relations at Easter Seals, who was on Harkin's staff from 1987 to 1991, believes that disability rights were initially considered outside the arena of civil rights. Eventually, she notes, the civil rights community, persuaded in part by Wright and Ralph Neas, became convinced that disability rights were civil rights.

With Weicker defeated in his 1988 reelection campaign and Coelho retired from the House in 1989, the baton was passed to Steny Hoyer, Ted Kennedy, and Tom Harkin. In the Senate, Kennedy chaired the Labor and Human Resources Committee, and Harkin, the Subcommittee on the Handicapped of the Labor and Human Resources Committee. Bobby Silverstein, Harkin's staff director and chief counsel of the Subcommittee on the Handicapped, who had drafted the second version of the ADA, tracked the section 504 regulations closely (Feldblum 2000a, 127). The final version of the ADA specifies that it should be interpreted according to the case law and regulations of the Rehabilitation Act.[36] The bill, introduced in modified form during the 101st Congress in May 1989, was presented as a civil rights measure, with members of Congress echoing the language heard in the debate over the 1964 Civil Rights Act.

Largely under Patrisha Wright's direction, a coalition of the disability community lobbied members of Congress on a bipartisan basis. According to a coalition member, Becky Ogle, director of government affairs of the Spina Bifida Association, they would meet every Monday at one o'clock on Capitol Hill to get their "marching orders" for the day, and one of their chief tasks was "to put a face on discrimination" (Ogle 2001). One congressional staffer described the process as being "tutored" by Wright, Arlene Mayerson, and Chai Feldblum, who were taking a leading role in explaining substantive provisions of the law to Congress and staffers.

Congressional Action

Harkin's former staff member Katy Beh Neas (2002) reports that the disability community was united on the need for federal legislation to prohibit discrimination on the basis of disability and that Harkin wanted a bill that could become law. Convincing the business community to sign on to the bill was a more difficult task, she says.

Much of the congressional debate revolved around fears that compliance with the ADA would overwhelm the business community with excessive costs and added paperwork. The bulk of this opposition came from associations representing small business owners, such as the National Federation of Independent Businesses (NFIB). Groups such as the National Association of Manufacturers and the U.S. Chamber of Commerce also expressed concern, but were not as vehement in their opposition (Silverstein 2000). Testifying before Harkin's Subcommittee on the Handicapped, a representative of the Chamber stated that although his group favored the goal of the bill, "the costs of this action would be enormous and obviously could have a disastrous impact upon many small businesses struggling to survive." The bill supporters countered that surveys showed that most accommodations for employees with disabilities were either free or cost less than five hundred dollars (*Congressional Quarterly*, May 13, 1989, 1122–23).

In contrast to its fairly smooth passage in the Senate, the bill had been in the House for almost a year, in part because, instead of a single Senate committee, the bill had to proceed through four House committees (and six subcommittees): Education and Labor, Energy and Commerce, Public Works and Transportation, and Judiciary in addition to the Rules Committee. Each committee had at least one subcommittee hearing, during which amendments were introduced and debated.

The recollection of then-House member Larry Craig (1999), Republican from Idaho, provides an insight into the House debate over the ADA.[37] One of the most important issues, coverage of disabilities, aroused little serious opposition in the House. However, some members of Congress, reflecting the concerns of the business community, were troubled about the "large pool from which potential litigants might be drawn" (Craig 1999, 213) as well as the cost of the accommodations that would have to be provided for the vast numbers of workers with disabilities. They debated limiting the bill to categories of disabilities such as vision, hearing, or mobility impairments, but there was little support for this option. Most of the House discussion over coverage of disabilities was whether alcoholism, drug addiction, and homosexuality should be classified as disabilities—none were.

William Dannemeyer, Republican from California, proposed amendments barring coverage of homosexuals regarded as having AIDS or HIV, excluding communicable diseases from coverage, and specifying that the act did not create rights based on sexual orientation. He said this last amendment was intended to avoid having the ADA "turned into a homosexual bill of rights" (*Congressional Quarterly,* May 5, 1990, 1335). These amendments were defeated.

The principal cause of concern in the House during debate over the ADA was the costliness of the accommodations that would be required, especially to small businesses and communities as well as public transportation companies, and what would constitute an "undue burden." This sentiment, often expressed as a fear that the law was too vague, was stated repeatedly by House members. The business community also expressed concern that ambiguities in the law would lead to uncertainty about the extent of their obligations. In response, Bill Richardson, Democrat from New Mexico, attempted to reassure them, noting that "whenever possible we have used terms of art from the 1964 Civil Rights Act and the Rehabilitation Act of 1973, phrases already interpreted in courts throughout this land so that business can know exactly what we mean" (*Congressional Record* 1990, H2427). Reaffirming this view, one of the primary sponsors of the bill, Major Owens, New York Democrat, explained, "there is a history of experience in implementing the concepts of this bill which will greatly facilitate the task of informing those with rights and responsibilities under this legislation as to what its provisions mean" (*Congressional Record* 1990, H2427–28).

A number of representatives proposed amendments setting limits on the dollar amount spent on compliance. Representative James Olin, Democrat from Virginia, offered an amendment to limit the employer's obligation at accommodation to 10 percent of an employee's salary (*Congressional Record* 1990, H2471). The majority, however, objected to this measure, saying it was preferable if the courts determined the reasonableness of the accommodation (O'Brien 2001, 175–76).

Another proposal sought to create a rebuttable presumption that a small business was in compliance with the law if it spent $1,500 on accommodations in the past three years; there were also several amendments to limit public transit costs. Tom Campbell, Republican from California, offered an amendment that would have delayed the effective date of the public accommodations section of the bill until eighteen months after the final regulations were issued, rather than eighteen months after the enactment of the bill; it was narrowly defeated (*Congressional Quarterly,* May 5, 1990, 1355). In the end, none of these limiting amendments obtained a majority of votes.

Perhaps the major controversy in Congress at the time, affecting not only the ADA, but other civil rights laws as well, revolved around the nature of available remedies. During the summer of 1989, the Bush administration and the ADA sponsors struck a deal in which the disability advocates acceded to omitting a provision that provided for compensatory and punitive damages to victims of employment discrimination and, instead, limited the employment discrimination remedies to those in the 1964 act: injunctive relief, back pay, and attorneys' fees. In return, the administration agreed to support broader coverage of the public accommodations section of the law than in the public accommodations section of the 1964 Civil Rights Act.[38]

Months later, however, Congress considered the Kennedy-Hawkins bill, introduced in February 1990, that would have allowed compensatory and, in some cases, punitive damages for Title VII litigants. The administration contended that it was not fair for ADA remedies to be pegged to this proposed expanded version of Title VII and sought to tie the ADA remedies to the existing Title VII remedies of injunctive relief, back pay, and attorneys' fees. Proponents of the ADA argued that if Kennedy-Hawkins were enacted, disability plaintiffs would be at a disadvantage compared to other civil rights litigants. They claimed that the original agreement was based on the understanding that ADA remedies would be consonant with Title VII remedies, whatever they were at the time. Underscoring the vision of the ADA as a civil rights measure, a Senate staffer contended, "the notion was that you should treat people with disabilities the same as you treat minorities and women . . . the clear message was one of parallelism" (*Congressional Quarterly,* February 24, 1990, 600).

An administration-supported amendment offered by Representative James Sensenbrenner Jr., Republican from Wisconsin (*Congressional Record*

1990, H2612–13), was narrowly defeated in the House Judiciary Subcommittee on Civil and Constitutional Rights in a 5–3 party-line vote (*Congressional Quarterly,* April 28, 1990, 1273). Objecting to the Sensenbrenner amendment, Representative Don Edwards, Democrat from California, called it "gross discrimination" if "women and minorities will get better treatment than persons with disabilities" (*Congressional Record* 1990, H2615). The amendment lost in the House in a 227 to 192 vote (*New York Times,* May 23, 1990).

Representative Tom DeLay, Republican from Texas, talked about the effect the law would have on small businesses, reminding his colleagues of the "incredible costs" that section 504 had imposed on the government and accused bill supporters of taking the same "deep pocket theory" evident in section 504 and applying it to private businesses (*Congressional Record* 1990, H2315). Craig (1999, 216–17), however, noted that although it may have appeared that all attempts to limit the reach of the bill were defeated, there were numerous provisions that protected business interests.

Congress inserted cost considerations into each section of the law: in the "reasonable accommodation" and "undue hardship" language in Title I, the "undue burden" defense in Title II, and the "reasonable modifications" and "readily achievable" standards in Title III. Additionally, only new or altered construction was subject to immediate accessibility requirements and there was a phase-in period for small businesses. Similarly, Hawkins pointed out that the "Senate receded on almost every point of difference [between the Senate and House versions], particularly those which amended the Senate-passed bill with provisions deemed important to business or other private interests" (*Congressional Record* 1990, H4615).

Reflecting the concern for conciliating business interests, Bush also attempted to assure the business community that their "fears that the ADA is too vague or too costly and will lead to an explosion of litigation are misplaced." By incorporating the standards of section 504; by allowing flexibility in meeting the requirements of the act, including the phase-in provisions; and by allowing cost to be a factor in determining whether an accommodation is reasonable or an alteration is readily achievable, he said, a "careful balance [has been] struck between the rights of individuals with disabilities and the legitimate interests of business" (Bush 1990b).

One of the most hotly contested issues in the House was an amendment proposed by Representative Jim Chapman, Democrat from Texas, and supported by the National Restaurant Association and the NFIB, which termed the vote on the matter a "key small business vote" (NCD, n.d.). The amendment would have permitted a food service facility "to refuse to assign an employee with an infectious or communicable disease of public health significance to a job involving food handling" in the absence of a direct threat to health or safety (*Congressional Record* 1990, S7437). After much debate, on May 22, 1990, the amendment narrowly passed the House in a vote of 199 to 187 (*New York Times,* May 23, 1990).[39] The House approved the final bill in a 403 to 20 vote.

On May 24, the House requested a conference, and the Speaker appointed twenty-two conferees to represent the House side. When the Senate met on June 6, Senator Jesse Helms, Republican from North Carolina, sought to have the Senate conferees include the language of the Chapman amendment in the final version of the bill, replacing a Senate version that offered broader protection to food service workers with AIDS or HIV. Admitting that there was no evidence that AIDS or HIV was transmittable though food or casual contact, Helms nevertheless termed this a key vote in support of small businesses because of the consequences of the public's perception of the health risk of such workers. "You can call it hysteria all you want to," Helms said, "but you better believe that the vast majority of people who eat in restaurants do not want to have their food prepared or handled by people who have AIDS or who are HIV positive" (*Congressional Record* 1990, S7437).

Arguing against the motion to instruct, Harkin (*Congressional Record* 1990, S7437) pointed out that the Senate-passed measure already removed "an individual with a currently contagious disease" who "poses a direct threat to the health or safety of other individuals" from the protection of the act. The Chapman amendment proposed to strike "the words 'poses a direct threat to others'" from the act, allowing a worker with a communicable disease that was not transmittable through food or other casual contact, such as AIDS, to be excluded from the protection of the law. Harkin cited medical evidence indicating "that there is not one case of AIDS or HIV ever coming from food handling or from airborne substances." Accepting this amendment, he warned, would undermine the integrity of the law because it would "codify unfounded fears and ignorance," allowing employers to act "not based on medical evidence that that individual poses a direct threat to other people but based on ignorance, based upon fear, based upon mythology" (*Congressional Record* 1990, S7437–38). In remarks made to the business leadership on March 29, 1990, Bush also spoke out against the amendment (*Congressional Record* 1990, S7442), saying "our goal is to turn irrational fear into rational acts." Amid procedural wrangling, the Senate adopted Helms's motion to instruct in a voice vote.

There were countervailing pressures at work during the conference. Although a majority of both houses favored the Chapman amendment, representatives of the disability community announced that they would withdraw their support for the law if it included the amendment. According to Dart (1993, xxiii), the disability community was willing to be "flexible in terms of time limits, remedies, and cases of undue hardship, [but] would publicly oppose an ADA that included any significant permanent exemptions of coverage." Ultimately, faced with the prospect of dooming the entire legislation, the majority of conferees of each house voted against including the amendment.[40]

In addition to the Chapman amendment, another contentious issue in conference was whether the mandate against discrimination should be enforced against Congress through internal mechanisms only or through the courts. Ultimately, the conferees reached a compromise that complaints against House policies or practices would be governed by the Office of Fair Employment Practices and, based on an amendment by Charles Grassley, Republican from Iowa, complaints against Senate procedures would initially go through an internal grievance process that could be followed by suit in federal court. Orrin Hatch, Utah Republican, supported Grassley's attempt to permit judicial review of ADA claims in the Senate, saying, "We shouldn't saddle the private sector with something we're not willing to saddle ourselves with" (*Congressional Quarterly,* June 30, 1990, 2071).

Despite this agreement, Senator Wendell Ford, Democrat from Kentucky, and several others successfully argued that judicial review of congressional actions would constitute a separation of powers violation. The bill was returned to conference on a voice vote, with a majority of the Senate indicating it supported Ford's amendment, which merely granted civil rights protection to Senate employees, over the Grassley version. The bill's second trip to conference allowed Helms to attempt to have conferees accept the Chapman amendment. He again failed, largely because of opposition from Hatch and Bob Dole, Republican from Kansas, who were now willing to enact the law without the Chapman amendment. Hatch proposed that the Secretary of Health and Human Services (HHS) compile an annual list of communicable and infectious diseases that could be transmitted through food handling. Restaurant operators would be able to remove people with these illnesses from food handling positions. This was accepted first in the Senate and later in conference. Dannemeyer's subsequent motion to recommit the bill to conference for a third time to restore the Chapman amendment language also failed to secure a majority (*Congressional Quarterly*, July 14, 1990, 2227–28; see NCD, n.d.).

With strong lobbying by business interests as well as members of the disability community, the conference report was approved in the House on July 12 with a 377 to 28 vote and in the Senate on July 13 in a 91 to 6 vote.[41] Thirteen days later, on July 26, 1990, in a ceremony before thousands gathered on the White House South Lawn, Bush signed the ADA. In his remarks on signing the act, he exclaimed, "Let the shameful wall of exclusion finally come tumbling down" (Bush 1990a). Standing close to the president, Justin Dart, considered the "father of the ADA," was handed the first pen used to sign the bill (*St. Louis Post-Dispatch*, July 28, 2002).[42] Speaking at the signing ceremony, Neas (1990, 7) proclaimed that "the civil rights community, the Congress and the public are finally beginning to understand that disability rights are civil rights—and that when one of us suffers discrimination, the rights of all of us are diminished."

The ADA became law in the midst of controversy surrounding Kennedy-Hawkins—enacted as the 1991 Civil Rights Act—over Bush's veto in 1990. Kennedy-Hawkins allowed victims of employment discrimination on the basis of race, sex, age, religion, *and* disability to demand jury trials and collect money damages in cases of unlawful intentional discrimination.[43]

Provisions of the Law

In justifying the law at the outset, Congress proclaimed that "some 43,000,000 Americans have one or more physical or mental disabilities, and this number is increasing as the population as a whole is growing older" (42 U.S.C. §12101(a)(1)). Explicitly depicted as a civil rights act, the ADA described discrimination against people with disabilities as "a serious and pervasive social problem." Analogizing people with disabilities to other groups subjected to historical discrimination, the law invoked the powerful language of footnote 4 in *United States v. Carolene Products* (1938) by characterizing "individuals with disabilities [as] a discrete and insular minority who have been faced with restrictions and limitations, subjected to a history of purposeful unequal treatment, and relegated to a position of political powerlessness in our society, based on characteristics that are beyond the control of such individuals and resulting from stereotypic assumptions" (42 U.S.C. §12101(a)(7)).

Discussing the "double standard" of judicial review arising out of footnote 4, Abraham and Perry (2003, 23; see also Ely 1980) describe the "special judicial protection" the courts have afforded to "unpopular racial, religious, and political minorities and other often helpless and small groups." By incorporating the language of footnote 4 into the act, Congress clearly intended to signal the courts to accord people with disabilities the preferred status granted other "discrete and insular minorities."

The civil rights theme continued with Congress declaring that "it is the purpose of this Act . . . to provide a clear and comprehensive national mandate for the elimination of discrimination against individuals with disabilities; to provide clear, strong, consistent, enforceable standards addressing discrimination against people with disabilities; [and] to ensure that the Federal Government plays a central role in enforcing the standards established in this Act on behalf of individuals with disabilities" (42 U.S.C. §12102(2)(A)(B)(C)).

The ADA defines a disability with a broad stroke, classifying "an individual with a disability" as a person with "a physical or mental impairment that substantially limits one or more of the major life activities" of an individual. The second part of the definition, "has a record of such an impairment," refers to an individual "who has a history of, or has been misclassified as having, a mental or physical impairment that substantially limits one or more major life activities." The third, "regarded as," prong applies to individuals who have no substantially limiting impairments but are treated as if they do, or their substantially limiting impairments result from the attitudes of others (42 U.S.C. §12102).[44] The purpose of the last part of the definition was to prevent discrimination based on stereotypical fears, biases, and perceptions about people with illnesses such as cancer, mental disorders, or asymptomatic HIV (Blanck 2000a, 204).[45] Equal Employment Opportunity Commission regulations define "major life activities" as "caring for oneself, performing manual tasks, walking, seeing, hearing, speaking, breathing, learning, and working" (29 C.F.R. Part 1630.2(I)).

The attempts to eliminate the "regarded as" prong in Congress were defeated with the explanation that it was necessary to protect people without disabilities, such as cancer survivors or burn victims, who might suffer discrimination because of stereotypes based on ignorance or fear (Burgdorf 1997). Because of the uncertainty of the number of persons within the "regarded as" prong, it was clear that Congress's finding of 43 million people with disabilities was very imprecise and intended as a floor rather than a ceiling (Bristo 2002).[46]

Seen by many as "the most important piece of disability policy in the 20th century" (Pfeiffer 1996a, 272), the ADA is wide-ranging, banning discrimination on the basis of disabilities in employment (Title I), in the delivery of state and local government services, including public transportation (Title II), in public accommodations (Title III), and in telecommunications (Title IV). Title V consists of miscellaneous provisions, including attorneys' fees, alternative dispute resolution, retaliation, consistency with state laws, and insurance underwriting. To ensure continuity between the legislative acts, Congress directed the courts and executive branch agencies to follow the legal interpretations and regulations of section 504 when implementing the ADA.

Within less than a year after its passage, the EEOC and the DOJ, the two primary agencies responsible for promulgating regulations, along with the Department of Transportation (DOT), had received almost four thousand comments and heard testimony from almost three thousand people. And on the one-year anniversary, they issued final rules: the EEOC in employment (Title I) and the DOJ in public services and programs in state and local governments (Title II) and public accommodations (Title III). Soon the DOT, the Architectural and Transportation Barriers Compliance Board, and the Federal Communications Commission also issued final rules. A wide range of agencies, such as HHS, Commerce, and the Small Business Administration, to name a few, were also implicated in implementing the ADA (Craig 1999, 219).

The ADA as a Civil Rights Law

Most members of the disability community reacted very positively to the ADA. Bristo (2002) says it "reflect[ed] a paradigm shift of disabled people redefining and reclaiming disability," replacing the medical model with a social and civil rights model. Although Dart (2001) qualifies his comment by saying "an advocate is never satisfied," he believes that, "relative to the rights mandates in the past," the ADA was a "profound success."

One activist cited a "different spirit" between section 504 and the ADA, proclaiming that the ADA renewed a spirit of ending second-class citizenship. Sheila Thomas-Akhtar (2001), formerly the civil rights information and technical assistance coordinator at Access Living in Chicago and now a paralegal in the Civil Rights and Disability Rights Bureaus of the Illinois attorney general's office, simply states that the law "changed her life." And according to Wright (2000), "the face of America changed dramatically because of the ADA." One respondent reported that, as a result of the ADA, more people with disabilities are "out and about." And Ogle (2001) says that, because of the ADA, people with disabilities "have the right to pursue the American dream." Feldblum (2000b) claims the ADA "changed awareness of people with disabilities, that they have a right to opportunity, rather than pity." Moreover, she states, society is more aware of physical accessibility for which the ADA is responsible, and it has made people with disabilities aware that they have rights in employment settings and can ask for accommodations. David Hanson, commissioner of the Mayor's Office for People with Disabilities in Chicago, characterizes the ADA's achievements as "monumental" (Hanson 2001). Katy Beh Neas (2002) proclaims the ADA the "Emancipation Proclamation for people with disabilities."

Although the new law was full of promises, it was also "vague and contradictory" (Switzer 2001, 629). Litigants soon learned that "the Act was not being interpreted as its drafters and supporters within the disability community had planned" (Krieger 2000, 7). Indeed, Diller (2000, 20) reports that "ADA advocates have looked on in horror as the case law has unfolded." Burris and Moss (2000, 31) suggest that a possible reason for the disparity between hope and reality was that although Congress identified the nation's aims as "assuring equality of opportunity, full participation, independent living, and economic self-sufficiency" for people with disabilities, the law was only directed at ending discrimination, a much narrower aim that, by itself, was unlikely to achieve the lofty goals of the disability community.

The framers of the ADA had expected the courts to base their interpretations on their experience with earlier antidiscrimination laws such as Title VII and the Age Discrimination in Employment Act (ADEA) of 1967, as well as the legislative intent, case law, and agency regulations of the 1973 Rehabilitation Act (Befort and Thomas 1999). Although some traced the problems of enforcement to the law's vague and somewhat ill-defined terms (see Pfeiffer 1996a), the activists who framed the ADA and championed it in court defended its vagueness as necessary. They believed it was their best chance to achieve a disability rights law and believed that Congress's intention of securing equal treatment for people with disabilities was clearly manifested.

Curtis Decker (2000), executive director of the National Association of Protection and Advocacy Systems (NAPAS), also believes that vagueness is not a problem; in his view, the flexibility within the law is advantageous.

Others agreed, expressing concern that absolute terms, such as dollar amounts or percentages, would have been subject to misinterpretation by the courts. Such laws are intentionally vague, one said. The problem, according to James Dickson, formerly at the National Organization on Disability (NOD) and currently at the American Association of People with Disabilities (AAPD), was not that the law was poorly drafted, but that there was a lack of political will to enforce it. "The terms are clear and the *Congressional Record* spoke to Congress's intent," he says (Dickson 2001).

When asked whether they view the ADA as a civil rights law, the disability rights advocates unhesitatingly proclaimed it a civil rights law. Wallace Winter, director of the Disability Law Project at the Legal Assistance Foundation of Chicago, observes that "many disability rights advocates pushing for the ADA derived their ideas and strategies from the civil rights leaders of the 1960s and '70s" (Winter 2002). "Certainly it is a civil rights bill," says Carolyn Osolinik (2001), a Ted Kennedy senior staffer for civil rights issues from 1981 until 1992, "we used other civil rights laws as models and analogies." Susan Henderson (2001), managing director of DREDF, analogizes the ADA to other civil rights bills in its effort to "break down barriers and attitudes." Frank Laski (2002), executive director of the Massachusetts Mental Health Legal Advisors Committee, emphasizes that "its origin and genesis is civil rights." But, he says, there are differences. The principle behind a traditional civil rights bill is "equality and a level playing field." The principle behind the ADA is "accommodations and affirmative steps." Thus, he states, you "can't simply end discrimination by treating a disabled person like everybody else." He observes that Title VII theory is not as useful in disability discrimination cases—largely because of accommodation issues—and that there has been more negative reaction to ADA litigation from employers and courts than to race and sex discrimination cases.

Others also differentiated the ADA from traditional laws guaranteeing equality. Stan Eichner, director of litigation of the Disability Law Center in Massachusetts, distinguishes it from other civil rights law, saying "since the ADA, in certain instances, imposes an affirmative obligation to provide reasonable accommodations, it is the only civil rights law where an organization might face liability for treating everyone exactly the same." He also notes that, "it is the only civil rights law in which rights are balanced against costs" (Eichner 2002). Breslin (2001) agrees that the ADA is a civil rights law, but says it is structurally different from other civil rights laws: first, because it specifies that discrimination can take physical forms (as in architectural barriers); and second, because equal employment and other opportunities may require accommodations. As a civil rights law, its impact, which is significant, will be limited because it only deals with the issue of discrimination, not the barriers that arise from economic structures. The ADA does not, nor is it intended to, deal with the problem of poverty among people with disabilities (except insofar as discrimination limits opportunities).

After pointing out that the ADA had followed the path of the traditional civil rights laws with civil disobedience and grass roots organizing, Robert Herman (2002), senior advocacy attorney for the Paralyzed Veterans of America, focuses on the differences between the ADA and those laws. The ADA, he says, requires society to ignore disabilities and, at the same time, to pay attention to them. The 1964 Civil Rights Act did not require positive action; but with the ADA, it is not sufficient to say to people with disabilities, "you can come into my restaurant, you have to build a ramp [for them]."

3 Disability Rights
and the Workplace

Title I, which took effect on July 26, 1992, applies to private employers, state and local governments, employment agencies, and labor unions; it prohibits discrimination "against a qualified individual with a disability because of the disability of such individual" in hiring, firing, and promotion, as well as "other terms, conditions, and privileges of employment" (42 U.S.C. §12112(a)). A "qualified individual with a disability" is one "who, with or without reasonable accommodation, can perform the essential functions of the employment position that such individual holds or desires" (42 U.S.C. §12111(8)).[1]

When a qualified employee or job applicant requests an accommodation, the employer must comply unless it "would impose an undue hardship on the operation of the business" (42 U.S.C. §12112 (b)(5)(A)). An undue hardship is "an action requiring significant difficulty or expense," based on the "nature and cost of the accommodation," and the size, financial resources, and nature of the business operation (42 U.S.C. §12111 (10)(A)(B)(i)(iii)). Additionally, employers may defend themselves against a charge of discrimination by showing that the selection criteria or qualification standard was "job-related and consistent with business necessity" or by showing that the applicant or employee "pose[s] a direct threat to the health and safety of other individuals in the workplace" (42 U.S.C. §12113 (a)(b)).

Disability and Employment

The most commonly cited evidence of the employment status of people with disabilities is a poll conducted by Harris Interactive (the Harris Poll) and commissioned by NOD. It provides a glimpse of the employment status of people with disabilities in the United States. Beginning in 1986, Harris began conducting surveys of a sample population of people with disabilities and comparing their responses to a sample of people without disabilities; the surveys were duplicated in 1994, 1998, and, most recently, in 2000. Questions in the 2000 *Survey of Americans with Disabilities* revolved around myriad lifestyle issues, including education, health care, access to transportation, income, and employment (NOD/Harris 2000).

The employment statistics confirm Congress's assessment of underemployment among people with disabilities. According to this survey, among working-age people eighteen to sixty-four without disabilities, 81 percent worked either full-time or part-time; the comparable figure for people with disabilities was 32 percent, a gap of 49 percent. Put another way, while eight in ten people without disabilities were employed at least part-time, only about three in ten people with disabilities worked at least part-time. Moreover, the employment rate of people with disabilities has been rather consistent, varying only by a few percentage points between years surveyed.

Among people with disabilities who are employed, about one-third (36 percent) reported being subject to discrimination in the workplace, most often being rejected for a job for which they were qualified. Perhaps the most interesting response was to a question to unemployed people about whether they preferred to be working: 67 percent of unemployed people with disabilities said they would prefer to be working, only 37 percent of unemployed people without disabilities said they wanted to be working. Not surprisingly, the income data confirm the employment picture: only 10 percent of people without disabilities had an annual household income of $15,000 or less; among people with disabilities, 29 percent had an annual household income of $15,000 or less. At the other end of the income scale, only 16 percent of people with disabilities reported having an annual household income of more than $50,000, compared to 39 percent of people without disabilities.

The Harris Poll data reveal a number of employment-related concerns among people with disabilities. Compared to people without disabilities, their earnings are lower, fewer are employed, and many face discrimination on the job, most often by being denied the job they seek. In discussing employment trends over time, the survey shows that although there has been some improvement in a few employment indicators over the last fourteen years, people with disabilities lag behind people without disabilities in employment and income status.

Discussing the employment status of people with disabilities following passage of the ADA, Stein (2000b, 315) notes that, despite the booming economy and declining unemployment rate in the 1990s, "unemployment of working-age individuals with disabilities appears not to have similarly diminished." He attributes this in part to a societal lack of understanding about the capabilities of people with disabilities and the need to combat discrimination. Schwochau and Blanck (2000, 272) state more forcefully that "the ADA's track record in improving employment opportunities for individuals with disabilities appears dismal."[2]

Despite the opportunity to seek relief in the courts, Moss and Malin (1998) argue that ADA lawsuits have not been very effective in combating discrimination because of the victims' unwillingness to sue. Based on the difficulty of proving discrimination and the restricted availability of damages, victims engage in a cost-benefit analysis and rationally conclude that there is little likelihood that they will benefit from a lawsuit; this is especially true for plaintiffs contemplating suit for a refusal to hire. These perceptions are further heightened by the court's tendency to encourage compromise solutions as well as the employer's ability to steer cases toward arbitration rather than litigation. As an alternative to litigation, Moss and Malin (1998) propose that the public sector fund the accommodations necessary to allow people with disabilities to work. However, in the current fiscal climate, it is unlikely that such a plan will be adopted, and whatever its drawbacks, litigation or the threat of litigation may be the most effective way to combat discrimination on the basis of disability.

Administrative Enforcement

Congress designated the EEOC as the lead agency with responsibility for regulatory and enforcement authority of the ADA. On July 26, 1991, one year after the law was enacted, the agency issued regulations, which, as directed by Congress, closely followed section 504 regulations.[3] Enforcement of the law by the EEOC began on July 26, 1992, when the employment discrimination provisions of the act became effective. According to the data compiled by the agency, there were 174,244 individual ADA charge filings from FY1992 to FY2002, out of a total of 896,243 employment discrimination charges filed with the EEOC during the decade.[4] By way of comparison, there were 179,809 Title VII charge receipts filed during this time (EEOC 2003a).

Following the model of existing federal antidiscrimination workplace procedures, Title I plaintiffs are required to file charges with the EEOC or a state or local fair employment practice agency before initiating court action.[5] From July 26, 1992, to September 30, 1995, EEOC data show that complaints about back impairments represented the largest category of charges filed with the EEOC (Stansky 1996, 68). When charges are filed, the agency investigates to determine if there is "reasonable cause" to believe discrimination has occurred. If so, the agency usually attempts to conciliate between the parties; if an investigation finds there is no reasonable cause to believe the discrimination occurred, the complaining party may seek judicial review.[6]

The agency was also given the authority to sue on its own. From FY1993 to FY2002, the EEOC filed (or intervened in a suit filed by a private plaintiff) in 491 ADA cases; as a basis of comparison, the agency filed suit or intervened in 2,265 Title VII suits, more than four times the number of ADA suits (EEOC 2003b).[7]

Title I and Civil Rights Remedies

Following the model of Title VII of the 1964 Civil Rights Act in acknowledging that racial discrimination impedes employment opportunities, the ADA recognizes that people with disabilities may be excluded from the workplace when employers are influenced by society's "stereotypes and inaccurate assumptions" about their inability to perform the job (Mudrick 1997, 56). As in Title VII, amended by the 1991 Civil Rights Act, successful Title I plaintiffs may receive injunctive relief, back pay, attorneys' fees, and, in some cases, compensatory and punitive damages.[8] Also, like Title VII, the ADA bars both disparate treatment (intentional discrimination) and disparate impact (adverse discriminatory effects). Plaintiffs in ADA cases may be awarded back pay in either case, but most courts only allow compensatory damages for disparate treatment claims. In adjudicating disparate treatment claims, the courts generally follow the procedure outlined in *McDonnell Douglas v. Green* (1973), although the Supreme Court has not spoken to this issue nor to the matter of the allocation of the burden of proof in ADA employment discrimination cases (Malloy 2001).[9]

In ADA cases, disparate treatment—commonly known as intentional discrimination—claims arise when plaintiffs assert that an employment decision was motivated by their disability; to defend against such charges, employers must show their actions were motivated by legitimate, nondiscriminatory reasons. The employee has an opportunity to prove that the employer's reason was merely a pretext for discrimination. Disparate impact claims involve allegations of neutral policies that adversely impact people with disabilities (Laing 2002, 917–18).[10]

Unlike Title VII, which allows persons of either sex and of all races to show an employer acted on the basis of sex or race, the ADA only applies to people with disabilities (Parmet 2003). Consequently, all ADA plaintiffs must initially prove they have a disability, that is, that they are within the class of persons Congress intended to protect in the law (Mudrick 1997; Feldblum 2000a; Wilkinson and Frieden 2000). Thus, before adjudicating the issue of discrimination, the court must determine if the plaintiff meets the definition of disability. This stage of the lawsuit has occupied the lion's share of attention, sowing confusion in the courts as well as among litigants about what constitutes a disability (Brown 2003, 118). One study indicated that more than 1,100 reported ADA cases involved consideration of the definition of disability and that two-thirds of the plaintiffs in these cases were considered not disabled (Edmonds 2002, 324).

In allowing employers to present "an undue hardship" defense, Congress empowered the courts to gauge the extent to which the physical environment must be altered or an alternative procedure established to allow an employee to function in the job (Miller 2000). Because such a determination is largely based on the cost of the accommodation relative to the income or assets of the business, a court's finding of discrimination will often vary with the nature of the plaintiff and the nature of the defendant.[11] By contrast, because Title VII does not permit a cost defense to a charge of discrimination, the size of the business does not affect the outcome of the case as long as it exceeds the statutory minimum. Additionally, remedying a Title VII violation may require the employer to compensate the victim of the discrimination, but it typically does not entail continuing costs in the form of accommodations.

The ADA requires employers to do more than merely cease discriminatory conduct; they must provide affirmative support, that is, accommodations, to enable people with disabilities to function in the workplace (Tucker 2001).[12] Employers must offer persons with disabilities accommodations that are not offered to people without disabilities. To secure "equality of opportunity, full participation, independent living, and economic self-sufficiency," the ADA is based on a principle of "structural equality" that mandates that employers treat people with disabilities differently from people without disabilities to achieve the equality encapsulated in the law (42 U.S.C. §12101 (a)(8); Krieger 2003, 3–4; see Karlan and Rutherglen 1996). Most employment discrimination laws compel equality of opportunity, which is described by Krieger (2000, 4–5) as "formal equality." The ADA embodies "structural equality," which not only requires an absence of discrimination, but in requiring "reasonable accommodation" mandates affirmative action to achieve an equality of result (see Scotch and Schriner 1997; Diller 2000; Batavia and Schriner 2001).

Interpreting the Law Narrowly

There is a consensus among most disability scholars and disability rights advocates that the federal courts, particularly the Supreme Court, are chiefly responsible for the constrained implementation of the ADA, and that neither Congress (for drafting a badly written statute), nor the federal agencies (for insufficient enforcement), nor the plaintiffs (for bringing nonmeritorious cases), nor the attorneys (for poor representation) bear primary responsibility for the ADA's failure to live up to the expectations of the disability community.

There are a number of theories that address the judiciary's reaction to disability claims in the employment arena. In her examination of workplace disability policy from World War II to the present, O'Brien (2001, 78) contends that the courts' constricted interpretation of Title I stems from the judiciary's adherence to the "whole man theory" of rehabilitation, a view "focused on barriers in the minds of disabled people." This 1950s approach to disability was characterized by a belief that normalcy for people with disabilities meant they must adjust themselves to society and overcome the obstacles hindering them, rather than requiring society to remove the barriers that prevent them from being fully engaged in it. In her view, the courts' acceptance of the whole man theory was translated into a belief that people with disabilities must adapt themselves to the workplace rather than the reverse.

She argues that beginning with its interpretation of disability rights under section 504, and continuing into ADA Title I litigation, the courts have forced disability plaintiffs to prove they are worthy of protection under the law, that is, that they are truly disabled according to some predetermined judicial standard. She attributes the poor showing of Title I plaintiffs to the judiciary's refusal to accept the ADA's guarantee of equal opportunity for people with disabilities. Indeed, she asserts, "according to a majority of justices on the Supreme Court, society had *reason* for prejudice because disabled people were 'different'" (O'Brien 2001, 139; emphasis in the original).[13]

Diller (2000) rejects a number of plausible interpretations about ADA Title I litigation, namely, that the claims filed are weak and frivolous, that the law is inherently flawed because of its vagueness, or that the judiciary has not had enough time to become acquainted with the law and, given time and greater experience in adjudicating ADA claims, the decisions will be more reflective of the legislative intent. In his view, none of these adequately explain the judicial record that so heavily favors employers. For example, if the statute were merely vague, the courts might not necessarily follow congressional intent, but they would not heavily tilt their decisions in one direction only—toward the employer. He contends that the best explanation for the judiciary's circumscribed interpretation of the ADA is "backlash" based on the courts' unwillingness to acquiesce in the basic premise of the law that employment discrimination on the basis of disability is a violation of the rights of disabled people (see also Krieger 2000).

Diller maintains that the courts believe the statute confers an unearned benefit on people with disabilities and they seek to ascertain whether the plaintiff has earned the benefit of the law rather than whether the defendant has deviated from it. He believes the courts are not favorably disposed toward civil rights litigation as a whole and their antipathy is heightened in ADA cases by their perception that plaintiffs demand affirmative action from employers rather than equality.

In his analysis of Title I litigation, Soifer (2000, 1292) similarly charges that the Court has misconstrued the statute's legislative intent and misapplied its text. Although Congress created a law with a clearly articulated view of discrimination on the basis of disability, Soifer believes that "the Court set out to prune the ADA's capacious definition" in its decisionmaking. Focusing on the Supreme Court's 1998–1999 term, he notes the contradiction between the Court's emphasis on individualized determinations of disability claimants and its willingness to bow to the employer's desire for bright lines and rules, in essence allowing them to "retain discretion to hire and fire as they wish" (Soifer 2000, 1302). In his eyes, the Title I cases reflect the Court's lack of concern for human dignity, in contrast to its concern for the dignity of the state embodied in its Eleventh Amendment decisions. Reiterating this theme, Soifer argues that in adhering to the principles of the "new federalism jurisprudence," the Court evidences more concern for states' rights than human rights, particularly the rights of disabled people. Additionally, he attributes part of the Court's narrowing construction of the ADA to the discomfort the justices may feel about people with disabilities and their inability to empathize with such plaintiffs. Returning to this topic several years later, Soifer (2003, 1290) accuses the majority on the Court of being "firmly unconvinced" that people with disabilities require legal protection—or at least believing that the federal government is barred from providing such protection.

Colker (2004, 48) lends her voice to the criticism of the courts as well for misinterpreting the law. She contends that ample documentation exists to clarify the statute's intent and "that the blame lies with the judiciary that has refused to educate itself to the history of this statute." Barring plaintiffs' access to the courtroom on the grounds that they are not disabled ignores the voluminous evidence that Congress intended the law to encompass a broad segment of society. Both scholar and advocates insist that there is substantial evidence that Congress intended the ADA to offer broad protection to persons with disabilities. Their position is supported by the *Congressional Record,* which documents that the controversy about the reach of the act was primarily limited to concerns about the extent to which the law encompassed drug users and persons with AIDS/HIV.

The Supreme Court and Title I Litigation

Although such criticisms apply to the federal courts generally, not surprisingly, the Supreme Court draws the most fire by setting the tone for ADA litigation. Table 3.1, which presents the employment discrimination rulings decided by the Supreme Court, shows that the Court has only ruled in the plaintiffs' favor in three cases.

Arbitration

In November 1998, the Court handed down its first ruling in an ADA employment case. *Wright v. Universal Maritime Service* (1998) presented a question about whether a general arbitration clause in a collective bargaining agreement required an employee to use the company's arbitration procedure for an alleged violation of the ADA. The employer argued that the collective bargaining agreement precluded the employee, Caesar Wright, from seeking judicial review of his ADA claim. In a decision announced by Justice Scalia, the Court unanimously rejected this position, holding that there was no "presumption of arbitrability" for an ADA claim such as Wright's (*Wright*

Table 3.1 Supreme Court employment discrimination cases, 1998–2003

Case	Year	Issue	Disposition
Wright	1998	Collective bargaining agreement and ADA suit	Pro-Plaintiff
Cleveland	1999	Disability benefits and ADA claim	Pro-Plaintiff
Sutton	1999	Mitigating measures and definition of disability	Pro-Defendant
Murphy	1999	Mitigating measures and definition of disability	Pro-Defendant
Kirkingburg	1999	Mitigating measures and definition of disability	Pro-Defendant
Garrett	2001	State immunity from suit for money damages	Pro-Defendant
Williams	2002	Definition of "substantial limitation on major life activity"	Pro-Defendant
Waffle House	2002	Arbitration agreement and EEOC suit	Pro-Plaintiff
Barnett	2002	Definition of "undue hardship"	Pro-Defendant
Echazabal	2002	Definition of "direct threat"	Pro-Defendant
Clackamas	2003	Definition of "employee"	Indeterminate
Hernandez	2003	Policy against rehiring employees terminated for workplace misconduct	Pro-Defendant

1998, 77). Scalia explained that the belief that most disputes between labor and management should be submitted to arbitration arises out of the Court's interpretation of the 1947 Labor Management Relations Act and is based on the premise that arbitrators are best qualified to interpret collective bargaining agreements. In this case, however, because the dispute revolved around interpretation of a federal statute rather than the collective bargaining agreement, arbitrators would have no special expertise. Although *Wright* arose from an employment discrimination action based on disability, because the Court's decision was grounded in its analysis of the collective bargaining agreement, the ruling was only tangentially related to a claim of right under the ADA.

Social Security Disability Insurance

The Court's next decision, *Cleveland v. Policy Management Systems* (1999), resolved a dispute among the circuits about whether beneficiaries of the Social Security Disability Insurance (SSDI) program were barred from filing suits for employment discrimination under the ADA. In January 1994, Carolyn Cleveland suffered a stroke and applied for SSDI benefits; fulfilling the requirements of the SSDI program, she claimed she was unable to work.[14] She returned to work in a few months and, when she informed the Social Security Administration, it denied her claim. A few months later, her employer fired her. When she reapplied for SSDI benefits, she was initially denied, but was eventually awarded them. A week before the agency reversal, she filed an ADA suit, claiming that her employer had refused to accommodate her disability. The appellate court affirmed the district court's grant of summary judgment for the employer, holding that Cleveland's ADA lawsuit for employment discrimination on the basis of disability was incompatible with her claim for SSDI benefits. To collect the SSDI benefits, the court said, she would have to show she was too disabled to work, and to win her Title I action, she would have to show she met the ADA's requirement of being able to work (*Cleveland* 1997).

The Supreme Court parsed the meaning of disability within the ADA and the Social Security Act and considered the intersection of the two laws. In a unanimous opinion delivered by Justice Stephen Breyer, the high court agreed that the language of the two statutes appeared to contradict each other, but held that "the two claims do not inherently conflict . . . because there are too many situations in which an SDI claim and an ADA claim can comfortably exist side by side" (*Cleveland* 1999, 802–3). The key to understanding the compatibility of these two statutes, Breyer said, is that under the ADA, a "qualified individual with a disability" may be able to perform the job if the disability is accommodated by the employer. Largely because of the pressure of millions of claims, the Social Security Administration does not consider the question of accommodation in determining an applicant's eligibility for SSDI.[15] Additionally, Breyer noted, even if the claims were conflicting, it is permissible to offer two alternative legal theories in a case and allow the court to decide which one to accept. The Court remanded the plaintiff's claim to the court below, ruling that the case should not have been dismissed out of hand, but that the plaintiff should have been given an opportunity to explain why her ADA and SSDI claims were not inconsistent.

Definition of Disability

Less than a month after *Cleveland* was decided, on June 22, 1999, the Court's rulings in three companion cases, known as the "*Sutton* trilogy," rocked disability rights advocates, who insisted that the analysis of mitigating measures was contrary to congressional intent as well as the EEOC regulations.[16]

In this trio of cases decided in 1999, the Court was asked to determine the meaning of disability within the act. Specifically, it had to decide whether an individual who took corrective measures to alleviate the effects of an impairment was not disabled and therefore outside the protection of the law. The first case arose when twin sisters, Karen Sutton and Kimberly Hinton, applied for the job of global airline pilot with United Air Lines. As the circuit court noted, they were qualified by the Federal Aviation Administration (FAA) to fly for regional commuter airlines, but they wanted to fly for a major airline (*Sutton v. United Air Lines* 1997). Although they reached the interview stage of the application process, they were told that because of their severe myopia (nearsightedness), they were not qualified for the position.[17] The airline required uncorrected vision of 20/100, and theirs was at least 20/200 in one eye and 20/400 in the other. When corrected with contact lenses, their vision was 20/20. They filed charges with the EEOC, claiming the airline discriminated against them on the basis of their disability. After receiving the requisite "right to sue" letter from the EEOC, they initiated a federal action, alleging that they were disabled because their myopia was an impairment that substantially limited the major life activity of seeing. They also claimed they were "regarded as" disabled by United in violation of the ADA because they were precluded from working in an entire class of jobs as global airline pilots, without any proof that the vision requirement was related to job performance or safety.

The district court dismissed the action, adopting the airline's view that because their visual impairment was correctable, they were not substantially limited in any major life activity and thus did not meet the definition of disability (*Sutton* 1996).[18] Nor, said the court, did they satisfy the "regarded as" prong of the definition of disability because the airline did not perceive them as substantially limited in performing a range of jobs, but only the single job of global airline pilot. The Tenth Circuit Court affirmed the lower court decision (*Sutton* 1997). The majority of circuits had ruled in the other direction, disagreeing with the Tenth on whether mitigating measures, including eyeglasses and contact lenses, negated a finding of disability.

Justice Sandra Day O'Connor announced the 7–2 opinion for the Court. She began by explaining that although the act authorized three federal agencies, the EEOC, DOJ, and DOT, to issue regulations to implement specific titles of the act, Congress had not delegated such responsibility for the general provisions of the law, including the definition of the word "disability."[19] The sisters had argued that the EEOC guidelines supported their position that disabilities are to be assessed in their uncorrected state, but the Court disagreed, finding that the guidelines were "an impermissible interpretation of the ADA" (*Sutton* 1999, 482).

Addressing the primary issue in the case, whether these job applicants were disabled within the meaning of the law, the Court emphasized that the decision hinged "on whether disability is to be determined with or without reference to corrective measures" (*Sutton* 1999, 481). The plaintiffs argued that because the statute itself did not provide the answer, the Court should defer to the EEOC's "Interpretive Guidance," which specified that mitigating measures should not be considered when deciding whether an individual is substantially limited in a major life activity. The airline maintained that because the law is written in the present tense, it "requires that the substantial limitations actually and presently exist" (*Sutton* 1999, 481). The Court agreed that the terms of the statute required a reviewing court to take mitigating measures into account when determining disability status and, because the statute was clear on this point, there was no need to look to legislative history or administrative guidance for the answer.

O'Connor cited three reasons which, taken together, formed the basis of the majority opinion. Applying grammatical tools of analysis, she explained that "the phrase substantially limits [a major life activity] appears in the Act as a present indicative verb form" and rejected the interpretation that disability arises from an impairment that "might, could, or would be substantially limiting if mitigating measures were not taken" (*Sutton* 1999, 482). She acknowledged that a person who takes corrective measures still has an impairment, but that the impairment is no longer substantially limiting once these measures are taken. Second, because the ADA requires courts to ascertain whether a disability exists "with respect to an individual," judges must make an individualized determination about whether the plaintiff is disabled, and not simply evaluate a group of people with the impairment in question. Thus, disability must be judged by the extent to which the impairment affects an individual, and not simply whether the individual has an impairment. Using the example of diabetes, she noted that individuals are not considered disabled merely because they have diabetes; the court must examine the course of the disease and the treatment, that is, the mitigating measures, to determine if the diabetes impairs a major life activity. Indeed, she added, by ignoring the effect of medical treatment on the individual, a court would not be able to consider any potential negative side effects that could increase the likelihood of a finding of disability.

O'Connor next pointed out the discrepancy between Congress's finding of 43 million people with disabilities and the estimated 100 million people in the nation who need vision correction, the 28 million plus people with hearing impairments, and the approximately 50 million who suffer from hypertension. If Congress had intended to include these three types of individuals within the meaning of disability, most of whom were able to mitigate the effects of their impairments, it would not have identified only 43 million people as disabled. She concluded by affirming the lower court ruling that the use of mitigating measures such as eyeglasses or contact lenses, correcting vision to 20/20, meant that the plaintiffs were not substantially limited and therefore not protected by the antidiscrimination provisions of the act.

Turning to the plaintiffs' argument that they satisfied the "regarded as" prong of the ADA, O'Connor said that employers may use physical criteria in making an employment decision as long as they do not make such a decision "based on a physical or mental impairment, real or imagined, that is regarded as substantially limiting a major life activity." She added, "an employer is free to decide that physical characteristics or medical conditions that do not rise to the level of an impairment —such as one's height, build, or singing voice—are preferable to others, just as it is free to decide that some limiting, but not *substantially* limiting, impairments make individuals less than ideally suited for a job" (*Sutton* 1999, 490–91).[20] She ended by questioning the validity of the EEOC's inclusion of "working" as a major life activity, but because the parties had not challenged it, the Court felt it was not required to determine how much deference the agency was due. Nevertheless, assuming the regulations were valid, she noted, an inability to perform the major life activity of working refers to a broad class of jobs rather than the one specific job of global airline pilot, as in the *Sutton* case.

In her concurring opinion, Justice Ruth Bader Ginsburg said that she was most persuaded by Congress's reference to 43 million people with disabilities, coupled with its characterization of them as a politically powerless "discrete and insular minority."[21] Because the number of people with correctable impairments, especially those with poor eyesight, vastly exceeded 43 million, she believed that Congress could not have intended to include such people within the protection of the ADA. Additionally, because people with such impairments straddle all economic and social classes, they had not been subjected to a history of discrimination and did not raise concerns about political powerlessness.

In a dissent joined by Justice Breyer, Justice John Paul Stevens began by acknowledging that Congress may not have intended to extend its definition of disability to people with poor vision such as these pilot applicants.

However, rejecting the textualist approach and applying the traditional rules of statutory interpretation, he emphasized that to effectuate the remedial purposes of the act, the Court "should give it a generous, rather than a miserly construction" (*Sutton* 1999, 495). After noting that his view was supported by eight of the nine circuits (and three administrative agencies), Stevens divided his analysis into two parts, asking first whether, as a general proposition, corrective measures should play a role in the determination of disability, and second, whether corrective measures such as eyeglasses or contact lenses should be considered.

He began by reviewing the ADA's three-part definition of disability, noting that an individual with a prosthesis, who, by compensating for the loss of a limb, was able to perform a job on a par with a person with full use of limbs, would not fall within any of the three parts of the Court's definition of disability. Such individuals would be denied the protection of the ADA even though Congress had clearly intended the law to apply to them.[22] In his view, the act should be interpreted as inquiring whether an impairment that limits or has limited the individual existed before it was corrected. "This reading," he noted, "avoids the counterintuitive conclusion that the ADA's safeguards vanish when individuals make themselves more employable by ascertaining ways to overcome their physical or mental limitations" (*Sutton* 1999, 499). And, unlike the majority, he felt that the Court should resolve any lingering ambiguity by referring to the statute's legislative history. In his review of the legislative history, he quoted from congressional committee reports, all of which specified that disabilities such as diabetes, epilepsy, heart disease, and hearing impairments fell within the first prong of the definition of disability, regardless of correction or medication. Moreover, he noted, the regulations and guidelines of the executive branch agencies fully supported this position.

Justice Stevens did not deny the airline's right to establish a vision standard, nor did he insist that these applicants must be hired. Rather, his point was that the plaintiffs must be given an opportunity to present their case in court, that is, they must be allowed to offer proof that the defendant's conduct was discriminatory. This case, he insisted, merely asked whether these plaintiffs were protected by the ADA. He concluded by saying that, "although I express no opinion on the ultimate merits of [the plaintiffs'] claim, I am persuaded that they have a disability covered by the ADA" (*Sutton* 1999, 513). Their claim should not have been dismissed; instead, the lower court should have judged the merits of their case and required the airline to articulate and defend its vision criteria in court.

Justice Breyer's brief dissent pointed out that when faced with a choice of including members of a class, some of whom Congress may not have wanted to include, or excluding those whom Congress clearly wanted to include, the majority had opted for the latter, even though "the statute's language, structure, basic purposes and history require us to choose the former" (*Sutton* 1999, 513).

In the second of the trilogy, *Murphy v. United Parcel Service* (1999), the Court was asked to decide if a man with hypertension was disabled within the meaning of the ADA. United Parcel Service (UPS) fired Vaughn Murphy from his position as a mechanic and driver after it discovered that his blood pressure exceeded the limits imposed by DOT for commercial drivers and he was precluded from obtaining DOT certification.

Murphy's Title I suit was dismissed when the district court granted the company's motion for summary judgment. The court held that in light of the ameliorating effect of his blood pressure medication, he was not disabled (*Murphy* 1996). The appellate court affirmed, agreeing that he was "not an individual with a disability within the meaning of the ADA" (*Murphy* 1998, 2).

O'Connor's opinion for the 7–2 Court narrowly framed the question as "whether, under the ADA, the determination of whether an individual's impairment 'substantially limits' one or more major life activities should be made without consideration of mitigating measures" (*Murphy* 1999, 521). Reiterating the rule just announced in *Sutton,* she upheld the lower court's award of summary judgment for the company. Moreover, she said, Murphy did not meet the "regarded as" prong of the definition of disability because that would have meant that UPS viewed his hypertension as a substantial limitation on a major life activity when, in fact, it was not. United Parcel Service had argued that it did not regard him as having a substantial limitation, but rather regarded him as unqualified because he was unable to meet the standard for DOT certification.[23] Asking whether this was merely a cover-up for the fact that UPS actually regarded Murphy as substantially limited in the major life activity of working, O'Connor concluded that it was not. At most, UPS regarded him incapable only of performing the particular job requiring DOT certification, that of a truck driver.

The last case, *Albertsons, Inc. v. Kirkingburg* (1999), addressed another question related to mitigating measures. Hallie Kirkingburg suffered from amblyopia in his left eye and effectively had monocular vision. When he was hired by the Albertsons grocery store chain, he was erroneously certified as meeting DOT's vision standard. Two years later, when he was retested, the doctor reported that he fell below the DOT standard and could not be recertified. He sought a waiver from DOT, but before any action was taken, Albertsons fired him on the grounds that he had not met the DOT standard for vision. Although he subsequently obtained the waiver, the store refused to rehire him.

Speaking for a unanimous Court, Justice David Souter cited the principal issue as being whether Kirkingburg's particular vision problem, amblyopia, was a physical impairment within the meaning of the ADA, that is, whether it substantially limited the major life activity of seeing.[24] Souter began by noting that the appellate court's definition of disability was too lenient; the lower court had allowed a mere difference in seeing to be translated into a substantial limitation in the major life activity of seeing. The court had also incorrectly discounted evidence that his brain compensated for his eye condition (considered a mitigating measure like medication or artificial devices) and thus failed to consider the effect of corrective measures in evaluating his claimed disability. And finally, by not assessing the specific manner and degree to which his sight was impaired, the circuit court had violated the ADA's requirement to consider an individual's limitation on a case-by-case basis. The ruling was for the defendant, with Souter saying that employers were entitled to rely on federal safety standards without having to defend their reliance on them.

These three decisions unleashed an outpouring of scholarly commentary, virtually all critical of the Court's narrow reading of the law. Feldblum (2000a, 106–8), one of the drafters of the ADA, argues that the Court had strayed from the widely accepted interpretation of the law under section 504 and, despite clear evidence of congressional intent, had misapplied the ADA. She compared the 1999 decisions to the precedent established by the lower courts in section 504 cases, maintaining that in the latter the courts had spent little time pondering the definition of "handicap" or assessing whether the plaintiff was really "handicapped." Their main concern was to determine if the employer's action was based on the individual's "handicap" and if the plaintiff was qualified for the job.

Quoting from the Senate Labor and Human Resources Committee report, Feldblum noted that the Senate had indicated its satisfaction with how the courts interpreted the term "handicap" in section 504 cases; moreover, it had considered and rejected attempts to narrow the definition of disability in the ADA beyond drug addiction and selected psychological and sexual disorders. She also cited the House Education and Labor Committee Report, showing that Congress had specifically intended to include diseases such as diabetes and epilepsy, even if controlled by medication, within the first prong of the definition of disability. In discussing these cases, Bristo (2002) reports that Tony Coelho, one of the framers of the ADA, commented to her that the Supreme Court had wrongly interpreted the law. "'Of course, I intended to cover myself,'" she quotes him saying.

Pointing to the same evidence of legislative intent, Parmet (2003) echoes this view, contending that the Court's approach to mitigating measures, which was diametrically opposed to Congress's, can best be explained by its adherence to the principle of textualism and its disregard for legislative and administrative interpretative statements. The Court, she said, has harkened back to an outmoded model of disability that preceded passage of section 504 in which individuals were easily classified as disabled or not disabled. But, as the legislative history indicates, Congress had a much broader perception of the class of people with disabilities, ranging from those who were totally disabled to those with impairments that could be mitigated by corrective measures. Although, in her view, most such individuals would satisfy the first part of the ADA definition of disability, if some courts were reluctant to consider such people disabled, they surely should agree that they met the third, "regarded as," prong. She concludes by summarizing the dilemma faced by people with disabilities: "if mitigating measures are considered, few, if any, of the millions of individuals who depend upon medication, prosthetic devices, or other means to function independently and successfully despite their impairments will be entitled to the benefits of the ADA." And, she continues, the door of the courthouse will only be open "to those with impairments that neither medical science nor human ingenuity can overcome" (130).

Whatever the merits of the plaintiffs' arguments in these three cases, the effect of the high court rulings was to render the ADA a nullity for many individuals. Selmi (2001, 567) characterizes the claims involved in these cases as "on the outer perimeter of the statute," indicating he was not surprised that the Court rejected them. His concern, however, is that the lower courts will rely on the *Sutton* trilogy to dismiss cases based on "claims nearly everyone would classify as involving disabilities," such as diabetes, epilepsy, and depression, by finding they do not fit within the definition of disability. He believes the judiciary's "bias" against the law is motivated by apprehension over the flood of litigation likely to ensue if the statute were more broadly defined.

State Immunity

Two years after the Court rocked the disability community with its narrow interpretation of the definition of disability, it handed down another Title I decision in *Board of Trustees of the University of Alabama v. Garrett* (2001). In this case, the state defended itself against the charge of discrimination by arguing that its sovereign immunity protected it from suit. The high court agreed, ruling that state employees are barred from bringing ADA suits for damages against state employers.

Substantial Limitation

In *Toyota Motor Manufacturing v. Williams* (2002), the Court resolved the issue of the proper standard for determining a substantial limitation in a major life activity. Ella Williams had been employed in Toyota's Kentucky manufacturing plant from 1990 until 1997. During that time, she developed bilateral carpal tunnel syndrome and bilateral tendonitis, affecting her ability to move her arms, wrists, and hands. After she was diagnosed, she worked in restricted activities for two years and then took medical leave and filed a claim with the Kentucky Workers' Compensation Board. She returned to work but soon filed suit, claiming Toyota was unwilling to accommodate her impairment. This suit was also settled and she returned to work in another capacity as part of the Quality Control Inspection Operations team, where she was able to perform two of the four tasks associated with the job. Two years later, Toyota announced that all members of the team would have to perform all tasks, requiring her to hold her arms above her head for long periods of time. Her condition flared up again and although there is a dispute about the sequence of events that followed, she eventually filed suit against Toyota.

The Sixth Circuit held that Williams's impairments were "sufficiently disabling," "analogous to having missing, damaged or deformed limbs that prevent her from doing the tasks associated with certain types of manual assembly line jobs" (*Williams v. Toyota Motor Manufacturing* 2000, 843). Based on this evidence, the court concluded she was substantially limited in a major life activity and her ability to perform household tasks or tend to her personal grooming did not undermine this conclusion.[25]

The Supreme Court reversed. Speaking for a unanimous Court, O'Connor pointed out that the appellate court had erroneously restricted its inquiry to her ability to perform tasks at work. The proper standard, she explained, began with the EEOC definition of a substantial limitation, but the regulations did not speak to the evidence needed to prove substantial limitation in the ability to perform manual tasks.[26] O'Connor first sought clarification from the dictionary, defining "substantial" as "considerable," "of central importance," "to a large degree," "major," and "important." Combining these elements, she concluded that major life activities were "activities that are of central importance to daily life" and cited congressional intent as the reason for "creat[ing] a demanding standard for qualifying as disabled" (*Toyota Motor Manufacturing v. Williams* 2002, 197). Echoing *Sutton*, she referred to the congressional finding of 43 million people with disabilities and maintained that if Congress had intended to include people unable to perform minor or isolated tasks within this group, the number of people with disabilities would have been a good deal higher.

The circuit court, she said, had erroneously limited its inquiry about the effect of her disability to the workplace only. Because the definition of disability applies to the entire act, not merely to Title I, the inquiry should not have been restricted to the workplace. Additionally, manual labor, especially that associated with a particular job, does not constitute the sum total, or even the most important, of such tasks in an individual's life; the courts must assess her overall ability to perform manual tasks. And because "household chores, bathing, and brushing one's teeth are among the types of manual tasks of central importance to people's daily lives," the lower court should have considered this evidence in determining whether Williams was substantially limited in the major life activity of performing manual tasks (*Toyota Motor Manufacturing v. Williams* 2002, 202).[27] Last, O'Connor said, although Williams could not fully engage in some of her former activities such as sweeping, dancing, and driving long distances, she had not shown she was unable to perform activities centrally important in the lives of a majority of people. Therefore, the appellate court erred in awarding her summary judgment on the issue of her disability.

Williams prompted a reaction from Hoyer, one of the prime congressional movers behind the ADA. He disputed O'Connor's interpretation of legislative intent, insisting that Congress had borrowed the language of the Rehabilitation Act in defining disability (or "handicap") because courts had "generously interpreted this definition. Moreover," he added, "we thought using established language would help us avoid a potentially divisive political debate over the definition of disabled" (*Washington Post,* January 20, 2002). Hoyer challenged the Court's definition of "substantially limited," insisting that Congress had not intended litigants to argue over whether plaintiffs were capable of performing mundane household chores or maintain personal grooming activities. Admitting it was impossible to divine the intent of the 535 members of Congress, he was sure most favored a broad interpretation of disability. Finally, he rejected the Court's reference to 43 million people with disabilities as a ceiling, when, in his view, the opposite was true; "the number we used wasn't designed to limit the effect of our legislation, but to show its breadth" (*Washington Post,* January 20, 2002). Decker (2000) also believes the courts have strayed from the legislature's intent and have a "misguided interpretation of what a disability is." Decisions such as the *Sutton* trilogy and *Williams* reflect the Court's constrained perspective on disability rights. The "Court's crabbed vision" (*Sutton* 1999, 513) of "major life activity" meant that people with impairments were forced to forfeit their protection under the act simply by continuing to live independently (see Annas 2003; Zucker 2003).

Although the Court did not address the issue of whether work was a major life activity in *Williams,* the majority denigrated the significance of her work by holding that the manual tasks she performed during working hours were not centrally important and that because she could brush her teeth and comb her hair, she was not substantially limited in her ability to perform manual tasks. According to the Court, because she could attend to her personal hygiene, she was not disabled and not entitled to the protection of the act, despite her inability to earn a living without an accommodation from her employer. The irony is that although there was no dispute that Williams's impairments interfered with her ability to work—a problem the ADA was intended to remedy—the Court's narrow perspective allowed her employer to evade its responsibility under the act.

The disability community has argued that Congress did not intend this result and that the 43 million, continually cited by the Court, was not intended as a limiting number. Indeed, in referring to the 43 million people with disabilities, Congress noted that "this number is increasing as the population as a whole is growing older."[28] Feldblum believes that the Court's position "illustrates the absurdity and illogic of the situation. . . . After this," she contends, "the only people who we know have a disability are those who are blind, deaf and in a wheelchair, and those who have HIV" (quoted in Savage 1999, 44). Many disability rights advocates have urged Congress to clarify and strengthen its intent and so prevent the Court from denying the guarantees of the antidiscrimination provisions of the act to millions of people. Thus far, Congress has not taken up this invitation.

Equal Employment Opportunity Commission Lawsuits

A week after *Williams* was announced, the Court handed down a 6–3 ruling in *EEOC v. Waffle House, Inc.* (2002). This case questioned whether an arbitration agreement between an employer and employee barred the EEOC from filing an ADA suit on the employee's behalf.

When he applied for a job at Waffle House, Eric Baker signed an agreement to submit all disputes or claims against his employer to binding arbitration. He was offered the job, but declined it, continuing his job search at another Waffle House. He accepted the job of grill operator without signing another application form. Shortly after he began working, he suffered a seizure and was fired soon thereafter. Although he did not sue or pursue arbitration, he filed a discrimination charge with the EEOC. After investigation, the agency unsuccessfully attempted conciliation and then filed suit against the company in its own name and on Baker's behalf, seeking an injunction against the company to cease its unlawful employment practices. Also, alleging intentional discrimination under Title I, the agency asked for relief to make Baker whole, including back pay, compensatory and punitive damages, and reinstatement; Baker was not a party to the suit.

In response to the EEOC's suit, Waffle House filed a motion to dismiss or, citing the Federal Arbitration Act (FAA), a petition to order the matter to arbitration; the district court judge declined to do either (*Waffle House* 1998).[29] The Fourth Circuit agreed that the EEOC was not bound by the provisions of the FAA, but, in an attempted compromise to give the arbitration agreement some weight, limited the available remedies to injunctive relief (*Waffle House* 1999).

With Justice Stevens writing the 6–3 opinion, the Court tracked the history of the EEOC's independent authority to litigate as well as to sue on behalf of victims of discrimination.[30] Because the EEOC's power to sue under the ADA was derived from Title VII, the Court evaluated the agency's statutory authority to sue for such "victim-specific" remedies under Title VII, as amended by the 1991 Civil Rights Act. The 1991 act authorized suits for injunctive and monetary relief by "complaining parties" under Title VII and the ADA for compensatory and punitive damages, and the Court concluded that this applied to both private individuals and the EEOC. The Court also assessed the effect of the FAA and held that, as a nonsignatory, the EEOC was not bound by the arbitration agreement between Baker and Waffle House. It also reversed the circuit court decision that the EEOC action was limited to injunctive relief only, ruling that the EEOC was empowered to seek all available remedies.

Writing for Chief Justice William Rehnquist and Justice Scalia, Justice Clarence Thomas objected to the decision for two reasons: it allowed the agency to sue on behalf of a party who was precluded from suing himself because of a valid arbitration agreement and it undercut the preference for arbitration inherent in the FAA.

Although this case was a victory for the disability community, the decision primarily turned on the Court's interpretation of legislative intent in authorizing the EEOC to have an independent litigating posture in Title VII and ADA cases (Naum 2002). There were scant references to the ADA in the ruling and those that were mentioned were only in passing. The Court rested the EEOC's ability to bring an ADA action on behalf of victims on its authority under the 1964 and 1991 Civil Rights Acts, not the Americans with Disabilities Act. Finally, in addressing the scope of the FAA, the Court balanced the policies behind the law against the power of the EEOC without directly considering the effect of the outcome on the ADA or on victims of disability discrimination.

Seniority Systems

A few months later, in *U.S. Airways, Inc. v. Barnett* (2002), the Court clarified when an accommodation to an employee becomes an undue hardship for an employer. The case revolved around an employee's request for an accommodation that conflicted with an established seniority system.

Robert Barnett had injured his back while working for U.S. Airways as a cargo handler. He applied for and received a mailroom assignment on the basis of his seniority. After two years, the airline declared the position vacant and invited senior employees to bid on it. Barnett asked to be allowed to stay in the mailroom because the ADA identifies "reassignment to a vacant position" as a type of reasonable accommodation (42 U.S.C. §1211). The airline refused to bypass the seniority system and he was soon removed from the position.

Announcing the 5–4 ruling, Justice Breyer rejected the airline's contention that equality principles required it to adhere to neutral operational rules and denied the request for an accommodation. In demanding that employers make reasonable accommodations for employees with disabilities, he explained, the act demands preferential treatment and companies are not absolved from accommodating them simply by pointing to the existence of a neutral rule to the contrary.

Clarifying the relationship between a "reasonable accommodation" and an "undue hardship," Breyer noted the lower courts' resolution of the problem approvingly: to avoid summary judgment for the employer, the employee must show that an accommodation appears reasonable while the employer must demonstrate that the accommodation would lead to an undue hardship. The issue in this case, he said, was the validity of the employee's showing that the accommodation was reasonable. The question for the Court to resolve was: does an otherwise reasonable accommodation become unreasonable when it requires the violation of a seniority system? "The answer to this question," Breyer said, "ordinarily is 'yes.'" And, he continued, it was unnecessary to assess the matter on a case-by-case basis "because it would not be reasonable in the run of cases that the assignment in question trump the rules of a seniority system. To the contrary, it will ordinarily be unreasonable for the assignment to prevail" (*Barnett* 2002, 403).

The Court cited its own precedent as well as lower court rulings in Title VII and Rehabilitation Act cases that supported its position. Although those cases involved collective bargaining agreements, the Court saw no reason to differentiate those seniority systems from one imposed by the company as in the case of U.S. Airways. Extolling the virtues of a seniority system for promoting fairness, uniformity, and stability, Breyer said that requiring an employer to defend the system on a case-by-case basis would undermine these principles. Because there was no indication in the ADA that Congress intended such a result, it is "ordinarily sufficient" for the employer to merely point to a seniority system to defeat a charge of discrimination. Leaving a small opening, Breyer said an employee was entitled to argue "special circumstances" existed that would make an accommodation reasonable despite a seniority system (*Barnett* 2002, 405).

Justices Scalia and Thomas dissented, arguing that the majority opinion introduced uncertainty by only creating a rebuttable presumption in favor of a seniority system. In their view, a seniority system is an evenhanded policy that does not burden an employee because of his or her disability; they criticized the opinion for leaving open the possibility that the ADA permitted neutral rules and practices, like seniority systems, to be challenged by employees seeking accommodation.

Justice Souter, writing for himself and Justice Ginsburg, cited the legislative history of the act in congressional committee reports and argued that the seniority system at issue in the case was not a defense to an ADA claim of discrimination. In Souter's view, Barnett had easily met his burden because this seniority system was, according to the airline's own policy, not even a contract because it could be altered at will by the employer. The burden therefore should have shifted to the airline to show that bypassing the seniority system would impose an undue hardship on it.

Ironically, by preferring the seniority system over the "reasonable accommodation" provision in *Barnett,* the majority ignored congressional intent as well as the plain language of the act. In contrast to Title VII, which explicitly exempts a valid seniority system from its antidiscrimination provisions, as noted by Souter, Congress rejected that approach in the ADA, merely stipulating that a seniority system was to be considered part of the calculus for determining the reasonableness of an accommodation to an employee (Pirius 2003; Nevin 2002).

Direct Threat

The last disability rights decision of the 2001–2002 term, *Chevron U.S.A. Inc. v. Echazabal* (2002), involved an interpretation of the "direct threat" affirmative defense. The issue was the validity of an EEOC regulation that permitted an employer to consider the threat to the employee himself as well as to the others in the workplace.[31]

The plaintiff in this case, Mario Echazabal, began working for independent contractors at a Chevron oil refinery in 1972. He first sought a full-time job with Chevron in 1992 and was offered a position, contingent upon passing a physical examination. When the examination turned up a liver abnormality, Chevron refused to hire him, but he continued to work for the contractor at the Chevron oil refinery. Three years later, he again applied with Chevron and his liver ailment was again revealed, this time as hepatitis C. Chevron ordered the independent contractor for whom Echazabal worked to remove him from the site and reassign him to a job without exposure to harmful solvents or chemicals. He was laid off in 1996.

Echazabal sued Chevron, claiming it violated the ADA by refusing to hire him because of his liver condition. The Ninth Circuit reversed the lower court's grant of summary judgment for Chevron. The appeals court held that the EEOC regulation expanding the "direct threat" defense to include danger to the employee as well as to co-workers exceeded the bounds of permissible rule making because the act only specified a direct threat to others (*Echazabal v. Chevron U.S.A. Inc.* 2000).

Speaking for a unanimous Court, Souter again parsed the statutory language. Relying on the canons of statutory interpretation, he evaluated Echazabal's argument that the "direct threat to others" language in the statute and the omission of a "direct threat to oneself" meant that only others had to be considered. After reviewing the text, Souter concluded that the statute did not mandate the exclusion of this provision and the EEOC regulation was a reasonable interpretation of the law, notwithstanding the charge that it exhibited the kind of paternalism in the workplace the ADA was intended to eradicate.[32]

Souter also noted there were policy reasons to support this position, citing the company's desire to avoid lost time for illness, excessive turnover, and fear of tort litigation. Most important, he maintained, the company was legitimately concerned about violating the 1970 Occupational Safety and Health Act (OSHA) requirement of providing a hazard-free workplace. Unpersuaded by Echazabal's argument that an employer is never prosecuted under OSHA for hiring an employee with a disability who was willing to assume the risk of the job, Souter said the EEOC acted properly in reconciling the competing interests of OSHA and the ADA. It struck the right balance by correctly perceiving that Congress did not intend to rule out consideration of risk to an employee on a certain job, "but was trying to get at refusals to give an even break to classes of disabled people, while claiming to act for their own good in reliance on untested and pretextual stereotypes." The EEOC regulation, he continued, "disallows just this sort of sham protection, through demands for a particularized enquiry into harms the employee would probably face"; it requires the "direct threat" defense to be substantiated by "a reasonable medical judgment that relies on the most current medical knowledge and/or the best available objective evidence" (*Chevron U.S.A. Inc. v. Echazabal* 2002, 85–86; 29 C.F.R. §1630.2 (r)).

The opinion prompted reaction from both sides. Not surprisingly, the business community approved the decision, with the Chamber of Commerce calling it "a major victory" (*New York Times,* June 11, 2002). On the other side, the AAPD president charged that "the court had once again demonstrated its fundamental hostility to disability rights in the workplace" (*New York Times,* June 11, 2002).

Although it is difficult to criticize an employer for showing concern for an employee's welfare, Chevron had allowed Echazabal to remain on the job for three years after learning of his liver abnormality and then suddenly had him excluded from the workplace. Indeed, he had worked at the Chevron site for more than twenty years, primarily as an employee of Chevron's independent contractors.

The majority opinion appears to conflict with the Court's ruling in *International Union, United Auto Workers v. Johnson Controls* (1991), in which it held that an employer could not exclude women of childbearing age from working in areas where toxic materials, such as lead, were used on the grounds of protecting their unborn children from harm or themselves from tort liability. Eschewing paternalism there, the Court had held that such a decision must be left to the child's parents. In *Echazabal,* however, the Court was unwilling to allow the employee to decide to undertake the risk. And ironically, after disdaining most EEOC interpretations of the law in other ADA cases, in this instance the Court found its interpretation reasonable, despite the absence of support from the text or evidence of congressional intent.

Partners as Employees

In early 2003, the Supreme Court declined to resolve the issue of whether the shareholder-directors of a professional corporation should be considered employees for purposes of the ADA, remanding the case to the lower court. *Clackamas Gastroenterology Associates, P.C. v. Wells* (2003) involved an ADA suit against a medical group by its bookkeeper, Deborah Anne Wells, who filed her action after being terminated. The issue presented to the Court was whether the four physicians who were shareholders (and owners) of the clinic should be treated as employees for the purposes of the lawsuit. If they were considered partners rather than employees, the clinic would have fewer than the requisite fifteen employees for ADA coverage.

In a 7–2 opinion announced by Stevens, the Supreme Court reversed the Ninth Circuit and remanded the case to allow the lower court to resolve the conflict. After indicating that the ADA was silent on this issue, the Supreme Court approvingly cited the EEOC compliance manual's list of six factors that should be used to determine whether a shareholder-director is an employee or partner; most were related to the degree of control, authority, and influence exercised by the individual. Assessing the district court's findings, the high court indicated that they "appear to weigh in favor of a conclusion that the four director-shareholder physicians in this case are *not* employees of the clinic" (*Clackamas* 2003, 1681; emphasis added). Writing for Breyer and herself, Justice Ginsburg expressed the view that the clinic should not be permitted to evade its responsibilities under the ADA.

Substance Abuse

At the end of its 2002 term, the Court decided *Raytheon Company v. Hernandez* (2003), which addressed the extent of an employer's obligation to recovering drug users. After testing positive for cocaine, a twenty-five-year employee, Joel Hernandez, was forced to resign from his job as a missile plant worker at Raytheon for workplace misconduct. He sought reinstatement after two years, informing the company of his previous employment and enclosing letters indicating he was in recovery. The employee in the personnel office who reviewed his file rejected his application on the basis of a company policy against rehiring employees terminated for misconduct. She claimed that she was unaware of the nature of his misconduct when she made her decision. Hernandez sued, claiming the company violated the ADA because its refusal to rehire him was motivated by the fact that he was a former drug addict. Moreover, even if the refusal to rehire him was based on a neutral employment policy, such a policy had a disparate impact on people with disabilities.[33]

The Ninth Circuit ruled that the company's "no rehire" policy was not a legitimate reason to refuse to reinstate him (*Hernandez v. Hughes Missile System Company* 2002).[34] The company had argued that its policy was unrelated to his disability, that is, his past drug addiction, because it treated all former employees fired for misconduct alike. The appeals court, however, held that the rule against hiring former employees terminated for misconduct violated the ADA when applied to persons like Hernandez, who were fired *only* for testing positive for drug use and not for other types of misbehavior. "If Hernandez is in fact no longer using drugs and has been successfully rehabilitated," the court stated, "he may not be denied re-employment simply because of his past record of drug addiction" (*Hernandez v. Hughes Missile System Company* 2002, 1036).

On appeal, the high court rejected the appellate court's analysis. Speaking for a unanimous Court, with Justices Souter and Breyer taking no part, Justice Thomas criticized the circuit court for applying disparate impact theory to a disparate treatment claim. According to Thomas, instead of determining whether the company's policy constituted a legitimate nondiscriminatory reason for refusing to rehire Hernandez (as it was obligated to do in a disparate treatment claim), the appellate court had improperly found that the company policy had a disparate impact on former drug users, thus "conflating the analytical framework for disparate-impact and disparate-treatment claims." The lower court, Thomas continued, should have found that such a neutral policy "is by definition, a legitimate nondiscriminatory reason under the ADA" (*Raytheon Company v. Hernandez* 2003, 519). The Court vacated the judgment of the appeals court and remanded the case with orders to apply the correct legal analysis to Hernandez's disparate treatment claim.

Taken together, these decisions indicate the Supreme Court's unwillingness to accept the broad parameters of the ADA's guarantees. Despite substantial evidence of congressional intent to the contrary, the Court has held that the employment discrimination provisions of the act should be narrowly interpreted to prevent the litigation that would likely follow a more expansive reading of the law. In just five years, the Court handed down twelve Title I decisions, with only three decided in the plaintiff's favor.[35] Moreover, these three rulings were only tangentially related to the disability rights guaranteed in the ADA. When the Court defined the terms of the act, it invariably chose a restrictive definition that limited its effectiveness, allowing the lower courts to dismiss suits, typically before considering the merits of the claim. As a result of its Title I rulings, the lower courts primarily focused on whether the plaintiff met the standard of disability rather than on whether the defendant had broken the law.

Title I Litigation in the Lower Federal Courts

Parry (1998) was the first empirical study of ADA Title I litigation. Intending to assess the truthfulness of the popular perception that "the law unfairly favors employees with disabilities over employers of persons with disabilities" and that "employers are unduly burdened by the ADA and . . . many employees with questionable disabilities receive favored treatment" (403), Parry's analysis was based on 760 cases decided between 1992 and 1997 (including one Supreme Court case).[36] He included only those in which one of the parties prevailed on the merits or the case was dismissed, the latter a victory for the employer, and found that employers prevailed in 92.1 percent of the rulings and employees prevailed in 7.9 percent (404). Parry also reported that employers were only slightly less successful in the 83,158 complaints to the EEOC during these years, with 86.4 percent of the cases resolved in the employer's favor. Similarly, Moss's (2000) study of EEOC charge filings through June 1995 confirmed that "only a small percentage of charges result in increased employment opportunities for people with disabilities" (132).

In subsequent years, Parry and Albright at the American Bar Association (ABA) Commission on Mental and Physical Disability Law updated the surveys of Title I decisions. Table 3.2 illustrates the outcome of the Title I cases leading to judicial resolution from 1992 to 2002. As table 3.2 indicates, the employers' success rates varied only slightly over the ten-year period, for the most part hovering at 95 percent. In their most successful year, Title I plaintiffs only succeeded in 5 percent of suits filed; in their worst year—2000, the year after the *Sutton* trilogy was decided—their success rate was less than 3 percent. The last column in the table represents the percentage of employee victories in all Title I cases, including those that were excluded from the database because no final resolution had been reached.

Colker (1999) examined appellate court rulings through July 1998. Unlike Parry, she included suits against public and private employers; however, although she does not report a breakdown of the types of defendants, most complaints of employment discrimination were filed against private employers. Like Parry, she was motivated by the desire to determine the validity of the numerous media reports that characterized ADA lawsuits as frivolous, saying they were brought by plaintiffs with no genuine impairments who were seeking unjust enrichment at the expense of employers.

Colker based her analysis on 475 ADA appellate decisions reported in Westlaw and found that the defendants prevailed in 376 rulings for a success rate of 84 percent. Relying on the cases appearing in the ABA trial court database, she also reported the outcome of the 615 employment discrimination cases decided by district courts. Here, defendants fared even better, prevailing in 570 decisions for a success rate of 93 percent.[37] Her findings, which are similar to Parry's, confirm that plaintiffs rarely prevail in ADA employment discrimination suits and that they have one of the worst success rates of any group of litigants, with only prisoners losing their cases as frequently.[38] She attributes these results largely to the judiciary's unwillingness to defer to agency guidelines and its reliance on summary judgments.

In a subsequent study, Colker extended the years of her analysis by examining all "nonpatently frivolous" discrimination cases decided at the appellate court level between August 3, 1994, and July 26, 1999. She identified the 720 appellate rulings and found that the defendants' success rate ranged from 83 percent in 1994 to 89 percent in 1997, with a mean average of 86.5 percent for all cases (Colker 2001, 259, table 7). Table 3.3 illustrates these findings.

Commenting on the outcome of these cases in a later study, Colker (2002, 223) sought to explain why "plaintiffs' lawyers make such large miscalculations in deciding which cases to appeal." In her view, the plaintiff's bar misjudged the likelihood of successful ADA appeals because of its experience in employment discrimination cases decided under section 504, in which they prevailed in approximately 35 percent of the cases. To confirm her belief, she measured the outcome of section 504 employment discrimination cases after 1994 and found that the defendants' success rate had risen dramatically, increasing by 23 percent.[39]

Taken together, the Colker and Parry data indicate that employment dis-

Table 3.2 Federal Title I litigation, 1992–2002

Year of decision	Total cases (no.)	No final decision	Final decision	Employer wins (no.)	Employer wins (%)	Employee wins (no.)	Employee wins (%)	Employee wins as % of total cases[a]
1992–1997	1,200	440	760	700	92.1	60	7.9	5.0
1998	408	111	297	279[b]	93.9	17	5.7	4.2
1999	434	130	304	291	95.7	13	4.3	3.0
2000	514	121	393	379	96.4	14	3.6	2.7
2001	429	101	328	314	95.7	14	4.3	3.3
2002	442	115	327	309	94.5	18	5.5	4.1

Source: Mental and Physical Disability Law Reporter, 1998–2003.
[a] Figures in this column calculated by the author. [b] This number was erroneously reported as 280 in the published article.

Table 3.3 Appellate employment discrimination litigation, 1994–1999

Year of Decision	Total cases (no.)	Employer wins (no.)	Employer wins (%)	Employee wins (no.)[a]	Employee wins (%)[a]
1994	6	5	83	1	17
1995	42	35	83	7	17
1996	114	96	84	18	16
1997	178	158	89	20	11
1998	219	189	86	30	14
1999	161	140	87	21	13

Source: Colker (2001, table 7).
Note: Data collected from August 3, 1994, to July 26, 1999.
[a] Figures in these columns calculated by the author.

crimination litigation has not furthered the goals of the disability community. Parry (1999) attributes most of the low success rate among Title I plaintiffs to the catch-22 of the ADA, that is, the requirement that the employee must have a "substantially limiting disability" yet, at the same time, be "qualified" to fulfill the needs of the job (see also O'Brien 2001; Diller 2000). He identifies a second catch-22 situation that contributed to the plaintiffs' poor showing in court. Plaintiffs who applied for or received state or federal disability insurance benefits were collaterally stopped from claiming discrimination under the ADA because, in accepting these benefits, they must have essentially admitted that they were incapable of working.[40] Finally, Parry cites the barrier imposed by the "undue hardship" defense in the act, which allows an employer to claim it is too expensive or disruptive to hire or retain the plaintiff as an employee.

He concludes that, despite the prevailing view of the ADA as a boon for employees, employers are actually favored in the law, in part because of procedural roadblocks that prevent plaintiffs from being heard on the merits and in part because the balance of equities swings in the employers' favor when they raise the defense of "undue hardship," which most often involves the cost of employing a person with disabilities.

Colker believes the defendants' success rate in the employment cases is largely attributable to the judiciary's abuse of summary judgment procedure. The court treats issues that should go to juries for factual determinations, such as the reasonableness of the accommodation, the nature of the employer's hardship, and the plaintiff's disability (especially the latter) as suitable for summary judgment and decides them as a matter of law. Plaintiffs are harmed by this, she believes, as studies have shown that plaintiffs in other types of employment discrimination litigation are more successful when their cases are decided by juries rather than the court (Colker 1999, 102). In her view, ADA plaintiffs are disadvantaged because of the court's willingness to treat a matter of fact as a matter of law. She also believes that the judiciary's unwillingness to defer to agency interpretations contributes to the heavy losses by ADA plaintiffs.

Willborn (2000, 103) also examined the pattern of ADA employment litigation, comparing it in part to the pattern of Title VII litigation.[41] Unlike the Colker and Parry studies, Willborn's analysis did not focus on the outcome of the cases. Instead, he divided the 605 ADA employment claims reported in Westlaw from July 26, 1992, to June 30, 1997, into types of claims: hiring, discharge, or accommodation, though the latter, he said, rarely represented a pure type. He found that, unlike in Title VII cases, ADA plaintiffs complaining of discriminatory discharges vastly outnumbered those charging employers with a refusal to hire. In the first five years of ADA employment litigation, the ratio between discharge and hiring cases was more than ten to one. In his view, the disproportionately low number of hiring cases compared to discharge cases suggests "that the Act has been used only sparingly" to address the primary concern noted by Congress in enacting the law, namely, the underemployment of persons with disabilities (Willborn 2000, 114).[42] He believes it would help effectuate the purpose of the act if the EEOC and public interest groups directed their energies to this area of the law; it might also provide greater incentives for litigants with hiring complaints to file suit against employers who refuse to hire them.

Despite Congress's intent to integrate people with disabilities into the workforce, the courts have been quite reluctant to interpret the ADA broadly and require employers to make the accommodations litigants seek.

4 Disability Rights
and Public Entities

Title II applies to state and local governments and the National Railroad Passenger Corporation (Amtrak), as well as any commuter authority designated in the Rail Passenger Service Act. It provides that "no qualified individual with a disability shall, by reason of such disability, be excluded from participation in or be denied the benefits of the services, programs, or activities of a public entity, or be subjected to discrimination by any such entity" (42 U.S.C. §12132). The law requires government entities to provide persons with disabilities an equal opportunity to receive or participate in programs, services, and activities, including recreation, social services, transportation, health care, and voting, to name just a few areas within the reach of the act.

A "qualified individual with a disability" is "an individual with a disability who, with or without reasonable modifications to rules, policies, or practices, the removal of architectural, communication, or transportation barriers, or the provision of auxiliary aids and services, meets the essential eligibility requirements for the receipt of services or the participation in programs or activities provided by a public entity."[1] Regulations promulgated by the DOJ require public entities to make services, programs, and activities in existing facilities "readily accessible to and usable by individuals with disabilities."[2] They do not have to take actions that "would result in a fundamental alteration . . . or in undue financial and administrative burdens" (28 C.F.R. §35.150(a)(3)). Newly designed, constructed, or altered facilities are governed by stricter accessibility standards and cannot claim a "fundamental alteration" or "undue burden" defense (28 C.F.R. §35.151).

Title II Litigation and Subnational Governments

Title II lawsuits have prompted concerns about the distribution of power between the federal government and subnational governments, and, more specifically, about the federal courts' intrusion into the fiscal autonomy of subnational entities. In adjudicating the claims of Title II litigants, the federal courts are instrumental in establishing the parameters of disability rights in state and local governments. By exercising supervisory authority over the disability policies of these government entities, federal judges are often viewed as encroaching into their policymaking arena, especially when ordering them to commit considerable resources to expand services and programs to comply with the mandate of nondiscrimination (see Pelka 1996; Clegg 1999). Not surprisingly therefore, as Percy (1993, 87) notes, some perceive the ADA as "another in a series of federal government actions that preempts the governing authority of state and local governments." The ADA has also been described as the "most costly piece of legislation for government . . . ever to hit this country" (Bauer 1993, 40). Its critics argue that the federal courts often ignore fiscal constraints and, notwithstanding the cost (undue burden) defense available to government bodies, impose unrealistic dictates on government agencies.

In investigating the impact of the undue burden defense on Title II cases, however, Jones (1995) found that the courts were generally unsympathetic to state and local governments, only siding with them in eight of twenty-eight cases. Jeffrey Rosen, general counsel and director of policy at the NCD, concurs, saying, "states very rarely win on cost issues" (Rosen 2000).[3]

Title II and Section 504

In part, the ADA was enacted because disability rights advocates believed that section 504 and its regulations were neither comprehensive nor well-enforced (Harrington 2000; see Burgdorf 1991). Additionally, as Percy (1993, 89) notes, a number of small communities do not receive federal funds. Title II, modeled after section 504, exceeds its scope because plaintiffs are not required to prove that defendants receive federal funding, removing one of the obstacles that plagued section 504 litigants. Title II brought a wide range of state and local government agencies and programs—such as athletic associations, state bar associations, state licensing agencies, voter registration boards, and municipal zoning boards—within its reach. Thus, the cost of complying with Title II has varied. Entities or programs in compliance with section 504 would have little additional expense; the cost for communities or programs outside the reach of section 504 would be far greater (Levitan and Pfeiffer 1992).

The ADA as an Unfunded Mandate

The 1970s ushered in an "era of regulatory federalism," during which the federal government imposed substantial financial commitments on subnational governments without providing adequate resources for implementation. Ironically, despite the antiregulatory rhetoric of the Reagan-Bush administrations, such laws actually increased during their tenure in office, outpacing deregulatory efforts. According to Conlan, Riggle, and Schwartz (1995, 24–25), state and local governments spent more than $10 billion between 1983 and 1992 to implement federal rules adopted during this period.

Termed "unfunded mandates," laws such as the Clean Air Act of 1970, the Clean Water Act of 1972, the Endangered Species Act of 1973, the Safe Drinking Water Act of 1974, and the Resource Conservation and Recovery Act of 1976, as well as the ADA, have had a significant impact on the fiscal policies of subnational governments at all levels (*Des Moines Register,* February 2, 1995). Numerous reports and studies have attested to the outlays required by such laws, calculating a price in the billions (see *Financial World,* April 11, 1995; *Congressional Digest,* March 1995, 69–71). Shortly after the ADA was enacted, Percy (1993, 103) cited estimates by the Congressional Budget Office (CBO) that it would cost state and local governments $20–30 million a year for several years for the purchase of accessible buses, $15 million a year to maintain the buses, and hundreds of millions more over the next thirty years to make train stations accessible.

Acknowledging the cost of unfunded mandates for subnational governments, St. George (1995, 13–14) nevertheless argues that they represent a legitimate, and possibly the most efficient, method of imposing uniform public policy standards. He also believes they provide subnational governments with an incentive to reduce the costs of such programs. Additionally, he points out that the federal government provides large subsidies to state and local governments to pay for services and programs, such as education and crime protection, that are traditionally the responsibility of these governments.[4]

Legislative history indicates that Congress paid much less attention to the potential costs of the ADA for state and local governments than to its burden on the business community. A few years after the ADA was enacted, however, during a December 1993 meeting of the National Conference of State Legislators in Washington, the chair of the Missouri House Budget Committee spoke of the difficulty of unfunded mandates in general and singled out the ADA, saying it "is just destroying us" (*Washington Times,* December 10, 1993). A study of 314 cities by Price Waterhouse for the U.S. Conference of Mayors found that ten existing mandates, including the ADA, cost $6.5 billion in FY1993. It was estimated that the price tag would be as high as $54 billion between 1994 and 1998 (Troy 1997, 141). The cost of the ADA alone was reported at more than $355 million in 1993 and estimated at more than $2 billion over the next four years (*Congressional Quarterly,* December 31, 1994, 3605).

After the 1994 congressional elections, in one of the first attempts to implement the Republican Party's "Contract with America," congressional leaders announced their intention to ease the burden of unfunded federal spending mandates, including the ADA, on subnational governments (Milani 2001).[5] On January 4, 1995, at the start of the new 104th Congress, two virtually identical bills were introduced (S1 and HR5), both aimed at alleviating the concerns of state and local governments about the cost of implementing federal mandates. Entitled the Unfunded Mandates Reform Act (UMRA) of 1995, the law aimed to curb federal laws and regulations that necessitated spending by subnational and tribal governments. Largely directed at environmental protection legislation, the UMRA was supported by numerous groups representing state and local governments. The principal sponsors of the bill were John Glenn, Democrat from Ohio, and Dirk Kempthorne, Republican from Idaho. Kempthorne cited a long list of associations and organizations supporting the bill, including the Conference of Mayors, the National Association of Counties, the National Conference of State Legislators, the National Governors Association, the Council of State Governments, and the Chamber of Commerce (*Federal Document Clearing House, Inc.,* January 19, 1995).

The bills were approved in Senate and House committees in early January. Governmental Affairs Committee Chair William Roth, Republican from Delaware, declared that although state and local governments appeared most concerned about the cost of environmental protection mandates, other federal requirements, including the ADA and the National Voter Registration Act, were "burdensome and costly" (*Congressional Record* 1995, S647). There was, however, also a consensus that laws protecting constitutional and civil rights must remain outside the reach of the act, in part because most members of Congress felt that the federal government had a duty to mandate such laws (St. George 1995). Roth stressed that his committee was aware of the unique nature of federal civil rights guarantees. He explained that,

> during the middle part of the 20th century, the arguments of those who opposed the national uniform extension of basic equal rights, protection, and opportunity to all individuals were based on a States rights philosophy. With the passage of the Civil Rights Acts of 1957 and 1964 and the Voting Rights Act of 1965, Congress rejected that argument out of hand as designed to thwart equal opportunity and to protect discriminatory, unjust and unfair practices in the treatment of individuals in certain parts of the country. The Committee therefore exempts Federal civil rights law from the requirements of this Act. (*Congressional Record* 1995, S649)

During the House debate over the bill, Owens stated that because people with disabilities were anxious about the effect of HR5 on the Medicaid program, he wanted to offer an amendment to exclude "any statute or regulation that acts to protect the health of [such] individuals" (*Congressional Record* 1995, H579). William Clinger, Republican from Pennsylvania and House manager of the bill, opposed the Owens amendment, arguing that the ADA "is unaffected by this legislation in any way, shape, or manner." He added, "there are some who would like to amend [it] because it in fact imposed some rather heavy burdens on our States and local communities to comply with the act in terms of retrofitting various things." Although he attempted to reassure disability rights advocates that the UMRA did not apply retroactively and would not affect future disability rights laws, he still believed that such laws should not be exempt from cost considerations (*Congressional Record* 1995, H580).

The final version of the UMRA excluded any law or regulation that enforced constitutional rights as well as one that "establishes or enforces any statutory rights that prohibit discrimination on the basis of race, color, religion, sex, national origin, age, handicap, or disability."[6] In prepared testimony before a joint hearing of the Senate Committees on Governmental Affairs and the Budget, Dart applauded the decision to exempt civil rights enforcement from the reach of the law, noting that state and local governments had been bound by section 504 policy for more than twenty years and if they had followed those rules they would likely be in compliance with the ADA. "It is those governments," he said, "that have done the least over this period that are now complaining the loudest" (*Federal Information Systems Corporation,* January 5, 1995).[7]

The Senate approved S1 in an 86–10 vote on January 27; a few days later, on February 1, HR5 passed in the House by a 360–74 vote. And on March 15 and 16, following intense partisan wrangling in conference, which resulted in a compromise permitting the courts to determine if the cost-benefit analysis were performed (but not to judge its thoroughness or accuracy), both chambers approved the conference report by even larger margins (*Congressional Quarterly,* April 15, 1995, 1087–89).

Signed by President Clinton on March 22, 1995, to take effect on January 1, 1996, the law defined a "federal intergovernmental mandate" as any provision that "would impose an enforceable duty" on a state, local, or tribal unit of government except funds granted "as a condition of federal assistance or a duty arising from participation in a voluntary Federal program."[8]

Amending the Congressional Budget and Impoundment Control Act of 1974, the UMRA required the CBO to estimate the impact on state, local, or tribal governments of any laws costing $50 million or more.[9] Additionally, it required the Advisory Commission on Intergovernmental Relations (ACIR) to review existing mandates and recommend ways to reduce their effect (*Congressional Quarterly,* April 15, 1995, 1087–89). Because the UMRA was only aimed at future mandates, it provided little relief for existing commitments. And by defining mandates narrowly, it had little effect on future mandates (Gullo and Kelly 1998, 381–82). Indeed, according to the ACIR director of government policy research, it would have affected only nine of the twenty-seven mandates enacted between 1981 and 1990. The remaining eighteen would have been exempt as civil rights acts or were tied to conditional grants; the nine that would have been affected were predominantly environmental protection laws (*Washington Post,* March 23, 1995; see Posner 1997).

Even though the ADA was beyond the reach of the UMRA, members of the disability community feared it might be targeted in the future. Their fears became more concrete when, in January 1996, the ACIR released a preliminary report that suggested trimming a number of existing mandated programs (Gullo and Kelly 1998, 386; see Posner 1997), including the ADA. The draft report, "The Role of Federal Mandates in Intergovernmental Relations: A Preliminary View and Comment," recommended excusing localities with insufficient funds from compliance with the ADA, designating a single federal agency to enforce the law, and eliminating private rights of action against state and local governments (*Disability Compliance Bulletin,* March 28, 1996). In addition to the ADA, other laws targeted for change included OSHA, parts of the Fair Labor Standards Act (FLSA), the Family and Medical Leave Act (FMLA), and the Clean Water Act. The agency advocated repealing or phasing out as many as fourteen mandates (*Washington Post,* March 8, 1996).

Representatives of social welfare and environmental groups, including disability advocates, protested the draft report during an ACIR conference. According to John Kincaid (1999, 322), "especially visible [during the protests] were wheelchair bound individuals." And Philip Dearborn, the ACIR's director of government research, credited disability advocates with "being instrumental in the removal of the ADA from the report"; another ACIR official depicted the ADA as "the most difficult issue for the commission to reach consensus" (*Disability Compliance Bulletin,* August 1, 1996).

The draft report was also criticized by the Clinton administration, whose spokesperson, Marcia Hale, the assistant to the president and director of intergovernmental affairs, contended that because the UMRA did not apply to civil rights laws, the commission should have excluded them from consideration. Moreover, Hale charged that the recommendations "would set back our efforts to guarantee equal rights for citizens with disabilities" (*Disability Compliance Bulletin,* March 28, 1996). Ultimately, because of political pressure, including reaction from the White House and negative public opinion, the recommendations in the preliminary report were not accepted by the commission.

Measuring Compliance

More than a decade ago, Holbrook and Percy (1992) wrote that political scientists were just beginning to study disability policymaking in the public sector. Most of the empirical work on the ADA, however, has focused on compliance issues related to Title I (see Pfeiffer and Finn 1995; Percy 2001; Switzer 2001). Only a few studies of implementation by public entities exist, most from the perspective of local governments as service providers (Pfeiffer 1996b; Pfeiffer and Finn 1997). Although they provide a glimpse into the perceptions of the "implementing population" (see Canon and Johnson 1999), because these studies draw upon the opinions of government officials and define compliance quite narrowly, they are, at best, imperfect measures of compliance with the law. Moreover, most seem to make little or no attempt to gauge the disability community's satisfaction with the progress of ADA implementation.

Pfeiffer and Finn (1995, 539) surveyed the state, local, and territorial government officials responsible for Title II services and programs. They asked questions about compliance, such as the extent to which the government had conducted the statutorily mandated self-evaluation program and assessed the accessibility of facilities as required by DOJ regulations. Based on the survey results, they concluded that "the ADA is being implemented on the state, territorial, and local government level." Two years later, Pfeiffer and Finn (1997, 771) wrote that, in their view, these governments were making good faith efforts toward implementation, and although the disability community might like more vigorous enforcement, Pfeiffer and Finn believed they were aware "that complete barrier removal and integration into society lies in the future." Similarly, Condrey and Brudney (1998, 41) surveyed personnel directors in the nation's largest municipal governments and found a high level of compliance with the "personnel-related aspects of the ADA," such as job descriptions, medical examinations, job advertisements, and testing.

Unlike the others, who based their studies on self-reporting, Switzer (2001) assessed the level of compliance in ten cities, measuring it by adherence to administrative requirements, such as the appointment of a disability coordinator. Not surprisingly, she found a higher rate of compliance in cities with disability coordinators who were committed to enforcing the ADA as a civil rights law. In contrast, cities with administrators who seemed to assume that the law was unlikely ever to be enforced had the lowest level of compliance.

Title II and Civil Rights Remedies

Litigation provides an opportunity, albeit indirect, to measure the "consumer's" (see Canon and Johnson 1999) satisfaction with the implementation of a law. Common to other civil rights laws, ADA litigation seeks vindication of a right as well as compensation for the wrong committed by the defendant. There are a number of factors related to the effectiveness of civil rights litigation: the reach of the law, the evidence necessary to establish proof of discriminatory conduct, the availability of remedies, and the range of permissible defenses (Tucker 2001). Litigants suing under Title II must prove they were discriminated against by the public entity on the basis of their disability; they must also overcome the statutory undue burden defense in which the courts weigh the reasonableness of the cost necessary to eradicate the discriminatory conduct or policies. Title II is silent on the question of damages, but specifies that it incorporates the relief available under section 504, which, in turn is "coextensive" with remedies available under Title VI of the 1964 Civil Rights Act, the section prohibiting discrimination on the basis of race or national origin by federally funded agencies.[10] Thus, following this complex web of legislative and judicial policy, Title II litigants are entitled to monetary damages as well as injunctive relief for violation of their rights. Special defenses available to public entities, such as immunity from money damages in the case of states, also play a role in Title II litigation. Mirroring section 504, the ADA specifies that prevailing parties are entitled to attorneys' fees and costs.

Common to other civil rights laws, the ADA is silent on the question of whether Title II plaintiffs must show discriminatory intent to obtain money damages and whether they are entitled to punitive damages. Most courts have concluded that money damages are only available in cases of intentional discrimination. A leading case on the question of damages is the Ninth Circuit decision in *Ferguson v. City of Phoenix* (1998). The plaintiffs were individuals with hearing impairments who sued the city for compensatory and punitive damages, claiming they were ineffectively served by the 9-1-1 emergency call system.[11]

After the district court denied the defendant's motion for summary judgment, the parties entered into a consent decree that left the question of damages open. Applying a "deliberate indifference" standard, the district court judge held that the plaintiffs had not proved the city had intentionally discriminated against them and rejected the plaintiffs' claim for money damages. On appeal, the plaintiffs argued that they had shown intentional discrimination, but in any event, they were entitled to damages even without such a showing.

The circuit court rejected both arguments, citing *Guardians Association v. Civil Service Commission of New York* (1983). Although a fractured ruling, *Guardians* has been interpreted to require proof of discriminatory intent to collect money damages in Title VI cases. The appellate court also cited *Franklin v. Gwinnet* (1992), a Title IX disparate treatment case, in which the Supreme Court had applied the long-standing principle that all appropriate remedies are available to litigants unless Congress explicitly states otherwise; the high court, however, never explicitly addressed whether damages were available in a disparate impact claim. Thus, the Ninth Circuit concluded that *Franklin* left the central holding of *Guardians* undisturbed. The majority of courts agreed with *Ferguson*. As the Second Circuit explained in *Garcia v. State University of New York Health Sciences Center* (2001), the prevailing view is that plaintiffs must show discriminatory intent, defined as deliberate indifference, to collect money damages in Title II cases (Paradis 2003).

Taking a contrary view, Buhai and Golden (2000, 1134), argue that the legislative history of the ADA indicates that "Congress did not intend to limit the award of compensatory damages only to victims of intentional discrimination." They point to *Alexander v. Choate* (1985, 295), in which the Court declared that Congress viewed "discrimination against the handicapped . . . to be most often the product, not of invidious animus, but rather of thoughtlessness and indifference—of benign neglect." However, although *Alexander* sanctioned disparate impact claims, it is less clear that it would have allowed plaintiffs to collect compensatory damages in such cases.

The Court ended the uncertainty about punitive damages in *Buckhannon Board and Care Home v. West Virginia Department of Health and Human Resources* (2001).

The Supreme Court and Title II Litigation

The Supreme Court has ruled on five Title II cases through 2004, and, as shown in table 4.1, three were decided in the plaintiff's favor. The cases show that the high court appears more willing to interpret Title II broadly, in contrast to its rulings in the Title I cases.

State Prison Systems

In *Pennsylvania Department of Corrections v. Yeskey* (1998), the Court was asked to decide whether the ADA applied to state prisons. The case arose when Ronald Yeskey was sentenced to prison for eighteen to thirty-six months despite a recommendation that as a first-time offender he be sent to a motivational boot camp that would have required him to serve only six

Table 4.1 Supreme Court Title II cases, 1998–2004

Case	Year	Issue	Disposition
Yeskey	1998	Applicability of Title II to state prisons	Pro-Plaintiff
Olmstead	1999	Integration of mentally disabled persons in community	Pro-Plaintiff
Buckhannon	2001	Availability of attorneys' fees in ADA litigation	Pro-Defendant
Barnes	2002	Availability of punitive damages in Title II	Pro-Defendant
Lane	2004	State immunity from money damages in Title II	Pro-Plaintiff

months before becoming eligible for parole. The prison authorities, citing his history of hypertension, refused to follow the recommendation. Yeskey, who eventually served thirty-two months, sued, claiming the state violated the ADA because it based his sentence on his disability. The lower court dismissed the case, holding that the ADA did not apply to state prisons. In *Yeskey v. Pennsylvania Department of Corrections* (1997), the Third Circuit reversed, finding that, according to DOJ regulations, the law explicitly applied to state prisons.

On appeal, Pennsylvania emphasized its traditional wide-ranging authority over prisons, which had long been recognized by the courts; it argued that courts should not defer to DOJ guidelines when they interfere with state sovereignty ("Brief for Petitioners," in *Pennsylvania Department of Corrections v Yeskey*) [12] The state contended that prisons were not typically considered providers of "services, programs, and activities," but were intended to isolate certain persons from the public, necessarily restricting their rights in the process. It added that the ADA was intended to integrate people with disabilities into public life, not to regulate conduct in prisons.

The circuits were divided on whether Congress had intended to include state prisons within the purview of the ADA. In *Amos v. Maryland Department of Public Safety & Correctional Services* (1997), for example, the Fourth Circuit cited federalism concerns and agreed with the state that the ADA was not intended to apply to state prisons, in part because its text was unclear.[13] After reviewing opinions in other circuits, the court concluded that "the statutory language does not bring to mind prisoners being held against their will, and therefore neither the ADA nor the Rehabilitation Act state with unmistakable clarity that the statutes apply to state prisons" (*Amos* 1997, 601). The Supreme Court granted *certiorari* and vacated and remanded the case in light of *Yeskey* (*Amos* 1998).

In his opinion for a unanimous Court, Justice Scalia observed that the text of the law was clearly applicable to state prisons and prisoners. He was not persuaded by the state's argument that prisons did not provide "services, programs, and benefits," he said, because they provide "recreational 'activities,' medical 'services,' and educational and vocational 'programs.'" Scalia emphasized that "the text of the ADA provides no basis for distinguishing these programs, services, and activities from those provided by public entities that are not prisons" (*Pennsylvania Department of Corrections v. Yeskey* 1998, 210). He rejected the view that because prisoners did not voluntarily participate in prison programs or activities, but were being held against their will, the statute did not apply to them.[14]

Integration

The ADA includes the legislative finding that "discrimination against individuals with disabilities persists in such critical areas as . . . institutionalization" (42 U.S.C. §12101(a)(3)). Tracking the language of section 504, the "integration regulation" of Title II requires a public entity to "administer services, programs, and activities in the most integrated setting appropriate to the needs of qualified individuals with disabilities" (28 C.F.R. §35.130(d)). Shortly after *Yeskey* was decided, the Supreme Court agreed to hear a case revolving around one of the core underpinnings of the law—the segregation and isolation of people with disabilities ("Brief of *Amicus Curiae* of the National Council on Disability," in *Olmstead v. L.C.*).

One of the most cited rulings in the litigation challenging state mental disability policy was the Third Circuit's decision in *Helen L. v. DiDario* (1995). The opinion was a triumph for the disability community when the appellate court held that Title II required the Pennsylvania Department of Public Welfare (DPW) to provide attendant care for the plaintiff in her own home rather than in a nursing home because the segregation was a form of illegal discrimination. The court rejected the state's argument that the ADA was aimed only at prohibiting discrimination between people with disabilities and people without disabilities, but did not rule out distinctions among disabilities. It also denied the state's claim that shifting to a home care arrangement would fundamentally alter the program. Because the goals of the ADA and the attendant care program were virtually identical, the court was not persuaded that complying with the ADA would force the state to alter the program, nor place an undue burden on the state. Indeed, the court thought it ironic that it would be more fiscally prudent to fulfill the plaintiff's request for home health care.

Olmstead arose in a suit brought by L. C. and E. W., two Georgia women with mental retardation and mental disorders who had voluntarily committed themselves to a state mental hospital, the Georgia Regional Hospital at Atlanta (GRH-A).[15] They claimed the state violated the ADA by keeping them confined in an institution for people with mental disabilities despite the judgments of numerous mental health professionals that they were capable of living in a community-based treatment program.

The state argued that lack of funding rather than discrimination on the basis of disability kept the women confined at GRH-A. Citing *Helen L.*, the Georgia District Court held "that under the ADA, unnecessary institutional segregation of the disabled constitutes discrimination per se, which cannot be justified by a lack of funding" (*L.C. v. Olmstead* 1997, 6). Indeed, the court found that institutional care was more expensive than the type of care sought by the plaintiffs.[16] Because there were existing community-based treatment programs, the court rejected the argument that supplying mental health services in a community-based setting would fundamentally alter the state's mental health program.[17] Mere administrative convenience, said the court, did not excuse the state's obligation to comply with the ADA.

The Eleventh Circuit also cited *Helen I.,* affirming the trial court's ruling that because community-based care was less costly than institutional care, the state's "purported lack of funds to provide community-based services to L. C. and E. W. was insufficient as a matter of law to establish that providing community-based care to plaintiffs would constitute a fundamental alteration" (*L.C. v. Olmstead* 1998, 904). The state could not defend itself against charges of discrimination by arguing that it was too costly to remedy the discrimination. However, the circuit court also ruled that the lower court did not sufficiently consider the extent to which community-based care would deplete the state's mental health budget and affect the services provided to others. Although community-based care is less expensive than institutional care, if the state must also maintain institutions for those who cannot be served in a community setting, the cost of operating two health care systems would fundamentally alter the state's mental health program.[18]

On appeal, the Supreme Court defined the term "discrimination" and addressed the scope of the state's cost-based defense. In a fractured 6–3 ruling, with Justices Scalia, Thomas, and Rehnquist dissenting, the high court substantially affirmed the appellate court.[19] In a ruling characterized as akin to *Brown v. Board of Education* (Colker 2000a, 654), Justice Ruth Bader Ginsburg's opinion for the Court forcefully stated that it was discriminatory to keep mentally disabled individuals in institutions against the advice of treatment professionals and against their will. Moreover, the Court settled an important question by holding that the law did not simply ban discrimination between people with disabilities and people without disabilities, it also banned discrimination among people with disabilities (Karger 1999, 1251).

Speaking for four of the six justices, Ginsburg objected to the appellate court's instruction to the lower court to allow cost as a defense "only in the most limited of circumstances" (*L.C. v. Olmstead* 1998, 902) because it failed to recognize the state's obligation to all citizens with mental disabilities. In her view, the "fundamental alteration" defense should be broadly defined to include expenditures for all state mental health services and not merely be based on a comparison of the cost of community-based care to the cost of

institutional care. A state should be permitted to argue that "in the allocation of available resources, immediate relief for the plaintiffs would be
inequitable" because it is responsible for the entire population of people
with mental disabilities (*Olmstead v. L.C.* 1999, 604). She suggested that a
state should be able to mount a successful "fundamental alteration" defense
by showing it had a "comprehensive working plan" for community-based
care "and a waiting list that moved at a reasonable pace" (*Olmstead v. L.C.*
1999, 605–6).

Justice Thomas's dissent for himself, Scalia, and Rehnquist argued that
the plaintiffs were not being discriminated against simply because they had
not been immediately placed in a community setting. He contended that
the statement "no qualified individual with a disability . . . shall . . . be subjected to discrimination" (42 U.S.C. §12132) prohibited states from differentiating between people with disabilities and people without disabilities, but
did not bar them from distinguishing among people with disabilities. In his
view, because congressional intent in the act was clear, it was unnecessary to
consider the DOJ regulation. He criticized the majority for undermining
state autonomy and its lack of concern for the state's role in the delivery of
health care services. The plaintiffs were not being discriminated against on
the basis of their disabilities, he said; the state's "limited resources" accounted for their continued institutionalization, and they "must wait their turn
for placement" (*Olmstead v. L.C.* 1999, 626).

Attorneys' Fees

After a two-year hiatus, the Court handed down a ruling in a Title II case
with broad implications for all litigants seeking to vindicate rights. *Buckhannon* (2001) arose when the state of West Virginia sought to enforce a law that
would have required the closure of such facilities as the Buckhannon Home.
The home sued in federal court under the ADA and the FHAA, but before the
trial commenced the state legislature repealed the law and the case was dismissed as moot. The home sought attorneys' fees, citing the "catalyst theory" recognized by most courts, in which plaintiffs are awarded attorneys'
fees when a lawsuit instigates a change in the defendant's policy or conduct.

Rejecting the "catalyst theory," the Supreme Court ruled that plaintiffs
were not entitled to fees when defendants voluntarily acquiesced in the
plaintiffs' claims or the parties reached a settlement agreement. To collect
fees, the suit must lead to a "material alteration of the legal relationship of the
parties" (*Buckhannon* 2001, 604). Plaintiffs were considered the prevailing
parties for fee-shifting purposes only if they won a judgment or entered into

a judicially sanctioned settlement. Plaintiffs who reached out-of-court settlements that resulted in policy changes, but whose claims were dismissed prior to adjudication, were ineligible for fees (Paradis 2003; Tebo 2003).

Although brought as a Title II case, the ruling was not limited to Title II actions, nor even to ADA litigation. The broad language of the decision will affect all actions in which attorneys' fees are awarded to prevailing parties, primarily in civil rights and environmental protection cases.[20] *Buckhannon* will likely also assume a special significance in statutes, such as Title III, in which the remedy is limited to injunctive relief (Kelly 2002).[21]

Punitive Damages

One year later, the Court addressed another unresolved issue in Title II (and section 504) litigation on which the circuits were split: the availability of punitive damages. In *County Centre v. Doe* (2001), the Third Circuit Court held that county governments were immune from punitive damages under Title II. But in *Gorman v. Easley* (2001), the Eighth Circuit handed down a contrary ruling.[22] Granting *certiorari* in the Eighth Circuit case, the Supreme Court resolved the conflict among the circuits in *Barnes v. Gorman* (2002).

The suit, brought under Title II and section 504, was filed by a paraplegic man who claimed he was injured by a Kansas City, Missouri, police officer during an arrest. The jury awarded him more than $1 million in compensatory damages and $1.2 million in punitive damages. The punitive damage award was vacated by the district court judge, who was reversed by the Eighth Circuit. The circuit court cited the Supreme Court's statement in *Gwinnet* (1992) that, barring a clear statement to the contrary, federal courts were authorized to award all appropriate relief. The appellate court reasoned that punitive damages were "an integral part of the common law tradition" and that Congress had not explicitly rejected this principle when enacting the ADA (*Gorman* 2001, 745).[23]

In a unanimous opinion, the Supreme Court reversed the Eighth Circuit. Announcing the opinion of the Court, Scalia traced the origin of section 504 and Title II remedies to Title VI. He explained that because Title VI is based on Congress's spending power authority, it embodied an agreement, or a "contract," between the federal government and the states. Under the agreement, states must be cognizant—either from the statutory language or because the remedy is traditionally available in breach of contract cases—of the fact that they may be liable for punitive damages when violating the terms of the contract. Because neither condition applies to Title VI, punitive damages are unavailable in Title VI, and inasmuch as Title II incorporates Title VI remedies, punitive damages are similarly barred in Title II suits. The majority over-rode Stevens's objection that, unlike Title VI, Title II does not derive from Congress's spending power and therefore merits a different analysis.

State Immunity

Despite the Supreme Court's explicit assertion that *Garrett* was limited to Title I, some circuits interpreted it to confer immunity on states in Title II suits as well.[24] Although the Supreme Court was poised to resolve this issue in the early part of 2003, the case was removed from its calendar after it had been scheduled for oral argument. A Tennessee case decided in May 2004, *Tennessee v. Lane* (2004), has provided a partial answer about the extent of the state's liability for money damages in Title II actions.

Title II Litigation in the Lower Federal Courts

My analysis of Title II litigation in the lower federal courts is based on all reported decisions through December 31, 2001, in which the lower court adjudicated a Title II claim against a public entity.[25] Following the reasoning of the Ninth Circuit in *Zimmerman v. Oregon Department of Justice* (1999), in which the court explained that employment was not a "service, program, or activity" within the meaning of Title II, the data exclude employment discrimination claims against public entities.[26]

After eliminating all cases outside the scope of the analysis, there were 442 Title II rulings, 116 in the appellate courts and 326 in the lower courts. To enable a comparison between decisions at the district and appellate court levels, the ruling was considered the unit of analysis, with cases at each court level counted individually.[27] The prevailing party varied by the court level: at the district court level, most rulings consisted of a decision on a defendant's motion to dismiss or for summary judgment.[28] The defendants were regarded as the prevailing parties if their motions were granted, if they won at trial, or if the plaintiffs' motions for summary judgment were denied. Plaintiffs were viewed as the prevailing parties if their motions for summary judgment were granted, if they won at trial, or if the defendants' motions for summary judgment or to dismiss were denied.[29]

The coding at the appellate level was more complex. Following the approach of most scholars, at the appellate court level the plaintiffs were coded as the prevailing parties if the court granted relief on one of their Title II claims or reversed the lower court ruling for the defendants and remanded the case to the court below for further adjudication.[30] Although the plaintiffs had not actually prevailed at this point, the remand gave them another opportunity to win in the court below or to settle the case. Conversely, the defendants were coded as losing if at least one plaintiff in the action succeeded in obtaining a favorable outcome on a significant element in the complaint or the outcome was indeterminate; the defendants were coded as winning if they succeeded in defeating the plaintiff's claim entirely. This methodology intentionally presents a "best case scenario" for the plaintiffs and a "worst case scenario" for the defendants, a scheme designed to ensure that defendants' victories were true victories.

Under this coding scheme, defendants prevailed in 53 percent of the rulings, with a success rate of 66 percent in the appellate courts and 48 percent in the lower courts. Figure 4.1 illustrates these results.

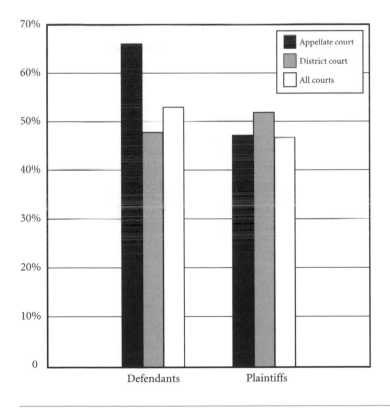

Fig. 4.1. Success of Title II litigants.

The defendants were also divided into state and nonstate actors to determine the effect of the immunity defense, available only to states. States were defendants in 254 cases and local government agencies in 188 cases.[31] Comparing the overall success rate of the state and nonstate governments, the state defendants prevailed in 59 percent of the rulings, while nonstate defendants prevailed in 46 percent. State defendants prevailed in 67 percent of the rulings in the circuits courts compared to 65 percent for nonstate defendants. The difference was greater in the district courts, with states prevailing in 55 percent of the rulings and nonstate defendants prevailing in only 39 percent of the rulings. These results are shown in figure 4.2.

To facilitate the analysis and determine whether the defendant's success rate in Title II litigation varied by the nature of the suit, the cases were divided into nine categories: (1) suits to remove *barriers* to accessibility—by in-

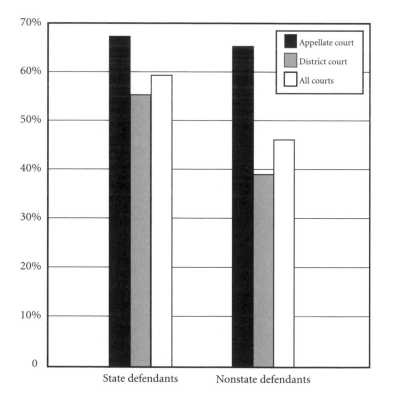

Fig. 4.2. Success of state and nonstate defendants in Title II litigation.

stalling building ramps and curb cuts—and to provide better access to public transportation; (2) suits against the *criminal justice* system for failing to accommodate disabilities during arrests, interrogations, and incarceration; (3) suits challenging the distribution of services and benefits in *health care* and *welfare* policies; (4) suits protesting expulsions and denials of licenses by state-funded institutions of *higher education* and professional licensing agencies; (5) suits demanding the *integration* of people with mental disabilities into local communities; (6) suits challenging fees for "handicapped" *parking* license plates or placards; (7) suits against *schools* or *athletic* associations challenging eligibility rules and other school policies;[32] (8) suits demanding *waivers* of government policies to accommodate disabilities; and (9) suits seeking to reverse decisions by *zoning* or planning boards. Figure 4.3 shows the number of rulings in each type of claim.[33]

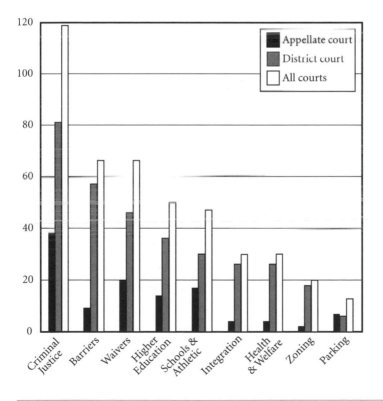

Fig. 4.3. Number of claims in Title II litigation.

As the figure illustrates, actions involving complaints against the criminal justice system, demands for waivers or accommodations, and suits to remove structural barriers to improve accessibility accounted for half of the Title II rulings, with the largest single category consisting of claims brought against prisons and law enforcement agencies. The success rate of the Title II defendants in each type of claim at each court level is shown in figure 4.4.

Figure 4.4 demonstrates that the outcome of the case varied by the level of court as well as by the type of claim. Most defendants were more successful at the appellate level—about 10–15 percentage points higher than in the district courts. The cases involving zoning, higher education, integration, and parking were the exceptions to this pattern, with defendants in these types of cases prevailing more frequently at the district court level. For the

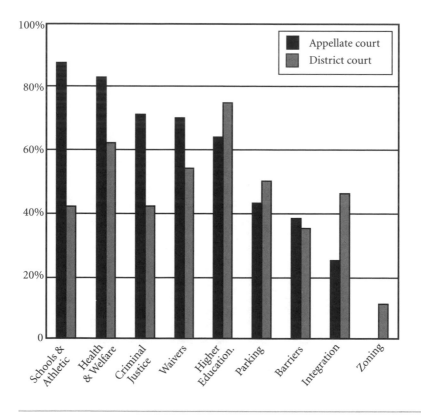

Fig. 4.4. Defendants' success in Title II cases by claim.

most part, defendants in cases involving zoning, structural barriers, parking, and integration were less successful than defendants in the other types of cases.

Consistent with Colker's (2000a) findings, the Title II defendants were more successful in the appellate courts, prevailing in 68 percent of those cases compared to 48 percent in the district courts, despite the fact that the coding scheme at the appellate level favored the plaintiffs. Perhaps this is not surprising, however, because, as Harrington (2000, 436) has noted, the federal courts have become less hospitable to civil rights plaintiffs at all levels, but especially at the appellate level. Perhaps also government agencies are more inclined to settle weaker cases than appeal when the plaintiff wins at the trial court level.

The difference between state and nonstate defendants is largely explained by the ability of the state defendants to invoke Eleventh Amendment immunity to shield themselves from liability.[34] And even when states do not formally claim immunity, federal judges may seek to avoid intruding into state disability policymaking. Perhaps, as well, the disparity in their success rates is attributable to the superior legal and financial resources of state governments compared to county and municipal governments and, especially, local school districts. The difference between state and nonstate defendants was not attributable to the type of cases in which they were involved. Although local governments were almost always the defendants in the zoning cases (with the lowest success rate), the integration claims and parking claims (in which defendants also fared badly) were brought against state defendants.

The cases demonstrate that the courts were more willing to impose costs on public agencies than on private employers. In contrast to the 80–90 percent success rate of defendants in Title I actions, public entities prevailed in only about half the cases (although more so at the appellate court level) that resulted in a ruling on the merits. One explanation for the difference in outcomes stems from the fact that Title I plaintiffs are more likely to be confronted with the catch-22 of ADA litigation in which they must show they have a "substantially limiting disability" and, at the same time, prove they are "qualified" to fulfill the needs of the position sought (see Parry 1998). Although the statute also requires Title II plaintiffs to show they have a qualifying disability, they were rarely challenged on this issue; moreover, they were not required to prove their qualifications. Being relieved of this burden, Title II plaintiffs were more successful than Title I plaintiffs. The courts were also more likely to favor plaintiffs with demonstrated physical disabilities who sought the removal of physical impediments to mobility, such as in the parking and structural barriers cases. Plaintiffs were less likely to prevail in cases, such as education, where they had to prove to the court's satisfaction that they were disabled within the meaning of the act.

Federal Court Policymaking

Judicial enforcement of a law depends in part on how expansively or narrowly lower courts interpret Supreme Court opinions, often based on such factors as the clarity and breadth of the majority opinion (see Canon and Johnson 1999). Thus, although the plaintiffs prevailed in *Yeskey* and *Olmstead,* because of the qualified nature of these rulings and the breadth of available defenses, these high court rulings have led to constrained interpretations of the law by the lower courts and other implementing bodies. And to the further dismay of disability advocates, some courts extended *Garrett* to bar damage actions against states, despite the high court's explicit disclaimer that its ruling did not apply to the issue of state sovereign immunity in Title II suits.

To demonstrate the role of the federal courts in implementing disability rights arising out ADA litigation, the remainder of this chapter presents an analysis of the case law in Title II claims, focusing on judicial interpretation of the act. Table 4.2 presents a summary of the number of cases and the defendants' success in each type of Title II claim.

Barriers

The third largest category of cases revolves around demands for the removal of structural barriers or better access to transportation.[35] The legislative history of the ADA clearly shows that Congress intended to facilitate the movement of individuals with impaired mobility. In statements on the Senate floor, senators such as Paul Simon, Democrat from Illinois, stressed that people with disabilities lacked access to transportation, housing, and other public facilities because of architectural and other structural barriers. He cited the 1987 Harris Poll, which showed that over half of the respondents reported mobility impairments (*Congressional Record* 1988, S5115–16).

The cases in this category revolved around allegations that the government neglected to install ramps or curb cuts on city streets or that the public transportation system failed to provide adequate transit or paratransit services. For the most part, the courts agreed with the plaintiffs that their demands were within the intended purposes of the act and were supported

Table 4.2 Title II claims in the lower federal courts, 1992–2001

| Type of claim | Appellate Court | | | District Court | | |
	Total cases (no.)	Defendant prevails (no.)	Defendant prevails (%)	Total cases (no.)	Defendant prevails (no.)	Defendant prevails (%)
Barriers	8	3	38	49	17	35
Criminal justice	38	27	71	81	34	42
Health care & welfare	6	5	83	34	21	62
Higher education	14	9	64	36	27	75
Integration	4	1	25	26	12	46
Parking	7	3	43	6	3	50
Schools & athletics	17	15	88	30	17	57
Waivers	20	14	70	46	25	54
Zoning	2	0	0	18	2	11

by the law and regulations. Addressing itself to the issue of curb cuts, the district court noted in *Ability Center of Greater Toledo v. City of Sandusky* (2001a, 591), that "during the enactment of the ADA, Congress expressed concern for the difficulties presented to disabled individuals by physical barriers . . . [and] specifically required state and local governments to provide curb cuts on public streets."

Another issue raised in these cases was whether construction projects to repair existing city streets or public buildings should be evaluated under the more stringent accessibility standard for new or altered construction or under the more lenient one for existing facilities; these judgments were commonly based on the extensiveness of the repair job. One of the leading cases in this area arose in a suit by plaintiffs with mobility impairments against the City of Philadelphia, which demanded that sidewalk curb cuts and ramps be installed as part of a resurfacing project.[36] The district court ruled that the resurfacing was an alteration and ordered the city to install curb cuts on streets resurfaced after January 26, 1992, the effective date of Title II. On appeal, the city disputed the lower court's definition of alteration, arguing, however, that if resurfacing were an alteration, it should be permitted to present evidence that the cost would impose an "undue burden."

The appellate court rejected both arguments, agreeing with the lower court that "by the city's own specifications," the resurfacing contracts were "not minor repairs or maintenance" (*Kinney v. Yerusalim* 1993, 1070). Underscoring the importance of curb cuts to the "usability" of the streets, the court held that the resurfacing "work is substantial, with substantial effect" and qualified as an alteration under the law (*Kinney* 1993, 1073). Finally, the court pointed out that although Congress clearly intended to ease the burden on government entities by allowing them to assert an "undue burden" defense in suits demanding changes to existing facilities, no such defense existed for new construction or alterations.

Another issue that arose in such suits revolved around the question of whether an organizational plaintiff, typically an advocacy group or service provider, had proper standing to sue under the "case or controversy" requirement of Article III of the Constitution. One of the first cases to address this issue, *Kessler Institute for Rehabilitation, Inc. v. Mayor and Council of Borough of Essex Falls* (1995), held that the plaintiff organization lacked standing because, according to the statute, only individuals with disabilities can sue public entities to enforce Title II.[37] Most courts, however, have permitted an organizational plaintiff to sue in its own right in ADA cases. In *Access Living v. Chicago Transit Authority* (2001b), the Chicago Transit Authority (CTA) sought summary judgment, arguing, among other things, that as an agency the plaintiff lacked standing. Citing case law and DOJ regulations, U.S. District Court Judge James Holderman explained that most courts had rejected this argument and allowed organizations serving the needs of people with disabilities to sue as long as they met the Article III standing requirements. Moreover, in the Seventh Circuit, organizations have standing if they can show they are required to divert their resources from their normal activities to fighting the defendant's discriminatory conduct. In this case, said the court, there was sufficient evidence that Access Living had devoted considerable resources to countering the CTA's discriminatory conduct that could have been used to accomplish its mission of counseling, referral, and advocacy.

Criminal Justice

The largest component of Title II rulings involves claims against agents of the criminal justice system—law enforcement agencies and prisons, predominantly the latter.[38] Although a victory for the plaintiff, *Yeskey* had left a number of questions unanswered. First, the ruling was limited to prisons, resulting in uncertainty about whether Title II applied to the entire range of law enforcement activities, including arrests and interrogations (Harrington 2000). Second, the Court failed to resolve an inconsistency with *Turner v. Safley* (1987), a previous ruling in a prisoner's rights case. In *Turner,* the Court had placed a heavy burden on a prisoner seeking to challenge a prison regulation, requiring the prison merely to show that the regulation "is reasonably related to legitimate penalogical interests" (*Turner* 1987, 96). *Yeskey* failed to clarify whether the principle established in *Turner* applied to ADA challenges as well, and it did not address the proper level of scrutiny for ADA claims against prisons.

In acknowledging that Congress intended the ADA to apply to prisons, *Yeskey* advanced disability rights, but the lower courts have been inconsistent in reconciling *Turner* with *Yeskey* (Lester 2003). For this reason, as well as the judiciary's overall reluctance to interfere with traditional state responsibilities for criminal justice, the victory in the high court has not translated into plaintiffs' gains in the lower courts. Indeed, the defendants' success rate in the lower courts in such cases rose after the high court ruling in *Yeskey*.[39]

In *Randolph v. Rogers* (1999), although state law required that prisoners with hearing impairments be provided with sign language assistance, the plaintiff was forced to attend his disciplinary hearing without it. Security trumped the ADA as the Eighth Circuit held that the district court should have considered prison security in deciding whether the state violated the ADA. The majority determined that the prison's refusal to comply with the plaintiff's request for a sign language interpreter was justified by its safety concerns.

Similarly, in *Clark v. Woods* (2001), a Texas district court accepted the defendant's argument that accommodating the prisoner's disability would pose a threat to the security of the institution and the safety of its personnel. It rejected the plaintiff's complaint that the prison's decision to curtail his contact visitations violated his rights under the ADA. Granting summary judgment to the Texas Department of Criminal Justice, the court was easily persuaded that the prison's decision to end the contact visits was based on its legitimate interest in furthering prison security.

Plaintiffs suing other agencies in the criminal justice system typically alleged they were subjected to discriminatory treatment during questioning or arrest, most often by being denied a sign language interpreter or suitable transportation to a jail facility. For the most part, the courts agreed that the ADA was applicable in such situations, allowing the plaintiffs to attempt to prove their charge of discrimination. One of the first cases to rule that an arrest was within the ambit of the ADA was *Barber v. Guay* (1995). In *Lewis v. Truitt* (1997), the court also agreed with the plaintiff that the ADA applied when officers arrested him for not responding suitably when they knew or should have known he had a hearing impairment. And in *Gorman v. Bartch* (1998), the court held that transporting a suspect to the police station constitutes a "service" within the reach of the ADA.

However, in *Hainze v. Richards* (2000), the Fifth Circuit departed from these "arrest" cases, deferring to the security concerns of the law enforcement agency. The plaintiff in this case had seemed intent on committing "suicide by cop," that is, provoking the police into shooting him. He was shot twice in the chest by sheriff's deputies after he walked toward them with a knife in his hand. He survived, and sued the sheriff's department on a variety of claims, including Title II, charging discrimination and failure to train officers adequately to protect persons with mental disabilities.

The court disagreed, however, ruling that the suspect "was not denied the benefits and protections of Williamson County's mental health training *by* the County, Sheriff Richards, or the officers. Rather, Hainze's assault of [the officer] with a deadly weapon denied him the benefits of that program" (*Hainze* 2000, 801; emphasis in the original). Moreover, the court held that, unlike a typical arrest case, a confrontation with a dangerous suspect such as this one was not within the purview of the ADA. "While the purpose of the

ADA is to prevent the discrimination of disabled individuals, we do not think Congress intended that the fulfillment of that objective be attained at the expense of the safety of the general public" (*Hainze* 2000, 801).

In addition to the defendants' success on the merits in the law enforcement cases, they also frequently succeeded in asserting immunity defenses based on the Eleventh Amendment. In *Kiman v. New Hampshire Department of Corrections* (2001), for example, decided after *Garrett,* the district court barred the plaintiff's claim against the state prison system, adopting the reasoning of three other circuits that *Garrett* immunized states from damage liability in Title II suits.[40]

Health Care and Welfare

The federal courts proved unreceptive to plaintiffs' demands for health care or welfare benefits. Although the rulings were based on a variety of legal grounds, the overriding reason was the court's unwillingness to override government decisions about the allocation of benefits or services. This was evident in *Doe v. Frommer* (1998), in which the Second Circuit Court dismissed a suit against the New York State Office of Vocational and Educational Services on the grounds that the plaintiff had not been discriminated against, and *Harris v. Oregon Health Sciences University* (1999), when the Oregon District Court dismissed the case, acceding to the state's argument that the patient required care beyond its ability to provide it. Furthermore, as illustrated in *Beno v. Shalala* (1993)—in which the plaintiff claimed discrimination in the termination of his welfare benefits—and *Adam v. Linn-Benton Housing Authority* (2001)—in which the plaintiff complained that denying her housing benefits was discriminatory—the courts were unwilling to permit plaintiffs to use the ADA as a vehicle to obtain or restore public assistance benefits. Consequently, in most such cases the courts held that either plaintiffs were not entitled to the benefits they sought or they had not been denied benefits. And in a number of 2001 cases, plaintiffs also lost when the courts extended *Garrett* to confer immunity on states under the Eleventh Amendment.

An important exception to the judiciary's general approach to health care and welfare claims was *Henrietta D. v. Guiliani* (2000), a district court ruling in a class action suit filed against the City of New York. This was a significant victory for disability rights advocates because the court viewed the ADA in concert with other statutory (and constitutional) guarantees, ruling that the plaintiffs were merely asking for benefits to which they were entitled under city and state law.

The plaintiffs in *Henrietta D.* were indigent city residents with AIDS or HIV who charged that the city, specifically the Division of AIDS Services and Income Support (DASIS), had failed in its responsibility to enable them to access public benefits, thereby violating the ADA as well as numerous state and federal laws.[41] In September 2000, following a bench trial, a district court judge found the city guilty of violating Title II in addition to other statutory and constitutional provisions and ordered injunctive relief. He noted that the assistance provided by DASIS was merely an accommodation to allow people with disabilities meaningful access to existing services and benefits.[42]

The court rejected the city's argument that the plaintiffs were seeking additional benefits and services not required by the ADA. "To the contrary," said the court, they only "seek meaningful access to the very same benefits and services . . . and only the modifications—such as intensive case management and low case manager-to-client ratios—required to ensure meaningful access to the same benefits and services" (*Henrietta D.* 2000, 212). Adopting a structural equality model, the court added that without these modifications, people with disabilities would be unable to achieve the equality of services that the ADA required the city to provide.

Higher Education

Plaintiffs who sued institutions of higher education and state licensing agencies sought accommodations, for the most part, in taking examinations or asked to be reinstated in graduate and professional schools. In such cases, the defendant argued, usually successfully, that the plaintiff was unqualified even with the accommodation or that providing the accommodation would fundamentally alter the program. In some cases, the defendant sought to dismiss the suit on the grounds that the plaintiff was not disabled. The courts accepted the defendant's analysis in most cases, adhering to the Supreme Court ruling in *Regents of University of Michigan v. Ewing* (1985) that courts should ordinarily defer to the academic judgments of university officials.

The Ninth Circuit case of *Zukle v. Regents of the University of California* (1999) exemplifies the deference courts typically show to institutions of higher education in ADA litigation. When the University of California, Davis, medical school dismissed the plaintiff for falling below its academic standards, she sued, citing the ADA regulation requiring a public entity to "make reasonable modifications in policies, practices, or procedures . . . to avoid discrimination on the basis of disability" (28 C.F.R. §35.130(b)(7)). The court explained that the plaintiff must initially prove that she is qualified and that a reasonable accommodation would allow her to satisfy the eligibility requirements. The school must show that the requested accommodation would fundamentally alter the program or that, even with the accommodation, she would be unable to meet its standards.[43] It added that the majority of circuits deferred to a school's judgment that a student is not academically qualified and that a reasonable accommodation is not available without a "fundamental alteration" in the program.

Deferring to the medical school's judgment about her academic qualifications, the court found that the plaintiff had been offered all the accommodations the medical school customarily offered students with learning disabilities and that she had still been unable to pass her courses. Thus, it concluded that she had not shown that she would be eligible for the program if provided with reasonable accommodations.

An example of the difficulty plaintiffs encountered in proving they are disabled is illustrated in *Panzer v. New York State Board of Law Examiners* (1994). Before taking the bar examination, the plaintiff had sought an injunction to allow him to take the test with a number of accommodations. His petition was denied after the board reviewed his reading test scores and consulted with a licensed psychologist. After failing the bar, he again requested accommodations and was again denied. After his appeal was rejected, he sued. The court, however, found that the board was entitled to rely on the opinion of its expert, who testified that the plaintiff did not have a learning disability.

After 1999, it became even more difficult for plaintiffs to prove they were disabled as the Court's Title I decisions began to affect the outcome of cases involving higher education; this was illustrated in a leading case against the New York State Bar Association. The suit arose after the plaintiff's request for "reasonable accommodations" when taking the New York State bar examination had been denied and she took it unsuccessfully five times. The issue under dispute in the case was whether she was disabled, that is, whether as a result of her impaired reading ability, she was substantially limited in the major life activity of working.

Following a twenty-one day bench trial, the district court judge found that the plaintiff was disabled within the meaning of the ADA and ordered a series of adjustments in her bar exam, including extra time, the use of a computer, and large print (*Bartlett v. New York State Board of Law Examiners* 1997). The judge rejected the state's argument that because she had been able to succeed academically by obtaining a Ph.D. in educational administration, she should be excluded from the protection of the ADA.

The Second Circuit differed with the lower court's analysis of the legal issues by finding the plaintiff substantially limited in the major life activity of reading compared to the average person (*Bartlett v. New York State Board of Law Examiners* 1998). The court, however, agreed with the trial court's conclusion that she was entitled to reasonable accommodations while taking the bar exam. However, a year later, after granting *certiorari* in *New York State Board of Law Examiners v. Bartlett* (1999), the Supreme Court vacated the appellate court's judgment and remanded the case for further consideration in light of its decisions in the 1999 trilogy of Title I cases and *Williams*.

On remand from the appellate court, the district court concluded that the plaintiff was substantially limited in the major life activity of reading, or, in the alternative, of working, and ordered the same accommodations it had ordered several years earlier (*Bartlett v. New York State Board of Law Examiners* 2001). Reviewing the voluminous expert testimony, the district court judge assessed the effect of "mitigating measures" and "corrective devices." The court limited its analysis to measures that affected her ability to read, excluding factors relating to other life activities. Based on her fatigue when reading, the length of time it took her to read and understand the material, and the limitations in word recognition, the judge believed she was disabled within the meaning of the act because, compared to most people, she was "substantially limited in the major life activity" of reading.

Similarly, in *Davis v. University of North Carolina at Wilmington* (2001), the plaintiff sued after her dismissal from a teacher's certificate program. Although the school offered to admit her to a master's program, she never applied. The university's motion for summary judgment was granted. On appeal, the circuit court focused its attention on the "regarded as" prong of the definition of disability. Although the court believed it possible that the university perceived her to be limited in her ability to perform her work, it found no evidence that it considered her to be "substantially limited" in a major life activity and unable to perform "a broad range of jobs." At most, the university regarded her as unable to teach, but because education offered a range of opportunities, the court held that she had not shown that the university considered her unable to perform a broad range of jobs. Because she was offered admission to a master's program, added the court, the university did not consider her ability to attend college substantially limited (assuming that it was a major life activity); at most, it considered her unable to complete the teacher certificate program. Thus, she had failed to meet the threshold requirement of proving she was disabled within the meaning of the ADA.

Integration

Although a relatively small number of suits were related to community-based living, the number of cases does not adequately portray the significance of the litigation effort in this area because many were class actions. Because the Third Circuit's interpretation of the integration mandate in *Helen L.* had become "the standard on which subsequent courts . . . relied" (Karger 1999, 1245), *Olmstead* had essentially ratified the prevailing view of the lower courts. However, *Olmstead* also provided an opportunity for states to argue in subsequent cases that fiscal considerations justified their failure to proceed with integration, that their limited resources were needed elsewhere (1260–61). Moreover, *Olmstead* afforded states a greater opportunity to claim that the high court had not set precise boundaries for the "fundamental alteration" or "reasonable modification" defenses (Smith and Calandrillo 2001, 702; see Cerreto 2001).

The limitations of the *Olmstead* decision were also evident in the slow pace with which the integration mandate was implemented following the ruling. A NAPAS report released in July 2000, a little over a year after *Olmstead* was decided, assessed state *Olmstead* plans and concluded that, although states were aware of the decision, "implementation efforts are sluggish at best. In fact," the report continued, "not a single state has an *Olmstead* plan that meets HHS recommendations [and] . . . waiting lists for community placement continue to grow rather than decrease in size" (NAPAS 2000, 1). Reflecting on the post-*Olmstead* era, Perlin's (2002, 261) "sad conclusion [was] that a decade after the passage of the ADA and in spite of *Olmstead*," much needed to be done for people with mental disabilities.

When plaintiffs sought judicial enforcement of the integration mandate following *Olmstead*, they found that the lower courts were not interpreting the high court ruling expansively.[44] *Williams v. Wasserman* (2001), a case brought against Maryland's Department of Health and Mental Hygiene, illustrates the difficulties the plaintiffs encountered when charging the state with denying community-based care. The state contended that because it could not establish community placements for all eligible patients, acquiescing to the demands of these plaintiffs would fundamentally alter the state's mental health program. After assessing the evidence, the court supported the state's good faith effort at allocating the available resources in its mental health program. Expressing sympathy for the plaintiffs, the court concluded, "the plaintiffs' pain and frustration was genuine and understandable; the defendants' efforts to provide a stable, safe, and caring environment also were genuine and commendable, if not always successful. In the end, the plaintiffs have not shown sufficient reason for the court to order the State of Maryland to do more" (638). In addition to interpreting *Olmstead* to allow states a great deal of latitude in determining the pace of integration, some circuits also expanded *Garrett* to permit states to escape from damage liability entirely.

Parking

The smallest number of claims revolved around challenges to the fees for disability parking placards or licenses, but as in many Title II cases, because they affected statewide policy, the impact was felt more widely than the number of cases would suggest. Although it seemed the ADA was clear on the issue, many states were charging for the right to participate in "handicapped" parking programs and the circuits were split over whether they should be permitted to do so (Groshong 2003, 811). The plaintiffs in these cases cited the language in the statute as well as a DOJ regulation that stated that a "public entity may not place a surcharge on a particular individual with a disability or any group of individuals with disabilities to cover the costs of measures, such as the provision of auxiliary aids or program accessibility, that are required to provide that individual with nondiscriminatory treatment required by the Act or this part" (28 C.F.R. §35.130(f)).

The leading case for the plaintiff's position, *Dare v. California Department of Motor Vehicles* (1999), involved a class of persons with disabilities who challenged a six dollar placard fee. They claimed it violated the ADA's prohibition against surcharges to offset the costs of programs required to avoid discriminating against people with disabilities. The court concluded that the surcharge constituted facial discrimination against people with disabilities, conflicting with the clear command of the ADA. "Charging disabled people for parking that would otherwise be free constitutes discrimination in the provision of access to public buildings, a measure required under the ADA" (*Dare* 1999, 1173).

In some circuits, however, defendants successfully argued that the federal courts lacked jurisdiction over the matter because the federal Tax Injunction Act (TIA) prohibited federal courts from "enjoin[ing], suspend[ing], or restrain[ing] the assessment, levy or collection of any tax under State law where a plain, speedy and efficient remedy may be had in the courts of such State" (28 U.S.C. §1341). Although there is a split among the circuits on this question, most circuits that have considered the issue have rejected the defendant's argument that the parking surcharge is a tax rather than a fee, and therefore outside the jurisdiction of the federal courts (Groshong 2003).

Hexom v. Oregon Department of Transportation (1999) illustrates the prevailing view among the lower courts in which the Ninth Circuit found that the $4.00 fee for parking placards and decals was a regulatory fee designed to pay for the costs of the program and impermissible under the ADA. But in *Hedgepath v. Tennessee Department of Safety* (2000), the Sixth Circuit concluded that the $20.50 fee to register a vehicle and purchase a placard was a general revenue-raising device, that is, a tax, and dismissed the case.

In addition to plaintiffs losing on the merits, however, they also lost when states successfully presented an immunity defense. In *Thompson v. Colorado* (2001), the appellate court reversed the magistrate judge's ruling that the ADA prohibited the state from imposing a parking fee, holding that the state was immune from suit on Eleventh Amendment grounds.

Schools and Athletics

The cases challenging school and athletic policies show that, as in the cases involving higher education and licensing, the courts were also disinclined to interfere with the judgments of school officials. Procedural obstacles in such cases also arose when the courts held that parents who file Title II suits against public school systems must first exhaust their administrative remedies under the IDEA. In *Babicz v. School Board of Broward County* (1998), for example, after the lower court dismissed the plaintiff's damage suit against the school board for lack of subject matter jurisdiction, the appellate court affirmed. Adopting the reasoning of the Second and Seventh Circuits, the Eleventh Circuit explained that litigants must exhaust IDEA administrative remedies before they can proceed with their ADA or section 504 claims to prevent them from circumventing the IDEA's ban on money damages.

Shirey v. City of Alexandria School Board (2000) illustrates another difficulty for plaintiffs challenging school policies toward children with disabilities. The issue in the case was an emergency evacuation policy. The parents cited two incidents in which their daughter was left in the building during an evacuation drill; once, she spent seventy minutes in the school during a bomb threat (although accompanied by an adult), and the second time, she had been alone for two minutes during a fire drill. The parents claimed these incidents violated her rights under the ADA and sought injunctive relief as well as compensatory and punitive damages. The lower court granted the defendant's motion for summary judgment and the Fourth Circuit affirmed. The appeals court explained that there was no dispute that the child was entitled to safe evacuation during an emergency, but the issue was whether she had been denied it on the basis of her disability. The court found that the school had developed a reasonable and safe plan prior to the fire drill and had successfully tested it and was therefore not liable for discrimination. In a footnote, the court indicated that it was "sympathetic to the child's distress during the confusion of a fire drill," but added that "the imperfect execution of an otherwise reasonable evacuation plan" did not constitute discrimination (*Shirey* 2000, 14n2). With respect to the bomb threat incident, the court found that she was discriminated against, but concluded that the remedy should be limited to injunctive relief, that is, the development of a safe evacuation plan and, since the school had already developed such a plan, no other action could be taken.

Another important issue in claims against schools and athletic associations revolved around eligibility rules that prevented children with disabilities from playing competitive sports. The ground rules in such cases were set out in an Eighth Circuit case, *Pottgen v. The Missouri High School Activities Association* (1994) and two Sixth Circuit decisions, *Sandison v. Michigan High School Athletic Association* (1995) and *McPherson v. Michigan High School Athletic Association* (1997). These cases involved young men with learning disabilities who exceeded the age- or semester-limit for playing interscholastic high school sports.[45]

In *Pottgen,* the plaintiff challenged the age limit that prevented him from playing baseball in his senior year. The court determined that the rule was essential to the baseball program and that a modification would be unreasonable. Similarly, in *Sandison,* the appellate court held that the age requirement was necessary for the sake of fair competition for runners and that modifying it was unreasonable because it would fundamentally alter the high school sports program by giving an unfair advantage to the older, more muscular runners. The court concluded that "the plaintiffs' respective learning disability does not prevent the two students from meeting the age requirement; the passage of time does" (*Sandison* 1995, 1033). And in *McPherson,* the appellate court rejected the plaintiff's challenge to an eight-semester limit for playing basketball. The court required the plaintiff to show either that the rule was formulated to exclude a player with a disability or that it was reasonable to accommodate him by waiving the rule. Following *Sandison,* the court held that a modification would be unreasonable because it would require a "fundamental alteration" of the sports program.

Waivers and Accommodations

The second largest category of cases consists of demands for waivers of government policies or accommodations. Such cases typically required the courts to determine whether Congress intended the ADA to ban the discriminatory effects of facially neutral laws. As the Ninth Circuit explained in *Crowder v. Hawaii* (1996), because the Supreme Court had interpreted section 504 to reach policies with a disparate impact on people with disabilities, most lower courts applied this reasoning to the ADA as well.

Although defendants were only moderately successful in these cases at the district court level, they fared very well at the appellate level. The prevailing view in the circuit courts was that the plaintiffs had failed to show that the government's conduct was discriminatory because there was no exclusion from services or denial of benefits. An example of the court's reasoning in such cases can be seen in *Atia v. New York City Housing Authority* (2001), in which the plaintiff had sought to install a second telephone line in his apartment to enable him to participate in an employment training program from his home via a computer. He had received permission from the building manager on the condition that the phone only use existing lines and cause no structural damage to the building.

When the telephone company was unable to install the line and adhere to the conditions, the plaintiff filed suit, arguing that the city violated the ADA by failing to accommodate his request to waive its policy against multiple telephone lines. The court, however, granted the defendant's motion for summary judgment, finding that the plaintiff presented no evidence that he was denied a benefit or service by the city, that is, that he was treated differently on the basis of his disability. "Specifically," said the court, "he has presented no evidence suggesting that other tenants were allowed to install second telephone lines without complying with the building's preconditions" (*Atia* 2001, 12).

In *Lightbourn v. County of El Paso* (2001), a class of plaintiffs with mobility and sight impairments sued the secretary of state of Texas for failing to accommodate their disabilities by ensuring the accessibility of polling places.[46] Following a bench trial, the lower court found that the "present system discriminates against the disabled" and ordered the parties to reach an agreement on the remedy (*Lightbourn* 1995, 1433). On appeal, however, the Fifth Circuit reversed, holding that the secretary of state had no such duty under Texas law or the ADA. Moreover, even if the secretary of state had breached his duty to maintain uniformity in the system, as required by Texas law, he would not have denied any benefit to the plaintiffs by doing so.

In another voting rights case, *Herschaft v. New York Board of Elections* (2001), the court also denied the plaintiff's claim against the Board of Elections that, because of his mental impairments, he should be granted an extension of the time allotted to independent candidates to gather signatures to get on the ballot for city council. Although the plaintiff was diagnosed as a paranoid schizophrenic, the court was unable to conclude that he was a qualified individual with a disability because there was insufficient evidence that he was limited in a major life activity. However, the court continued, even if he were disabled, he was not being excluded from participating in the election. Additionally, even if he were being excluded, his demand to modify the election procedure was unreasonable.

Dadian v. Village of Wilmette (2001) illustrates how some plaintiffs were able to persuade a jury that they had been discriminated against by the local government's failure to grant their request for an accommodation. These plaintiffs were an elderly couple who sought an exemption from a local ordinance to allow them to build an attached garage onto the front of their house. Concerned about the danger of backing out onto the street from a front driveway, the village board refused to grant their request. The Seventh Circuit upheld the jury verdict in the plaintiffs' favor, ruling that they had presented sufficient evidence to allow a jury to find they were disabled and that, by refusing to allow the exemption, the village had failed to accommodate them.

Zoning Claims

Most of the suits contesting zoning regulations or decisions were brought by organizations seeking to operate rehabilitation centers or mental health clinics in a downtown or commercial setting. When zoning boards or town councils denied their petitions for permits, typically because of opposition to the facility's clientele from businesses or residents in the area, they brought a Title II suit against the city, claiming the rejection was discriminatory because it was based on their clients' disabilities. In the early stages of this litigation, the plaintiffs were forced to rebut the defendants' argument that Title II did not apply to zoning policies (see *Wisconsin Correctional Service v. City of Milwaukee* 2001). In some cases the defendants also argued, for the most part unsuccessfully, that the plaintiff organization lacked standing to bring suit (see *Access Living* 2001b).

The leading case establishing that the ADA was applicable to zoning claims was *Innovative Health Systems, Inc. v. City of White Plains* (1997). The case arose when Innovative Health Systems (IHS) sought to relocate its outpatient drug- and alcohol-rehabilitation program to a larger, more convenient site in downtown White Plains, a city just outside New York. Two would-be neighbors of the IHS Center, a mall and cooperative association, objected to the proposed site because of the nature of the IHS clients and the predicted effect on the property values. After public hearings were held, IHS was denied a permit to move to the new facility.

IHS sued under the ADA and section 504, seeking a preliminary injunction. Among other things, the city argued that zoning decisions were not within the bounds of the ADA or section 504. The district court disagreed and granted IHS the injunction. On appeal, the circuit court rejected the city's argument that the antidiscrimination provisions of Title II did not apply to zoning. Echoing the lower court, the appellate court explained that "both the ADA and the Rehabilitation Act clearly encompass zoning decisions by the City because making such decisions is a normal function of a government entity." The court continued, the "ADA's coverage [is not limited] to conduct that occurs in the 'programs, services, or activities' of the City. Rather it is a catch-all phrase that prohibits all discrimination by a public entity, regardless of the context, and that should avoid the very type of hairsplitting arguments the City attempts to make here" (*Innovative Health Systems* 1997, 44–45). Moreover, said the court, both the legislative intent and the DOJ regulations manifestly supported this interpretation.

When zoning boards deny permits to agencies serving people with disabilities, they typically do so when prospective neighbors argue that the facility will harm their neighborhood, often using stereotypical and inflammatory language about the clientele that will be served in the facility. When such rhetoric is spoken at public meetings or appears in news stories, plaintiffs present it as evidence of discrimination on the basis of disability. In *Pathways Psychosocial v. Town of Leonardtown, Maryland* (2001), as in *Innovative Health Systems,* the city refused to allow a nonprofit agency serving people with disabilities to move to a downtown location. The move was desirable because, among other things, the new location made it eligible for state revitalization funds. After approving a resolution to endorse the move, the town council rescinded it, in part because of opposition from a council member who had called other council members, claiming that "'Pathways' clients would be a public nuisance' and would 'urinate in public,' 'get drunk,' 'be exhibitionists,' and 'be violent'" (*Pathways Psychosocial* 2001, 776).

After failing to acquire a permit for another location, the agency sued for damages and injunctive relief. The plaintiffs charged that discrimination prompted the town's actions, citing the events leading up to its decision, as well as actions and words of some members of the town council. The court concurred, noting that council members "agree[d] with or respond[ed] directly to community opposition based on the fears and stereotypes of mentally disabled people" (*Pathways Psychosocial* 2001, 783). The court added that it considered the city's justifications for its actions a pretext for discrimination. Based on these findings, the court concluded that the plaintiffs had provided sufficient evidence to defeat the city's motion for summary judgment.

Although the courts have generally been more willing to rule in favor of the Title II plaintiffs than the Title I plaintiffs, the record of success in suits against state and local public entities does not indicate strong judicial support for the ADA.

5 Disability Rights

and Public Accommodations

Title III provides that "no individual shall be discriminated against on the basis of disability in the full and equal enjoyment of the goods, services, facilities, privileges, advantages, or accommodations of any place of public accommodation by any person who owns, leases (or leases to), or operates a place of public accommodation" (42 U.S.C. §12182(a)). Derived from Congress's authority to regulate interstate commerce, it identifies twelve types of facilities as public accommodations, including places of lodging, recreation, sales, education, and entertainment; within each category there are examples of businesses or enterprises such as hotels and inns; museums and libraries; restaurants and bars; parks and zoos; day care centers; homeless shelters; bowling alleys and golf courses; movies, theaters, and concert halls; grocery stores and shopping centers; Laundromats and banks; and private schools. Although the categories are limited to twelve, the kinds of establishments within each category are not fixed. The operation of the establishments must affect commerce, and entities controlled by religious organizations and private clubs are outside the reach of Title III. In part because of the specificity with which places are identified in the statute, courts are divided over whether Congress intended the law to cover physical places only, or whether it had a broader perspective in mind.[1]

Owners and operators covered by the act must make "reasonable modifications" in policies and practices to make goods, services, and accommodations available to people with disabilities unless the modification would "fundamentally alter" their nature; they must also ensure that no person with disabilities is excluded or treated differently because of the absence of auxiliary aids and services unless providing such aids would "fundamentally alter" the nature of the goods and services or result in an "undue burden."

Title III and Civil Rights Remedies

Although Title III "plays an enormously important role in the integration of individuals with disabilities into society" (Colker 2000b, 377), it has received the least attention of the three major parts of the act. Prior to the ADA, the laws explicitly prohibiting discrimination on the basis of disability in the private sector—the ACAA of 1986 and the FHAA of 1988—were restricted to the housing and airline industries (Hermanek 1994, 459). In modeling the ADA on the 1964 Civil Rights Act, Congress explicitly replicated Title II, the public accommodations section of the 1964 law that bans discrimination in accommodations on the basis of race and national origin. Title III broke new ground by including a wide range of privately owned retail and service establishments as well as commercial facilities, such as factories and warehouses, within its reach.[2]

During legislative debate over Title III, some members of Congress predicted that it would precipitate a flood of litigation—accompanied by demands for outrageous attorneys' fees—against the owners of small businesses. They expressed apprehension over the potential costs, noting that a damage award would add to the expense of compliance and drive small establishments out of business because, unlike larger enterprises, they would be unable to pass the costs onto consumers. Their fear was reflected in remarks made by Hatch, who stressed that although the bill exempted the "mom-and-pop grocery store" from its employment discrimination provisions, it did not relieve even the smallest shop from accommodating customers with disabilities (U.S. Senate Committee on Labor and Human Resources 1989, 97).[3] Speaking on the Senate floor, Dale Bumpers, Democrat from Arkansas, approved the law, yet warned that "we are obligated here to weigh the interest of the rights of the handicapped, which ought to be total, against what is obviously going to be quite a burden for a lot of small business people" (*Congressional Record* 1989, S10761).

The availability of money damages in civil rights laws is mixed. Although damage awards are unavailable under Title II of the 1964 Civil Rights Act, the 1968 housing legislation authorizes plaintiffs to sue for compensatory and punitive damages and, in 1988, when the law was amended to include discrimination on the basis of disability, the cap on punitive damages was lifted (Milani 2001, 151). According to Osolinik (2001), the "big concern" among members of Congress during the congressional debate over Title III was over damages, specifically, "the scope of coverage versus damages." Speaking for the White House, Attorney General Dick Thornburgh testified before Congress that Title III should emulate the remedial framework of Title II (of the 1964 act) and exclude both compensatory and punitive damages. To ensure its passage, the members of Congress eventually compromised; they restricted the remedy to injunctive relief (although allowing attorneys' fees and litigation expenses), but expanded the scope of coverage in the law to all retail and service establishments. In contrast, Title II of the 1964 Civil Rights Act only applies to establishments selling food, lodging, and entertainment (Weber 1995).[4] As Osolinik explained, because more types of establishments discriminated against people with disabilities, the list of places covered by the ADA needed to be longer than the list of places in Title II. Harkin, the chief sponsor of the bill in the Senate, accepted the compromise reluctantly, warning that ADA supporters "would consider any amendment that pertains to either of these two aspects of the legislation an amendment designed to destroy this fragile compromise" (*Congressional Record* 1989, S10714).

Colker (2000b, 394–95) has argued that Title III should have adopted the remedial provisions of the FHAA and allowed prevailing plaintiffs to recover compensatory and punitive damages in addition to injunctive relief.[5] She contends that the limited remedy has been detrimental to effective enforcement of the act: first, it has reduced the incentive for individuals to file suit against violators of the law; and second, it has reduced the incentive for compliance when the only punishment for noncompliance is an injunction requiring defendants to do what they are obligated to do in the first place. Colker's view is shared by others. Laura Miller (2002), managing attorney at Equip for Equality in Chicago, believes that the absence of damages in Title III has reduced incentives to comply with the law in cases of existing construction. Sullivan (1995, 1142–43) also notes that "many private businesses have delayed Title III compliance, waiting to be challenged on their noncompliance before instituting change."

Reflecting its concern for the cost to business owners, Congress limited the ADA's mandate on accessibility of existing structures, looking toward an ultimate goal of accessibility rather than a present one (Kelly 2002, 365). Owners of existing facilities are only obligated to remove structural and communication barriers when "such removal is readily achievable" (42 U.S.C. §12182(b)(2)(A)(iv)), meaning "easily accomplishable and able to be carried out without much difficulty or expense."[6] When such barriers cannot be easily removed, owners must make their goods and services available through "other readily achievable means" (42 U.S.C. §12182(b)(2)(A)(v)).

According to a report by the Senate Committee on Labor and Human Resources, the "readily achievable" standard was adopted as a middle ground between requiring the removal of all structural barriers in existing facilities or exempting all existing facilities from the reach of the law. The committee noted that it was easier for defendants to satisfy this standard than the "undue hardship" (Title I) or "undue burden" (Title II) standards, thus excusing owners of public accommodations from complying even if the requisite change would be less burdensome than an "undue burden" (U.S. Senate Committee on Labor and Human Resources 1989, 65–66). By instructing courts to consider the defendant's financial resources as well as the cost of the renovation in determining whether a structural modification is "readily achievable," the law allows a defendant to argue that the changes are too costly.[7]

The ADA Notification Act

In the decade following passage of the ADA, a backlash began to emerge, characterized by complaints that the "wrong people" were taking advantage of the law (NCD 1999, 13). The negative publicity was fueled by media reports that portrayed plaintiffs as filing fraudulent or excessive claims against small businesses struggling to survive (see Colker 1999; Percy 2000; Fleischer and Zames 2001; Milani 2001). One example was a story that appeared in the *Milwaukee Journal Sentinel* (October 8, 2000), which charged that "the ADA has created yet another layer of regulations that impose unnecessary costs on businesses, spawn more unnecessary litigation and create another cash bonanza for opportunistic trial lawyers." In addressing the validity of these popular perceptions of Title III lawsuits, Milani (2001, 176) observed that such charges were exaggerated and, although some attorneys may have sought high fees, there was little evidence that courts had granted outrageous fee awards in Title III cases.

In February 2000, shortly before the ten-year anniversary of the passage of the ADA, two Florida House Republicans, Clay Shaw and Mark Foley, introduced a bill to allow owners of businesses and commercial facilities to correct ADA violations before allowing plaintiffs to file suit against them. The ADA Notification Act, HR3590, would have amended the remedy provision of Title III to require a would-be plaintiff to serve written notice (in person or by registered mail) of their intent to sue an owner of a public accommodation; the notice would have to specify the location and date of the violation as well as inform the putative defendant that the suit could not be filed until ninety days had passed.[8] The law would have denied federal court jurisdiction to any Title III claim filed before the ninety days had expired.[9] In September 2000, an identical bill was introduced in the Senate as S3122 by Tim Hutchinson, Republican from Arkansas.

According to its sponsors, the bills were intended to stem the tide of litigation against unsuspecting business owners. These suits, they charged, were brought by avaricious attorneys who were more interested in lining their pockets than representing their clients and, because the violations were cured as soon as the lawsuits were filed, the lawyers sought large fees for doing little work. Additionally, the supporters argued, attorneys' fees have made it increasingly difficult for owners to meet their obligations under the law because they have diverted funds that could have been used to comply with the law.

In his opening statement on May 18, 2000, before the Subcommittee on the Constitution of the House Judiciary Committee, Representative Charles Canady, Republican from Florida, expressed concern that "the progress brought about by the ADA is being threatened by a growing number of lawyers who are generating large sums in legal fees for pointing out often simple fixes that would bring properties into compliance with the ADA" (U.S. House Committee on the Judiciary 2000b). Testifying in favor of the bill, Foley talked about "rogue attorneys" who "shake down thousands of businesses"; he characterized the fees collected in Title III suits as "legal extortion" and called the ADA a "cash cow" and "an equal opportunity employment act for lawyers." He expounded on how unfair the law was for owners of small businesses who "can barely afford clerks" and who, unaware of their obligations under Title III, are being victimized by greedy attorneys (U.S. House Committee on the Judiciary 2000e).

The most prominent witness at the hearings was Clint Eastwood, the actor and former mayor of Carmel, California. In 1997, he was the defendant in a lawsuit brought against him as owner of Mission Ranch Hotel in Carmel. The plaintiff had cited a number of ADA violations in her complaint, including the inaccessibility of the bathrooms. Eastwood contested her claim and prolonged litigation ensued. At the trial in September 2000, Eastwood testified that he had not been completely cognizant of his obligations under the ADA and that he was working to make the hotel accessible. Moreover, he contended that he should have been made aware of any ADA violations before the plaintiff filed suit. Diane zum Brunnen, the plaintiff in the Eastwood case, had sent him two letters, including one by certified mail that had been returned, complaining of the ADA violations. He admitted to the jury that he refused to open the letters, which, according to him, was a common practice among Hollywood personalities. Based on his own testimony, as Milani (2001, 179–80) observes, he had notice of the violations (or would have had notice had he opened the letters) and was given an opportunity to make his property accessible before the suit was filed.

Following a week-long trial, after determining that there were violations on Eastwood's property, a federal jury declined to award the plaintiff the $25,000 damages she sought under state law, thus depriving her attorneys of $577,000 in fees (*San Francisco Chronicle,* September 30, 2000).[10] After this experience, Eastwood sought to testify in support of the bill to counter such lawsuits, which he called "a racket and a scam, . . . a legal scam" (*Boston Herald,* May 19, 2000).

During the committee hearings, witnesses who testified against the bill argued that it would encourage businesses to simply ignore the law and wait for a Title III suit to be filed before complying. They stressed that the threat of having to pay a plaintiff's attorneys' fees was the only financial incentive for business owners to comply with the accessibility provisions of the law, predicting that if HR3590 were enacted, business owners would simply wait for a notice of an intent to sue before bringing their premises into compliance with the law (U.S. House Committee on the Judiciary 2000a). Moreover, they pointed out, attorneys were already reluctant to accept Title III cases because of the unavailability of money damages, and the proposed law would make them even more reluctant.[11] The opponents also complained that it was unjust to single out people with disabilities and force them to give notice of a violation before they could file a lawsuit (U.S. House Committee on the Judiciary 2000d). And because businesses had ten years to bring their premises into compliance with the ADA, the extra ninety days' notice was unwarranted and counterproductive to the purpose of the law (U.S. House Committee on the Judiciary 2000c).

Despite the publicity provoked by Eastwood's support for the bill, HR3590 was not acted on by Congress in 2000. A year later, in both March and April 2001, supporters attempted to breathe new life into it by introducing two companion bills in the Senate (S782, by Daniel Inouye, Democrat from Hawaii) and the House (HR914, by Foley). Each was referred to committee, but no action was taken. Foley again introduced the same measure as

HR728 in February 2003; again, the bill was sent to committee and has languished there.

Although the legislative effort to curb Title III litigation had failed, disability advocates feared that the Court's decision in *Buckhannon* (2001) would accomplish the same goal, with defendants settling cases and thereby depriving the plaintiffs' attorneys of their fees. They believed that by making attorneys reluctant to take on Title III cases, *Buckhannon* would frustrate Congress's aim of encouraging private enforcement of the law (Kelly 2002).

The Supreme Court and Title III Litigation

The Supreme Court has decided only two Title III cases through 2004. As table 5.1 demonstrates, the plaintiff prevailed in each case. The rulings, however, were fairly limited in scope and did not greatly advance the remedial purposes of the act.

Asymptomatic HIV

The high court addressed its first Title III issue in a case revolving around a dentist's right to refuse office treatment to a patient with HIV. The action arose when Dr. Randon Bragdon, a Bangor, Maine, dentist, declined to treat Sidney Abbott in his office after she indicated that she was HIV-positive.[12] He informed her that he treated patients with HIV at the local hospital; however, although he would only charge his normal fee, she would have to pay the hospital costs.

Ruling in her lawsuit, the district court cited other lower court rulings as well as the DOJ interpretive guidelines. The court held that because asymptomatic HIV was a physical impairment that "substantially limited a major life activity," in her case reproduction, she was disabled within the meaning of the act (*Abbott v. Bragdon* 1995, 586).[13] The court noted that over a decade before, the Supreme Court had determined that discrimination against indi-

Table 5.1 Supreme Court Title III cases, 1998–2001

Case	Year	Issue	Disposition
Abbott	1998	Applicability of ADA to asymptomatic HIV	Pro-Plaintiff
Martin	2001	Applicability of ADA to rules of professional golf	Pro-Plaintiff

viduals with contagious diseases violated the 1973 Rehabilitation Act. Mindful of the high court's instruction in *Arline* (1987, 288) that courts should normally "defer to the reasonable medical judgments of public health officials," the lower court reviewed the 1991 American Dental Association Policy on HIV and the 1993 Centers for Disease Control (CDC) Dentistry Guidelines on the use of protective measures in dental offices. Based on this evidence, the court concluded that office treatment did not constitute a "direct threat" to the dentist and awarded her summary judgment.[14]

The appellate court affirmed, agreeing that her HIV-positive status—whether symptomatic or asymptomatic—was a physical impairment under the ADA because it affected the major life activity of reproduction. Additionally, the court agreed that his evidence to support his claim about the danger of transmitting HIV during office treatment was insufficient to deny her motion for summary judgment. The court indicated it was cognizant of the "difficulty of the choices that the ADA compels healthcare professionals such as Dr. Bragdon to make." Perhaps in light of this, the court cautioned that its ruling should not be broadly interpreted and that there must be a "case-by-case inquiry into a service provider's responsibilities to treat HIV-positive patients" (*Abbott v. Bragdon* 1997, 949).

In a fractured 5–4 ruling, with Justice Anthony Kennedy announcing the opinion for himself and Justices Stevens, Souter, Ginsburg, and Breyer, the Court upheld the courts below. The majority found that Abbott was within the reach of the ADA because her HIV status was an impairment that substantially limited the "major life activity" of reproduction.[15] The Court cited judicial and administrative interpretations of the 1973 Rehabilitation Act and the ADA to bolster its conclusion that asymptomatic HIV infection was a disability within the meaning of the ADA.

The high court departed from the lower courts, however, in assessing Brandon's "direct threat" defense. It traced the origin of the direct threat exception to its holding in *Arline* (1987, 287) that the Rehabilitation Act did not require employers to hire persons who were at "significant risk of communicating an infectious disease to others in the workplace" unless reasonable accommodations would abolish the risk. It noted that Congress indicated its acceptance of this interpretation by amending the 1973 act and the FHA to incorporate this language and, of course, by including it within the ADA as well. Again, citing *Arline*, the Court explained that the risk "must be determined from the standpoint of the person who refuses the treatment or accommodation, and the risk assessment must be based on medical or other objective evidence" (*Bragdon v. Abbott* 1998, 649).

The majority generally approved of the circuit court's appraisal of the medical evidence, but objected to its reliance on the Dental Association policy and the CDC guidelines in concluding there were no issues of fact to be determined.[16] In the Court's view, the Dental Association was not qualified as a public health association and the guidelines did not assess the risk of contagion sufficiently. Indicating some skepticism about the defendant's ability to present sufficient evidence to defeat the motion for summary judgment, the Court remanded the case to allow the appellate court to reevaluate the degree of risk involved in the office treatment of her cavity.

On remand, as instructed by the high court, the circuit court reexamined both policies and reaffirmed the district court's summary judgment award for the plaintiff. The court found that the CDC guidelines sufficiently appraised the risk of contamination involved when using universal precautions; it also determined that the Dental Association policy was not based on ethical or moral standards, as it had been characterized, but was grounded in scientific fact. Again, warning of the "case-specific nature of [its] determination," the First Circuit ruled in Abbott's favor (*Abbott v. Bragdon* 1999, 90).

The Supreme Court had interpreted Title III expansively in *Abbott,* in part by declaring, over the objections of the dissent, that reproduction was a major life activity. Moreover, in determining that HIV was a physical impairment that limited the major life activity of reproduction and was a disability within the meaning of the ADA, the Court enlarged the scope of the ADA's protection. However, in remanding the case, the Court allowed the health provider to buttress his argument that treating her in his office threatened his safety. Moreover, when the appellate court had upheld the lower court's award of summary judgment for Abbott, it cautiously pointed out the limits of its holding.

Professional Golf

More recently, in a Title III decision handed down in May 2001, the Court interpreted the meaning of the "fundamental alteration" defense in sports competitions. The case concerned the use of a motorized cart in tournament golf by professional golfer Casey Martin. The primary issue was whether Martin's request for a waiver of the "walking rule" during tournament play constituted a "fundamental alteration" of the game. The two circuits that had ruled on this issue were split: the Seventh Circuit opinion, *Olinger v. United States Golf Association* (2000), supported the association, while the Ninth Circuit, in *Martin v. PGA Tour, Inc.* (2000), ruled in favor of the golfer.

Olinger was decided by the Seventh Circuit the day after *Martin* was decided by the Ninth Circuit.

Golfer Ford Olinger suffered from a degenerative disease that acutely hindered his ability to walk, and he asked to be allowed to ride in a golf cart in the qualification rounds for the U.S. Open, the premier golf tournament in the United States. The United States Golf Association (USGA) refused, arguing that the ADA was not applicable to the tournament and, even if it were, using a golf cart would fundamentally alter the game. He sued. The lower court ruled in the USGA's favor and the appellate court affirmed.[17] In a paean to the game of golf and its champions, the Seventh Circuit discussed the rule against golf carts in tournament play, explaining the importance the USGA placed on walking the course. Although it was undecided whether the U.S. Open was a public accommodation within the meaning of the ADA, the court accepted the USGA's argument that the game would be fundamentally altered if it allowed players to use golf carts because it would lessen the mental and physical stresses that are integral to major golf tournaments.

In contrast, the Ninth Circuit affirmed the lower court ruling in Martin's favor. The facts were virtually identical: Martin had a severe circulatory disorder in his right leg and when the Professional Golf Association (PGA) denied his request to use a golf cart during a "qualifying school" competition associated with a PGA Tour, he sued. He won a preliminary injunction, enabling him to use the cart, and subsequently won at trial, the judge concluding that the golf cart was a reasonable accommodation that did not fundamentally alter the game.

On appeal, the circuit court held that, as a matter of law, the PGA Tour competition was a public accommodation within Title III; indeed, it noted that golf courses are listed as examples of places of recreation in the statute.[18] The court rejected the argument that a golf course is a "mixed" public accommodation (a point also raised by the USGA in *Olinger*) and that the law only covered spectators "behind the ropes," not competitors. Finally, the appeals court agreed with the lower court that the use of the golf cart was "necessary" and "reasonable." And because it would not affect "the central competition in shot-making," it would not fundamentally alter the game (*Martin v. PGA Tour, Inc.* 2000, 1000).

The Supreme Court resolved the conflict among the circuits in *PGA Tour, Inc. v. Martin* (2001), affirming the Ninth Circuit in a 7–2 decision. There was little that was new in Stevens's majority opinion. In quick succession, he rejected the PGA's arguments that the law was not applicable because it was a private club and that Martin was a "provider" rather than a customer or client.[19] He simply noted that the PGA was an accommodation that offered the public the opportunity to watch as well as compete and Title III did not allow it to discriminate against individuals in either category. Because the PGA had agreed that in order for Martin to play it must allow him to use the cart, the Court's decision turned on whether a waiver of the no-walking rule would be a "fundamental alteration" of the game.

Echoing the lower court opinions, the Court agreed "that shot-making has been the essence of golf since early in its history" (*PGA Tour, Inc. v. Martin* 2001, 685n39) and that "the walking rule is at best peripheral to the nature of the [PGA's] athletic events, and thus it might be waived in individual cases without working a fundamental alteration" (689). The fact that he would still be subjected to the stress and physical strain from the unavoidable walking involved in the game, even with a cart, convinced the Court that permitting him to ride during tournament play would not fundamentally alter the play of the game. Thus, the Court allowed Martin access to the game, but was careful not to give him an edge over the competition (Warden 2002, 689–90).

Scalia and Thomas dissented, arguing that the Court should not decide what is essential to the game and what is not. They disagreed with the majority's interpretation that the ADA encompassed practitioners of the game, like Martin, and objected to its effrontery in determining that walking is not a key element of the game. In their view, a tournament is not a public accommodation and Martin is neither a customer nor a client. They maintained that the ADA only bars business owners (such as the PGA) from denying a person access to products or services that are offered to others; it does not require them to provide different products or services for individuals with disabilities. Just as one cannot order a bookstore to stock a certain number of Braille books, the PGA "store" can set the rules and if the public objects, they will not buy at the PGA "store."

Martin was a victory for disability rights advocates (see Shannon 2001). However, despite the extensive coverage given to it in the popular press, as well as scholarly journals, accompanied by predictions of a sea change in the nature of sports competition, it is unlikely to have much effect on other professional sports competitions or athletes. For suits of this nature to succeed, plaintiffs must show that an accommodation is necessary to enable them to compete and that it does not significantly affect the game or play of other athletes. As Stevens noted, few had sought this kind of waiver in professional golf since Martin's initial inquiry because, not surprisingly, most athletes did not have his severe disability nor did they have the qualifications to allow them to compete in major tournament play (Warden 2002).

Title III Litigation in the Lower Federal Courts

Surveying Title III litigation, Colker (2000b, 400) identified only twenty-five appellate court cases decided through July 1998, just 5 percent of all reported appellate ADA cases.[20] Despite predictions of a flood of litigation against "mom and pop" store owners brought by "greedy clients" and their "avaricious lawyers," there have been fewer Title III suits than Title I or II suits. Moreover, as Sullivan (1995, 1117) comments, the courts have "interpreted its [Title III's] provisions . . . with minimal adverse impact on private organizations."

Reporting the outcome of the cases in her study, Colker notes that, as in Title I actions, the Title III defendants were quite successful, prevailing at a rate of 72 percent in the circuit courts. Based on these results as well as the paucity of cases, she concludes that "plaintiffs have a somewhat easier time prevailing under ADA Title III than ADA Title I, but are not very inclined even to attempt litigation under ADA Title III." Thus, in her view, "Title III has been less successful than was originally hoped" (Colker 2000b, 379).[21]

My analysis of Title III litigation in the lower federal courts is based on all reported decisions through December 31, 2001, in which the lower court adjudicated a Title III suit against a public accommodation. After excluding the nongermane cases, there were 247 Title III rulings, 46 in the appellate courts, 201 in the lower courts.[22] These findings confirm Colker's (2000b) of the relative scarcity of Title III cases. Following the method used in the Title II cases, the ruling was the unit of analysis, with cases at each court level counted individually and the determination of the prevailing party varying by the court level. Based on this coding scheme, the defendants prevailed in 55 percent of the rulings, with a 70 percent success rate in the appellate courts and a 52 percent success rate in the trial courts. The results are shown in figure 5.1.

To facilitate the analysis in assessing whether the defendant's success rate in Title III litigation varied by the nature of the suit, the cases were divided into five types of claims: (1) challenges to *athletic rules and regulations;* (2) demands to remove structural *barriers* to buildings and increase access to facilities; (3) suits against private *educational* institutions and professional licensing agencies; (4) complaints about the denial of *goods and services* to persons with contagious or disfiguring diseases, mental disabilities, and

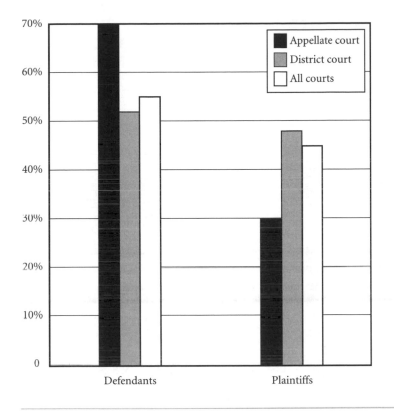

Fig. 5.1. Success of Title III litigants.

hearing impairments; and (5) suits against *insurance* companies to eliminate disparities in health insurance policies.

Figure 5.2, illustrating the number of rulings in each type of Title III claim, demonstrates that complaints related to structural barriers, insurance carriers, and denial of goods and services comprised more than three-quarters of the Title III rulings in the lower courts; the other three types accounted for less than one-quarter of the cases.

The defendants' success rate in each type of Title III claim in each court level is shown in figure 5.3. As this figure indicates, defendants in most types of claims did very well at the appellate court level, with none losing more than half the cases; three types of defendants prevailed at least 70 percent of the time in the circuit courts. Although the defendants were less successful in the district courts than in the appellate courts, with the exception of one

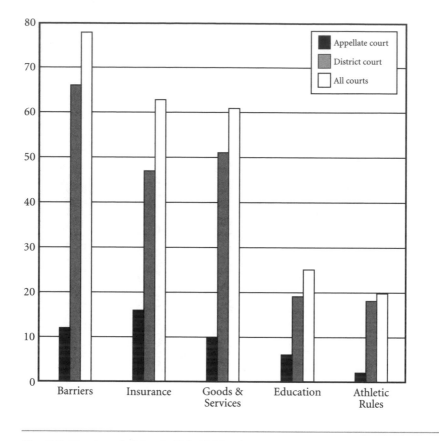

Fig. 5.2. Number of claims in Title III litigation.

type of defendant, they prevailed in at least half the cases—even in the trial courts. The only category in which the defendants did not prevail in the majority of lower court rulings involved physical barriers.

Defendants were initially divided into three types: businesses, universities, and other; businesses were further classified as large or small enterprises. To maximize the number of small business owners, in the event of ambiguity the business was coded as "small." Even under this coding scheme, designed to maximize the number of small enterprises, fewer than 10 percent of the rulings pertained to small businesses, most involving the denial of goods and services. The majority of defendants in such cases were sole practitioner doctors and dentists, but there were also a dry cleaner, a beauty shop, and a few restaurants and shops.

The defendants' success rate in the appellate courts—despite a coding scheme that favored plaintiffs—suggests that defendants chose their appeals wisely, perhaps preferring to settle weaker cases rather than appealing to a higher court when the plaintiffs won at the trial court level. But the Title III defendants were not as successful as those in the employment discrimination cases. In part, this is because, unlike plaintiffs in employment discrimination suits, Title III plaintiffs generally do not have to prove they are disabled and that they are qualified for a job at the same time. In some cases, however, primarily involving education claims, when the courts required Title III plaintiffs to prove they were within the ADA's definition of disability in addition to proving their qualifications, the defendants were more successful.

Finally, contrary to the predictions that the law would devastate small business owners, such defendants, whose fate was of great concern to mem-

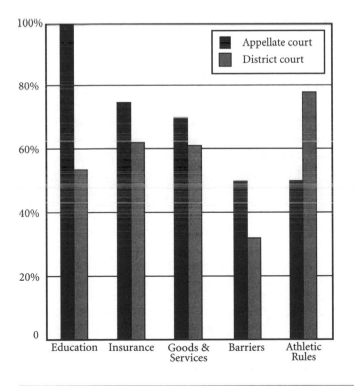

Fig. 5.3. Defendants' success in Title III litigation by claim.

bers of Congress during their deliberations, were not targeted in Title III litigation. The warnings about excessive litigation against them were greatly exaggerated. Because plaintiffs may hesitate to sue mom-and-pop businesses in their own neighborhood or such businesses may be more likely to comply with the law, the cases show that most of the Title III lawsuits are aimed at large-scale corporations and companies, defendants who barely received mention during congressional debate over the bill.

Federal Court Policymaking

Because *Martin* and *Abbott* did not address issues of major importance in Title III law, the lower courts have been relatively unconstrained by the high court in their interpretations of the act. Title III defendants have been substantially aided by the remedial framework of the law. The responsibility may lie with the courts for their narrow interpretation of the law (as Colker 2000b argues) or with Congress for excluding damage claims. Whatever the reason, the cases demonstrate that the "fragile compromise" forged by the disability community and the Bush administration in 1990 has been a significant factor in the litigation.

Citing a variety of legal grounds, the courts rule that they lack jurisdiction, that the cases are moot, or that the plaintiffs lack standing (see Milani 2004). Nearly 25 percent of the Title III rulings in this study in which the defendants prevailed at the district court level were dismissed, and almost 10 percent at the appellate court level, on grounds stemming from the limitation on damages. These constraints on access to the courts have proved to be formidable obstacles to interpreting the statute to effectuate its remedial purpose.

In a substantial number of cases, despite credible allegations of the defendant's discriminatory conduct, the courts dismissed the case, holding that injunctive relief was inappropriate because the plaintiff lacked standing. The rule of standing has three requirements: plaintiffs must show they have suffered an "injury in fact"; there is a causal relationship between the injury and the defendant's conduct; and the relief granted by the court will likely provide a remedy for the injury. The plaintiff bears the burden of proof (*Lujan v. Defenders of Wildlife* 1992, 560–61).[23] To establish standing for injunctive relief, plaintiffs must show they "will suffer an injury in fact which is (a) concrete and particularized and (b) actual or imminent, not conjectural or hypothetical" (*Tyler v. The Kansas Lottery* 1998, 1224). As the Supreme

Court explained in *City of Los Angeles v. Lyons* (1983, quoting *O'Shea v. Littleton* 1974, 495-96), to show an injury in fact, "past exposure to illegal conduct does not in itself show a present case or controversy regarding injunctive relief . . . if unaccompanied by any continuing, present adverse effects."[24] In ADA cases, as a Maryland district court noted, "a plaintiff does not have standing to obtain injunctive relief if he cannot demonstrate a likelihood that he will suffer future discrimination at the hands of the defendant" (*Levy v. Mote* 2000).[25] Summing up the law, a Florida district court judge stressed that Title III plaintiffs would be denied injunctive relief unless they showed they "actually suffered–and will again–suffer discrimination in violation of Title III" (*Access Now v. South Florida Stadium Corporation* 2001, 1365).

Title III Litigation Claims and Judicial Interpretation

The analysis of the lower federal court rulings in the five types of claims illustrates the way in which judicial interpretation has affected the implementation of Title III. Table 5.2 presents a summary of the number of cases and the defendants' success in each category of Title III claims.

Athletic Rules

Before rulings on the merits in cases involving suits against such defendants as the National Collegiate Athletic Association (NCAA), the National Football League (NFL), and the PGA, the courts have to resolve a number of threshold questions. The first is whether the defendant organization is a "place of public accommodation." The courts are divided on this, but most hold that the term applies only to physical structures. Some have adopted a broader view that it is unnecessary to specify a physical location where the discrimination occurred, and some (borrowing from Title II case law) have crafted a compromise in which organizations "closely connected to a specific facility" were considered within Title III (Stowe 2000, 319).

Ellit v. U.S.A. Hockey (1996) illustrates the narrow view in which the court dismissed a complaint against a youth hockey league because the suit did not allege that the child was denied access to the ice rink, the place where the hockey was played. Similarly, in *Stoutenborough v. National Football League* (1995), individuals with hearing impairments sued the NFL and a number of television stations to enjoin the policy of blacking out football games that had not been sold out. They argued that the practice was dis-

Table 5.2 Title III claims in the lower federal courts, 1993–2001

Type of claim	Appellate Court			District Court		
	Total cases (no.)	Defendant prevails (no.)	Defendant prevails (%)	Total cases (no.)	Defendant prevails (no.)	Defendant prevails (%)
Athletic rules	2	1	50	18	14	78
Barriers	12	6	50	66	21	32
Education	6	6	100	19	10	53
Goods & services	10	7	70	51	31	61
Insurance	16	12	75	47	29	62

criminatory because they were only able to access televised games. Although the circuit court agreed with the plaintiffs that the television broadcasts were a service of a public accommodation, it rejected the claim. Citing the plain language of the statute, the court found that Title III did not apply because the defendants were not within one of the twelve categories identified as public accommodations. Strictly adhering to the text, the court emphasized that the law defined "places of public accommodation" as facilities or structures. Thus, although the football games were played in a "place of public accommodation," the broadcasts did not constitute a "place" and were therefore outside the reach of Title III.

A California district court took the opposite position in *Shultz v. Hemet Pony League* (1996), in which a child's baseball league denied a request to allow an eleven-year-old child with cerebral palsy to play in a younger age bracket. Here, the court ruled that it was unnecessary to target a physical structure in making a Title III claim of discrimination. *Ganden v. National Collegiate Athletic Association* (1996), a case brought against the NCAA by a student with a learning disability, represented the middle ground in which the Illinois district court held that an organization may be considered a "place of public accommodation" if it is closely tied to a physical structure.

In some cases, such as *Matthews v. National Collegiate Athletic Association* (2001), the limitation on remedies led to the court's holding that even if the plaintiff were to prevail and the defendant were ordered to waive its rules or accommodate the plaintiff, the injunction would serve no purpose because the plaintiff had no eligibility left. In this case, the district court held that although the plaintiff had proven his claim for discrimination under Title III, he lacked standing to sue because an injunction would permit him to play beyond the time limit governing play of all student athletes.

In other cases, the defendant successfully availed itself of the "fundamental alteration" defense, arguing that waiving eligibility requirements to allow the plaintiffs to participate in a sport would fundamentally alter the game. Although the Supreme Court had resolved this for professional golfers in *Martin,* the district court came to a different conclusion in *Gander* (1996). It found that relaxing the minimum grade point average and waiving a core course requirement would not fundamentally alter the game, but it ruled against the plaintiff when it looked beyond the game to assess the purpose of the requirement. Upon considering this the court held that waiving the rules would fundamentally alter the NCAA's purpose of ensuring that high school players succeeded in college (see Weston 1999).

Barriers

Most of the complaints received by the DOJ in the early years of the ADA revolved around the removal of structural barriers (Hermanek 1994, 467). During congressional testimony, representatives of the disability rights community reported being segregated from society because of the inaccessibility of stores, restaurants, and workplaces; according to the Harris Poll conducted at that time, a substantial number of respondents claimed they were limited by structural barriers or inaccessible transit systems (Shapiro 1994, 106). Congress's commitment to removing such obstacles to allow people with mobility impairments to move about in society was evident in the statute, making it likely that, as in the Title II cases, judges would be sympathetic to the complaints of plaintiffs such as these. Additionally, because individuals with impaired mobility, especially wheelchair users, are a highly visible and vocal segment of the disability community, they are also more likely to be able to capture media attention and have access to legal resources to represent their claims in court (Fleischer and Zames 2001, chap. 5). As Jo Holzer (2001), executive director of the Council for Disability Rights, puts it, "the wheelchair is the international symbol for disability and has virtually become the symbol for the whole movement."

It is not surprising that the largest category of Title III claims consisted of complaints about structural barriers or other impediments to mobility in stores, restaurants, hotels, cruise ships, medical facilities, sports arenas, and concert halls; nor is it surprising that the defendants had one of the lowest rates of success in these cases. Additionally, the plaintiffs were often assisted in these cases by the United States participating as intervenor or amicus curiae. Although having the solicitor general on the plaintiff's side did not guarantee success, it often helped. Of the six circuit court rulings in such cases in which the plaintiff prevailed, the United States played a role in five.[26]

The plaintiffs, primarily individuals with wheelchairs, were aided in these cases by the fact that their legal arguments were supported by DOJ regulations as well as the ADA Accessibility Guidelines for Buildings and Facilities (ADAAG).[27] In *Independent Living Resources v. Oregon Arena Corporation* (1998), for example, the plaintiffs alleged numerous ADA violations and prevailed on most issues when the court adhered closely to the applicable regulations about wheelchair spaces and seating requirements.[28] The principal issue in this case related to the failure to maintain a sufficient number of aisle seats and wheelchair spaces in the Rose Garden, a multipurpose indoor arena in Portland, Oregon, that is used primarily for Portland Trail Blazer (basketball) and Portland Winter Hawks (hockey) games, but also for concerts, ice shows, and circuses.

The DOJ regulations required arenas and stadiums to modify a certain number of aisle seats so that they had removable armrests to enable persons with mobility impairments, including wheelchair users, to sit in them. The magistrate found that although the arena held 191 of these aisle seats, as required under ADAAG, only 14 were accessible to wheelchairs; the others required climbing up a few steps to get to them. The problem was exacerbated because season ticket holders were located in these areas and the arena was contractually obligated to renew their seats on demand.

According to the judge, the question was "whether those seats must actually be available for use by persons with disabilities, or whether it is sufficient that the defendant built 191 seats with removable armrests." He concluded by saying, "common sense suggests that the first interpretation is correct" (*Independent Living Resources* 1998, 1172), adding that he was not requiring all 191 seats to be reserved for persons with disabilities, but that ticket-selling procedures must ensure that they would be available when needed by such individuals.[29]

Many of the cases involving physical barriers were straightforward. In *Lieber v. Macy's West, Inc.* (1999), for example, the plaintiffs complained of a number of ADA violations, including barriers at sales counters, inaccessible fitting rooms and restrooms, inadequate aisle clearances, and narrow entrances. The major focus of the case was on the aisles that prevented persons with mobility impairments from reaching the merchandise. Because the store was engaged in a renovation project costing more than $100 million, the court applied the rules of "altered construction" and refused to allow a "readily achievable" defense.

After extensive findings of fact, although the court acknowledged that Macy's had made some efforts to comply with the law, there were still a few remaining obstacles. It ordered Macy's to modify the entrances to the building as well as the fitting rooms, sales counters, and restrooms; the store was also required to make the display merchandise more accessible by widening the aisles to allow wheelchair users to reach the merchandise on display.[30]

Similarly, in *Leiken v. Squaw Valley Ski Corporation* (1994), the plaintiffs sought a preliminary injunction to force the resort to abandon its "no wheelchair" policy. The case arose when two wheelchair users were not permitted to avail themselves of the activities at Squaw Valley's High Camp Bath and Tennis Club, a recreational resort complex with tennis, skiing, ice skating, and swimming facilities. The camp, renovated in 1989 before Title III went into effect, was only accessible by cable car, a two-car aerial train. One of the plaintiffs had been allowed to ride up the mountain to the camp, but could not use any facilities there; the other was not even permitted on the train.

The class action suit cited numerous ADA violations at the resort and asked the court to order it to make its facilities accessible. The suit mentioned, among other things, the inaccessibility of the parking lot, the cable car, the mountain camp, and the restrooms. The court agreed, but noted that the injunction would only require Squaw Valley to sell train tickets to all individuals, including wheelchair users, who wanted to ride up the mountain and prevent it from unconditionally banning them from its facilities. Interpreting the applicable DOJ regulations, the court concluded that there were no legitimate safety concerns to justify the policy; rather, it believed the policy stemmed from generalizations and stereotypical images of people with disabilities.

In some cases, despite clear instances of ADA violations, defendants, especially at the appellate level, prevailed by successfully arguing they were not proper defendants under the act; that is, they were not "owners or operators" of the premises in the dispute (Langer 1999/2000; Stowe 2000). Such cases arose when a plaintiff sued a parent company that, in turn, pointed to a franchising or licensing agreement and argued that the franchisee or licensee was the proper defendant.

The leading case illustrating this situation is *Neff v. American Dairy Queen* (1995). The plaintiff filed suit against the American Dairy Queen (ADQ) Corporation, claiming it was liable for the ADA violations at the two San Antonio Dairy Queens. The corporation contended that its franchisee, R&S Dairy Queens, Inc., operated the San Antonio stores. Neff cited the franchising agreement that required R&S Dairy Queens to obtain approval from ADQ before making structural changes in the buildings as evidence that ADQ operated the stores. The lower court granted the defendant's motion for summary judgment, concluding that the franchise agreement only permitted the corporation to veto proposed modifications to the building, but not to order them. Therefore, ADQ was not an "operator" within the meaning of the ADA.

On appeal, the plaintiff argued that summary judgment was inappropriate because there was "a genuine issue of material fact" about whether ADQ owned those stores. The Fifth Circuit noted that this was a case of first impression in the circuit and limited itself to the narrow question of "whether a franchiser with limited control over a franchisee's store 'operates a place of public accommodation' within the meaning" of the ADA (*Neff* 1995, 1066). The court further restricted its inquiry to determining whether ADQ could order its franchisees to modify their facilities to make them more accessible, ignoring the broader issue of ADQ's control over other areas such as equipment, uniform design, and trademarks. The appellate court affirmed the lower court, concluding that the language of the agreement indicated that because ADQ lacked the power to force R&S to remove structural barriers that hindered the mobility of people with disabilities, it did not operate the San Antonio stores.[31]

Citing *Neff* (1995), a California district court dismissed a complaint against the Days Inn corporation in *United States of America v. Days Inn of America* (1998). As the franchisor, the motel chain argued that it was not a proper defendant in the lawsuit and not responsible for the design and construction of Days Inn of Willows, California. The court agreed, finding that, as in *Neff*, the franchisor did not exercise control over the discriminatory conditions on the premises. Although the "readily achievable" defense did not play a significant role in defendants' victories, there were a few instances when the defendants were able to convince the court that removing a physical obstacle or renovating a facility was too costly.[32] In *Alford v. Bistro Restaurant* (2000), for example, the plaintiffs sued a local restaurant, charging that its front steps and inaccessible restroom violated the ADA. The restaurant claimed that it qualified as an existing structure under the act because it had not been renovated since January 26, 1992, although the wooden slats in an alternative pathway had been replaced by bricks after that date. The court agreed with the defendant that the replacement was not an alteration and applied the "readily achievable" test used in existing structures. Based on the estimates provided by each side for the expense of removing the barriers, the court found that the cost of renovating the restroom was greater than the Bistro's annual net income and was therefore not "readily achievable" as a matter of law. However, because a ramp to the front door was estimated to cost only about 10 percent of the restaurant's net income, the court denied the defendant's motion for summary judgment.[33]

Education

The cases in the education category were prompted by several types of complaints about education and testing policies. The courts were often sympathetic to parents requesting that their children be admitted or reinstated to a school, mostly in cases with younger children. They were less sympathetic, however, when the claims had implications for the educational programs. In such cases, the defendants' success, as in the Title II cases involving education, was primarily attributable to the courts' reluctance to render judgments about the plaintiffs' qualifications as students. Additionally, in these types of claims, the courts often applied the legal analysis associated with Title I, dismissing cases on the grounds that the plaintiffs were not disabled within the meaning of the act.

Plaintiffs were more likely to prevail when the exclusion was based on noneducational reasons. In *Alvarez v. Fountainhead, Inc.* (1999), for example, a four-year-old child was excluded from preschool because the school's "no medications" policy did not allow him to bring his asthma inhaler to school. The plaintiffs asked the court to order the school to rescind the policy and train its staff in the use of the inhaler, arguing that unless it did, the child would be unable to gain the benefits of a preschool education. The court rejected the school's argument that accommodating his disability would fundamentally alter its educational program; in the court's view, "requiring teachers to recognize symptoms of wheezing" (*Alvarez* 1999, 1052) was within their normal range of responsibility. Nor, given his doctor's statement that the teacher training would only take a short time, would the accommodation impose "an undue burden" on the school. Based on these factors, the court granted the plaintiff's motion for a preliminary injunction.

Similarly, in *Bercovitch v. Baldwin School* (1997), a private school indefinitely suspended an eleven-year-old child for misbehavior. Although he was not suspended because of his disability, once he was diagnosed with attention-deficit/hyperactivity disorder (ADHD), the school had an obligation under the ADA to readmit him and accommodate his disability. Thus, the court concluded that he had met the requirements for a preliminary injunction and ordered the school to allow him back with proper medication and treatment.[34]

The rulings in these two cases were somewhat anomalous because the courts were generally unwilling to find for plaintiffs who challenged their dismissals from schools for failing grades despite their claims that the grades resulted from their disabilities. In such cases, the courts typically found the plaintiffs were not qualified or not disabled within the meaning of the ADA, or that the defendants' actions were not based on their disabilities.[35]

In another case involving ADHD, the court rejected the plaintiff's plea for a permanent injunction to readmit him to school after he was expelled because of his grades.[36] *Axelrod v. Phillips Academy, Andover* (1999) challenged a student's expulsion from the prestigious high school, the plaintiff arguing that his poor grades resulted from the school's failure to accommodate his disability. After a nine-day trial, the court found that he had a disability, ADHD, but that the school's attempts to accommodate him were adequate, that he had been warned repeatedly, and that his academic record stemmed from his failure to "perform the required school work"; in sum, that he was "not otherwise qualified" (*Axelrod* 1999, 83).

Similarly, in *El Kouni v. Trustees of Boston University* (2001), the court denied the plaintiff's request for an injunction to expunge his records to allow him to seek readmission to the MD/PhD program that had dismissed him. Quoting from *Southeastern Community College v. Davis* (1979), the court found that although the plaintiff was disabled and the university had accommodated his disability by allowing him extra time on examinations, he was not qualified for the program because he had failed to show there was a reasonable accommodation that would enable him to succeed. Citing *Regents of University of Michigan v. Ewing* (1985), the court noted that it was expected to defer to the school's academic judgments.

In *Amir v. St. Louis University* (1999), the court found the university's action was not based on the plaintiff's disability. He had charged that he was dismissed from St. Louis University's (SLU) medical school because of his mental disability, obsessive compulsive disorder (OCD). The court found, however, that although his OCD met the statutory definition of disability, there was "simply a lack of evidence that [his] disability served as a factor motivating any of SLU's adverse decisions" (*Amir* 1999, 1028). Also citing *Ewing* (1985), the court expressed its reluctance to interfere with the school's academic decisions.

In a number of cases, the courts also found that the plaintiffs were not disabled. In *Gardiner v. Mercyhurst College* (1995), one of the early Title III cases, the plaintiff sought admission into a police training program. The court found that the plaintiff's mental condition may have been an impairment, but that it did not substantially limit the major life activity of working; at most, it limited his ability to be a police officer. And in *Ballard v. Kinkaid School* (2000), the plaintiff sought readmission to the private college preparatory school he had been attending for six years; he had been dismissed when his grades fell below the school's academic standards. The plaintiff claimed he had a disability, a visual disorder known as Irlen syndrome. The court, however, found that although Irlen syndrome might have been an impairment, it did not substantially limit his major life activities of reading and learning as determined by his passing grades and standardized test scores at his new school.

Finally, in cases involving national medical and law licensing examinations, the plaintiffs claimed they failed because their disabilities had not been accommodated when they had sought more time on the examinations or to take them in more accessible locations. Their claims were often rejected by the lower courts, which followed the Supreme Court's lead in defining disability narrowly.

A leading Title III case involving such a challenge to an educational policy, *Gonzales v. National Board of Medical Examiners* (2000) illustrates the court's approach. The plaintiff had asked the National Board of Medical Examiners (NBME) to accommodate his learning disability by giving him extended time to complete the United States Medical Licensing Examination.[37] He provided medical records to support his claim of a disability and, based in part on these, the medical school had allowed him additional time on examinations as well as other accommodations. Based on its expert's evaluation that he did not have a learning disability, the NBME denied his request. After two attempts and two failures, he sought a preliminary injunction. Following a four-day trial, the lower court denied the injunction, finding that he was not disabled because he was not substantially impaired in the "major life activity" of working.[38] The circuit court panel reviewed the conflicting expert opinions and assessed his academic success and performance on other multiple choice tests. In a 2–1 decision, it concluded that his impairments did not substantially limit him in performing the major life activities of reading, writing, and working, and that the lower court was correct in denying the injunction.

The dissent objected to the majority's refusal to consider him disabled, arguing that it was irrelevant that he achieved reasonably good grades in school and average scores on standardized tests because these were not "major life activities." The "major life activity" at issue was reading, in which he was impaired compared to most people. The judge contended that the majority's reliance on the Title I trilogy was misplaced. The plaintiff in *Kirkingburg* (1999) had been able to correct his disability, but the plaintiff in *Gonzales* maintained that despite his best efforts, he was unable to read as well as he needed to—as well as the average person. He added that, despite the expert opinion to the contrary, the record did not support the conclusion that the plaintiff was not disabled. Turning the tables on the "deference" argument, he emphasized that the plaintiff "has apparently satisfied the faculty of one of this country's preeminent medical schools that he would make a very good physician, and I have little doubt that the faculty of the University of Michigan Medical School are better judges than I of who ought to be allowed to practice medicine" (*Gonzales* 2000, 637).

Goods and Services

Claims revolving around the denial of goods and services included a diverse lot of businesses, such as department stores, day care centers, restaurants, hospitals, medical and dental offices, cable television companies, beauty parlors, wine shops, and grocery stores. The cases were brought by plaintiffs with a variety of disabilities, including hearing and visual impairments, autism, asthma, facial disfigurements, degenerative spine diseases, skin disorders, HIV, and AIDS.

Many of these cases were affected by the court's approach to the rule of standing; although plaintiffs in almost all types of Title III cases were affected by this, cases involving the denial of access to goods and services predominated. To satisfy the case or controversy requirement of Article III, the courts required the Title III plaintiffs to allege they would return to seek the services of the health care provider that had declined to treat them or to visit the restaurant or store that had barred or failed to accommodate them.

A leading case illustrating the obstacle caused by the standing requirement, *Aikins v. St. Helena Hospital* (1994), involved a claim that the hospital had not provided the plaintiff with sign language assistance. In dismissing her complaint, the court noted that she had not shown she was "likely to use the hospital in the near future, nor that defendants are likely to discriminate against her when she does" (*Aikins* 1994, 1134). A Maryland district court ruled on a similar claim involving a plaintiff with a hearing impairment who sued the hospital for not offering him a sign language interpreter during his stay following a motorcycle accident. The judge dismissed the case for lack of standing, citing *Proctor v. Prince George's Hospital Center* (1998, 7), in which the complaint was dismissed because the plaintiffs had not alleged that they would suffer "a real and immediate threat of future harm from [the] defendant, and not merely a conjectural or hypothetical threat."

In dismissing these suits before adjudicating the plaintiffs' claims on the merits, the courts do not reach the question whether the hospitals are guilty of discrimination. A year later, similar facts were alleged in *Toschia Falls v. Prince George's Hospital Center* (1999). Despite repeated requests, the hospital failed to provide sign language assistance to a young patient during her hospital stay. Citing *Aikins* and *Proctor,* the Maryland district court judge granted the defendant summary judgment on the Title III claim, ruling that there was no continuing act of discrimination against the child and, based on her mother's deposition, it was extremely unlikely that she would ever return to the hospital for treatment.

The effect of the court's strict interpretation of the standing requirement in Title III cases was also shown in two cases decided four years apart. The first, *Plumley v. Landmark Chevrolet, Inc.* (1997), involved a suit by George Plumley, whose wife was substituted as plaintiff at his death. Plumley, who suffered from AIDS, was called vicious names by a salesman at a car dealership. His suits for slander, emotional distress, and Title III were all dismissed by the lower court, which ruled that the action did not survive his death. The appellate court upheld the lower court on the Title III claim, ruling that to satisfy *Lyons,* the plaintiff "must show that there is a real or immediate threat that he will be wronged again." And because he had died, the court said, "it is unlikely that Landmark will wrong Plumley again" (312).

The case of *Blake v. Southcoast Health System, Inc.* (2001) starkly illustrates the importance of the standing requirement. The district court made little attempt to conceal its outrage at the defendant's conduct, which had caused the death of Betty Ann Blake, a fifty-year-old woman with multiple disabilities. She had been rushed to the hospital after choking on a piece of food and died there after more than twenty-four hours of slow strangulation, with numerous hospital personnel ignoring her suffering throughout. The court flatly concluded that the cause of her death was discrimination by the hospital and its staff on the basis of her disability.

The defendants moved to dismiss the suit brought by her parents and her estate, arguing that the estate had no standing to sue because Betty Ann was dead and could not be harmed in the future. "Under the *Lyons* standing standard," the court reluctantly concluded, "the fact that the defendants' discriminatory malpractice killed Betty Ann seemingly leads to the conclusion that the Estate cannot show any risk of future harm. Yet," it continued, citing *Plumley,* "application of the *Lyons* standard to this case is unsettling, because it allows the most egregious cases of institutional disability discrimination in violation of the ADA to continue unabated" (*Blake* 2001, 132). Describing her death as "unconscionable" and "agonizing" and one that "our society would not mete out even to the most monstrous war criminal sentenced to be hanged," the court determined that there was no "loophole" to justify an injunction that would prevent this kind of behavior in the future. Although he was clearly loath to do so, the judge dismissed the claim (137), but directed the clerk of the court to send the opinion to the attorney general for appropriate action.

Another obstacle plaintiffs confronted in cases complaining of the denial of access to goods and services arose from the court's narrow interpretation of a "place of public accommodation." In *Torres v. AT&T Broadband* (2001, 1037), the court dismissed the plaintiff's claim against AT&T, ruling that "the plaintiff's contention that digital cable services constitute a place of public accommodation is contrary to the plain language of the statute and its implementing regulations . . . because a digital cable system is not analogous to any of the examples or categories [in Title III]."

The issue litigated in *Neff* (1995), whether a parent company controlled its franchisee for purposes of ADA litigation, reappeared in an Eighth Circuit case, *Pona v. Cecil Whittaker's Inc.* (1998). The plaintiff in this case was asked to leave a pizzeria because she was accompanied by her service dog; the defendant, Cecil Whittaker's Inc., claimed that as the franchisor it was not responsible for the operation of the pizza restaurant. The lower court agreed and granted summary judgment. On appeal, the appellate court affirmed, citing *Neff*. The court held that Cecil Whittaker's did not have the authority to control access to the restaurant. It did not find it significant that Cecil Whittaker's president apparently advised the manager of the pizzeria to refuse the plaintiff entry because it "doesn't look good for the franchise" (*Pona* 1998, 1036). Although there was some dispute over whether he had actually made such a statement, the court believed that even if he did, it was insufficient to show that the corporation operated the restaurant or that the president controlled the manager's behavior.

Insurance

The most contentious (and most unsettled) legal issues, arguably, appeared in claims involving health insurance policies. For the most part, these cases challenged disparities between coverage of physical and mental disabilities and benefit restrictions on persons with AIDS or HIV. A threshold issue for the courts was whether Title III only protected those entering the physical structure, that is, the insurance office, from which the policy emanated. Although disputes over the meaning of "place of public accommodation" arose in other Title III cases, it was most often litigated in cases involving insurance claims (Stowe 2000, 299).

One of the first cases to address this issue was *Carparts Distribution Center v. Automotive Wholesaler's Association of New England* (1994). The plaintiff, who had been diagnosed with HIV and subsequently died of AIDS, was both an owner and employee of Carparts Distribution Center. His self-insured medical reimbursement plan was offered by Automotive Wholesaler's Association of New England (AWANE). After he was diagnosed, the plan was amended to cap benefits at $25,000 for AIDS-related diseases, while retaining the $1 million cap for all other illnesses. He sued under Titles I and III, claiming that the disparity in benefits was discriminatory. Following complex pretrial motions, the district court dismissed the claim on the grounds that the defendant was not a "place of public accommodation" within the meaning of the law. On appeal, the First Circuit reversed the lower court on procedural grounds and remanded the case, offering "guidance" to the court in interpreting the law.

After noting that the defendants may be liable under both Title I and Title III, the appeals court enumerated examples of public accommodations in the statute, emphasizing "travel service," "shoe repair service," "insurance office," and "other service establishments."[39] It concluded that the "plain meaning of the terms do not require 'public accommodations' to have physical structures for persons to enter. [And] even if the meaning of 'public accommodation' is not plain, it is at worst, ambiguous" (*Carparts* 1994, 19). Focusing on the example of a travel service, the court reasoned that the legislature knew that such establishments conduct business by mail or phone. By including them within Title III, Congress had clearly indicated it did not intend the "absurd" result of applying Title III to only those people who entered the premises while failing to cover those who availed themselves of the agency's services in some other way. Expressing doubt about the plaintiff's ability to show that the law extended to the content of the policy, the court reiterated that Congress did not intend to limit Title III to businesses that occupy a physical space and protect only those customers who enter it. Although the Second Circuit in *Pallozzi v. Allstate Life Insurance Company* (1999) and the Seventh Circuit in *Doe v. Mutual of Omaha* (1999) adopted this interpretation of Title III, no circuit court has flatly held that Title III governs the content of insurance policies (Ziegler 2002, 845n33).

The Sixth Circuit reached the opposite conclusion in *Parker v. Metropolitan Life Insurance Company* (1997). This plaintiff was employed by Schering-Plough Health Care Products, which offered long-term disability insurance to its employees through Metropolitan Life Insurance Company (MetLife). When the plaintiff became disabled because of a severe depression after about ten years on the job, she began to collect disability benefits. After her benefits ceased—at twenty-four months—she sued her former employer and the insurance company under Titles I and III, charging them with discrimination because individuals with physical disabilities were able to receive benefits until they reached sixty-five.

The district court had granted the defendant's motion for summary judgment, holding that she could not sue the insurance company under Title III because the law only regulated access to goods and services, not the content of insurance policies (*Parker* 1995).[40] A Sixth Circuit panel disagreed, concluding that Title III "prohibits discrimination in the contents of the goods and services offered at places of public accommodation, rather than just discrimination in terms of physical access to places of public accommodation." It found that Title III applies to insurance products because "insurance products are 'goods' or 'services' provided by a 'person' who owns a 'public accommodation'" (*Parker* 1996, 187–88).

After a rehearing *en banc,* the Sixth Circuit reversed the panel, reinstating the district court ruling. The appeals court cited *Stoutenborough v. National Football League* (1995), which held that the NFL was not liable under Title III for television broadcasts because they were a service rather than a place. It explained that Parker's disability policy was "not covered by Title III because Title III covers only physical places"; it added, however, that it "expressed no opinion as to whether a plaintiff must physically enter a public accommodation to bring suit under Title III as opposed to merely accessing, by some other means, a service or good provided by a public accommodation" (*Parker* 1997, 1011n3). Moreover, the court added, because Title III does not apply to the contents of the goods and services offered by the public accommodation, merely their availability, the prohibition against discrimination on the basis of disability does not encompass the terms of the policy. The Third Circuit in *Ford v. Schering-Plough Corporation* (1998) and the Ninth Circuit in *Weyer v. Twentieth Century Fox Film Corporation* (2000) also adopted this narrow interpretation of "place of public accommodation."

The courts are also divided over the interpretation of the "safe harbor" provision of the law (42 U.S.C. §12201c; Ziegler 2002). This section provides that Titles I through III "shall not be construed to prohibit or restrict . . . an insurer . . . from underwriting risks, classifying risks, or administering such risks that are based on or not inconsistent with State law" and that this exception "shall not be used as a subterfuge to evade the purposes" of Titles I and III. Most courts interpret this provision narrowly to bar ADA claims against insurers unless the policy violates state law or is a "subterfuge" to avoid the purposes of the ADA. Others have simply held that this provision does not apply to any insurance plans and policies that predated the ADA (Cole 2003, 876–77). Most courts have also refused to hold that insurers cannot discriminate in the content of policies, rejecting plaintiffs' arguments that Congress intended to foreclose disability-based distinctions and benefit caps, absent actuarial data to justify them. Indeed, in the Seventh Circuit decision of *Doe v. Mutual of Omaha* (1999, 558), the court upheld the insurer's right to limit benefits for policyholders with AIDS even though the company was unable to show it was "consistent with sound actuarial principles, actual or reasonably anticipated experience, bona fide risk classification, or state law."

Another unresolved conflict over interpretation of the law relates to differential benefits between physical and mental disabilities. Most circuit courts that have addressed this question have decided that the ADA does not prescribe equality among types of disabilities (Signorello 2001). Ironically, a 1996 law, the Mental Health Parity Act (MHPA), which was enacted to prevent disparities in insurance practices, was used to support this narrow reading of the ADA. The MHPA prohibited insurance companies and employers that provided mental health benefits from differentiating between mental and physical disabilities in lifetime caps and annual limits.[41] The courts have interpreted this to mean that by enacting the MHPA, Congress was assuming that the ADA did not govern disparities between mental and physical disabilities in the content of insurance policies (Martinson 1998, 376).

These lower court rulings indicate that the judiciary has not interpreted Title III expansively, especially when they involved large expenditures—as in the insurance cases. Plaintiffs were often hindered in their efforts to challenge businesses by the courts' reliance on jurisdictional doctrines, arising in part out of the limitations on damages in the law.

6 Disability Rights
and State Sovereignty

In recent years, Supreme Court decisionmaking has been guided by a "new federalism" jurisprudence that has expanded state sovereignty at the expense of the federal government's policymaking and enforcement authority (see Cross and Tiller 2000; Farber 2000; Mezey 2000).[1] This jurisprudence has had a divisive impact on the nation and, internally, "few issues have divided the Rehnquist Court as deeply and visibly as federalism concerns" (Heinrich 2000, 1275). To indicate the significance of this decisionmaking for the legislative prerogative, the Court ruled that Congress transcended its constitutional power five times during the 2000–2001 term, four times during the 1999–2000 term, and a total of twenty-nine times since the 1994–1995 terms (Colker and Brudney 2001, 80–81).

Not surprisingly, given its significance, the new federalism decisionmaking has attracted attention from scholars who have commented on its implications for federal-state relationships as well as for individual rights. Noonan (2002, 2) argues that federalism is a "misnomer" and it would be more "accurate" to refer to the principle driving the Court as "states' rights." Colker and Brudney (2001, 87), however, do not believe that the Court is primarily motivated by a desire to advance the interests of the states; in their view, "dissing [disrespecting] Congress" is an important element of the Rehnquist Court's "recent judicial activism." Garbus (2002, 121) agrees, depicting "the federalism issue as camouflage for states stepping on people's rights"; he is even more frank about calling it a "battle over race, class, religion, money, and power."

Whatever its motivation, in advancing the principle of state sovereignty, frequently by enhancing the immunity defense offered by the Eleventh Amendment, the Court has diminished Congress's authority to enforce federal civil rights laws and created uncertainty about the effectiveness of statutes, such as the ADA, that guarantee individual rights.[2] The new federalism jurisprudence adversely affects civil rights litigants by denying them an opportunity to secure the full panoply of federal remedies when their federally protected rights are violated.

The Eleventh Amendment and State Sovereign Immunity

The Court's primary, although not exclusive, means for advancing its new federalism policy has been the Eleventh Amendment, a once arcane legal tool intended to shield states from legal liability for their actions. "In a series of decisions announced between 1996 and 2002, the Court has brought state sovereign immunity under the Eleventh Amendment back from the dead" (Melnick 2003, 110).

The Eleventh Amendment provides that "the Judicial power of the United States shall not be construed to extend to any suit in law or equity, commenced or prosecuted against one of the United States by Citizens of another State, or by Citizens or Subjects of any Foreign State." It was ratified in 1798 to overturn *Chisholm v. Georgia* (1793), in which the Court held that a citizen of South Carolina was permitted to sue the State of Georgia in a dispute over a bond debt, overriding the state's defense of sovereign immunity.

The Court broadened the scope of the Eleventh Amendment in *Hans v. Louisiana* (1890), another case involving a dispute arising out of a state's indebtedness to its bond holders. Although the plain language of the amendment only applies to suits against a state by citizens of another state, the state argued that the federal courts lacked constitutional authority to hear cases brought by citizens against any state without its consent. The Supreme Court agreed, expanding the concept of state sovereignty by ruling that the Eleventh Amendment also conferred immunity on states in suits brought by their own citizens. Despite the broad statement in *Hans,* however, states do not have immunity in all cases. Suits may be brought against states by the federal government or by other states; states may also waive their immunity and consent to be sued. Additionally, state immunity does not extend to instrumentalities of the state, such as a city or county agency, unless a court determines that it is an "Arm of the State."

The protection offered states by the Eleventh Amendment is grounded in the doctrine of sovereign immunity, a principle establishing that states are shielded from suit without their consent. In *Ex Parte Young* (1908), the Court retreated from the principle of sovereign immunity by ruling that the Eleventh Amendment does not bar federal courts from ordering injunctive relief in suits against state officials.[3] Applying a legal fiction, the Court held that suits for prospective injunctive relief against state officers in their official capacities do not constitute suits against the state and therefore do not conflict with the immunity guaranteed by the Eleventh Amendment.[4] *Young* has helped ensure that states cannot escape compliance with federal law by cloaking themselves in immunity.[5]

The Court further restricted state immunity in *Fitzpatrick v. Bitzer* (1976), a case arising out of an employment discrimination suit against the state under Title VII of the 1964 Civil Rights Act. The state had argued that the Eleventh Amendment shielded it from suit in federal court, but the Court ruled that the Fourteenth Amendment, which was intended to alter the relationship between the federal government and the states, vitiated the state's Eleventh Amendment immunity. The Court explained that the enabling provision of the Fourteenth Amendment, section 5, gave Congress the authority to enforce the guarantees of the Fourteenth Amendment. But, when enacting a statute under its section 5 authority, Congress must clearly indicate its intent to abrogate state sovereign immunity.[6] A plurality opinion in *Pennsylvania v. Union Gas Company* (1989) created another exception to the Eleventh Amendment, allowing Congress to revoke state immunity in laws enacted under the interstate commerce clause.

Abrogating State Sovereign Immunity

One of the first manifestations of the new federalism decisionmaking was *Seminole Tribe of Florida v. Florida* (1996), in which the Court reconsidered the extent to which the state should be insulated from liability when sued in federal court. The case revolved around a dispute between the Seminole Indians and the state over the location of gambling casinos. The Seminoles filed suit, citing the state's violation of the 1988 Indian Gaming Regulatory Act, a law requiring states to enter into good faith negotiation with Native Americans to create gaming compacts (Herpers 1997). The state asserted an immunity defense, claiming it was shielded by the Eleventh Amendment and that Congress had overstepped its power in authorizing tribal governments to sue states. More than half the states supported Florida's position in the high court.

Announcing the opinion of the Court for a 5–4 majority, Rehnquist acknowledged that less than a decade earlier, in *Union Gas* (1989), a plurality had conferred power on Congress to rescind state immunity in interstate commerce legislation.[7] But, he said, *Union Gas* was not dispositive because it was a plurality opinion and the rationale expressed by the plurality was inconsistent with accepted interpretations of federalism principles.

Rehnquist articulated two standards for determining whether Congress had the authority to repeal state immunity: first, it must have "unequivocally expressed its intent to abrogate the immunity"; second, it must have done so "pursuant to a valid exercise of power" (*Seminole Tribe* 1996, 54). By expressly overruling *Union Gas,* the Court confirmed that Congress was only permitted to revoke state immunity in laws validly enacted under section 5 of the Fourteenth Amendment. In what would become a familiar refrain from "new federalism" dissenters, Stevens expressed concern that the limitations placed on congressional authority would prevent Congress from "providing a federal forum for a broad range of actions against states" (*Seminole Tribe* 1996, 77).

A year later, *City of Boerne v. Flores* (1997) specified the limits of Congress's enforcement power under section 5 of the Fourteenth Amendment by interpreting the recently enacted Religious Freedom Restoration Act (RFRA). The case arose in a challenge to the RFRA, a law reversing the Court's ruling in *Employment Division, Department of Human Resources of Oregon v. Smith* (1990). *Smith* had rejected a free exercise challenge to an Oregon law that purported to infringe on the religious practices of Native Americans. The Court held that states were not required to offer a compelling justification for neutral laws of general applicability that affected religious practices. The RFRA reinstated the "compelling state interest" test in free exercise cases.

A church leader in Boerne, Texas, sued the city for refusing to grant a building permit to his church; citing RFRA, he claimed that the city infringed on his exercise of religion without a compelling government interest. The majority opinion began by noting that Congress's constitutional authority under section 5 is limited to "remedial and preventive" legislation. Conceding that the line between enforcing existing rights and creating new ones is often elusive, the Court articulated the test for section 5 legislation: "there must be a congruence and proportionality between the injury to be prevented or remedied and the means adopted to that end" (*City of Boerne* 1997, 520).[8] To satisfy this standard, there must be a legislative finding that states committed constitutional abuses and the law may not impose a stricter standard of conduct on states than had existed previously.[9]

The Court acknowledged that under section 5, which authorizes Congress to enforce rights guaranteed in section 1 of the amendment, "legislation which deters or remedies constitutional violations can fall within the scope of Congress's enforcement power even if in the process it prohibits conduct which is not itself unconstitutional and intrudes into 'legislative spheres of autonomy previously reserved to the States'" (*City of Boerne* 1997, 519).[10] But Congress's enforcement authority, while extensive, is not absolute. And by altering the substantive meaning of the First Amendment, the legislature had overstepped the bounds of its authority under section 5. Echoing the words of John Marshall, the Court reminded Congress that the final authority to interpret legislative power under the Constitution resides in the judiciary.[11]

Although poorly defined, the "congruence and proportionality" test became the standard for determining whether Congress had properly relied on section 5 to abrogate the state's Eleventh Amendment immunity in suits seeking money damages. Shortly after *City of Boerne*, the Court again raised the bar of state immunity in *Alden v. Maine* (1999). The Court held that the Eleventh Amendment protected states from suit without consent in state, as well as federal, court. When a group of Maine employees sued the state under the Fair Labor Standards Act of 1938, the Court ruled that if they were barred from the federal courts on Eleventh Amendment grounds, they could not circumvent the state's sovereign immunity by suing in state court. Dissenting, Souter criticized the majority for allowing states to escape liability for violating federal rights established by Congress as part of its proper exercise of authority under Article I.

The day *Alden* was announced, the Court further expanded state immunity by curtailing Congress's authority to hold states accountable in suits for unfair trade practices and patent infringement. In these cases, the Court addressed Congress's authority to compel states to respond to private suits for false advertising and patent violations. In *Florida Prepaid Postsecondary Education Expense Board v. College Savings Bank* (1999), the 5–4 majority held that Congress exceeded its authority in enacting the Patent and Plant Variety Protection Remedy Clarification Act of 1992, a federal law subjecting states to private suits for patent infringement. The Court determined that the second prong of the *Seminole Tribe* test had not been satisfied because there was insufficient evidence of state infringement on patent rights for the law to be considered "remedial." In *College Savings Bank v. Florida Prepaid Postsecondary Education Expense Board* (1999), the same 5–4 majority ruled that the Trademark Remedy Clarification Act of 1992, a law declaring that states engaging in interstate marketing are subject to private suit under the 1946 Trademark Act, was also unconstitutional because it was not aimed at protecting property interests within the scope of the due process clause of the Fourteenth Amendment.

These rulings substantiated the fears expressed in Stevens's *Seminole Tribe* dissent in which he had warned that the majority opinion would impair the federal government's ability to provide relief for state violations of federal law.

The New Federalism and Age Discrimination

Taken together, these new federalism rulings signaled the Court's inclination to exercise heightened scrutiny over Congress's policymaking authority, with the Eleventh Amendment the primary vehicle for insulating states from damage liability. Over the next several years, the federal courts were increasingly drawn into the conflict over states' rights as litigants sought to hold states accountable for discriminatory job actions (Royer 2001).[12]

The first indication that the new federalism jurisprudence would shelter states from civil rights lawsuits appeared on January 11, 2000, when the Court handed down its decision in *Kimel v. Florida Board of Regents* (2000), a ruling potentially affecting more than five million employees.[13] The Age Discrimination in Employment Act was enacted in 1967 under Congress's authority to regulate interstate commerce. It made it unlawful to "to refuse to hire or to discharge an individual or otherwise discriminate against any individual with respect to his [or her] compensation, terms, conditions, or privileges of employment, because of such individual's age" (29 U.S.C. §623(a)(1)).

The law was initially limited to private sector employment; in 1974 it was extended to state employment policies as part of the 1974 FLSA amendments. By characterizing states and their subdivisions as employers, the amended version allowed public sector employees to sue for age discrimination (Durham 1999).[14] However, although it is reasonable to assume Congress intended to permit individuals to seek money damages, the ADEA did not expressly abrogate state immunity.[15]

Congress's authority to provide a damage remedy for age discrimination in state employment was soon tested when three suits were filed against the Florida Department of Corrections and state universities in Alabama and Florida, the plaintiffs alleging they were denied pay increases and promotions because of their age.[16] The states moved to dismiss the monetary claims, arguing they were immune under the Eleventh Amendment; they did not, however, challenge Congress's authority to regulate state employers under the ADEA nor the employees' right to sue for injunctive relief under the *Young* doctrine. The Florida plaintiffs survived the state's motion to dismiss because the courts held that Congress had the authority to revoke the state's immunity in ADEA suits. The Alabama plaintiff's case was dismissed, with the court ruling that although Congress had intended to abrogate state immunity, it did not have the authority to do so (Cooper 2000).

On appeal, the three cases were consolidated by the Eleventh Circuit, and a divided court held that although it was likely Congress had meant to extend the damage remedy to states, the ADEA did not contain a sufficiently clear statement of its intent to abrogate state immunity in damage suits (*Kimel v. Florida Board of Regents* 1998). The majority based its decision on two grounds: first, the law did not explicitly refer to Eleventh Amendment immunity; and second, it did not affirm that employees could sue states in federal court.[17] Conceding that Congress's intent might be inferred and that other circuits had reached the opposite conclusion, the three judge panel ruled that the ADEA failed to satisfy the "clear statement" rule.[18]

The Supreme Court's opinion was divided into two parts. Speaking for the majority, Justice O'Connor disagreed with the circuit panel and found that the ADEA satisfied the first prong of the *Seminole Tribe* test.[19] By incorporating the provisions of the FLSA into the ADEA, Congress had clearly manifested its intent to allow ADEA litigants to seek money damages from states. She added that most circuits had rejected state immunity claims in ADEA suits.

In the second part of the analysis, O'Connor conceded that Congress had a broad grant of affirmative authority to legislate under section 5, but emphasized that although it may "prohibit a somewhat broader swath of conduct" than the prohibitions in the Fourteenth Amendment, it may do so only "to remedy or deter" unconstitutional action (*Kimel* 2000, 81). Conceding that it was difficult to distinguish between remedial and substantive legislation, O'Connor reiterated the holding in *City of Boerne* (1997): although section 5 granted Congress wide latitude to enact remedial legislation, the courts alone were authorized to alter the substantive meaning of the Fourteenth Amendment.

The question to be determined was whether section 5 allowed Congress to legislatively expand the scope of individual rights guaranteed by the Fourteenth Amendment. Under the Court's interpretation of the equal protection clause of the Fourteenth Amendment, states could distinguish among people on the basis of age as long as the distinctions were reasonably related to legitimate state interests. However, because the ADEA prevented states from making reasonable employment decisions based on age, it exceeded the bounds of Congress's authority under section 5, as it was "disproportionate to any unconstitutional conduct that conceivably could be targeted by the Act" (*Kimel* 2000, 83).

O'Connor examined the legislative history of the ADEA to determine whether Congress had documented unconstitutional acts of age discrimination by states. She concluded that "Congress never identified any pattern of age discrimination by the States, much less any discrimination whatsoever that rose to the level of constitutional violation" (*Kimel* 2000, 89). Instead, she noted, the evidence consisted of isolated statements and anecdotal evidence of allegedly discriminatory conduct. This record led the majority to believe that "Congress's 1974 extension of the Act to States was an unwarranted response to a perhaps inconsequential problem" (89). Reflecting the Supreme Court's new federalism jurisprudence and its commitment to state autonomy, *Kimel* reinforced state sovereignty at the expense of federal civil rights guarantees and reasserted the Court's authority over Congress as the final interpreter of constitutional values.

The New Federalism and Disability Rights

The ADA presented another opportunity for states to argue that the Eleventh Amendment shielded them from liability in civil rights suits. Unlike the ADEA, however, the ADA explicitly deprived states of immunity in both state and federal court. Moreover, the ADA did not distinguish between state and nonstate employers, making both liable for money damages and injunctive relief (42 U.S.C. §12202).

In his suit against the Florida Department of Corrections, Wellington Dickson, a department employee, had also alleged discrimination on the basis of disability, a Title I claim. The Eleventh Circuit rejected the state's argument that it was cloaked in state immunity, holding that Congress had properly abrogated immunity in the ADA. The Supreme Court had not addressed Dickson's ADA claim in *Kimel;* it had intended to consider it with an appeal of an Eighth Circuit Title II decision, *Alsbrook v. City of Maumelle* (1999). In *Alsbrook,* the appellate court had ruled that Congress lacked the authority to abrogate state immunity in ADA suits against state employers. *Dickson* and *Alsbrook* were scheduled for briefing and argument on April 26, 2000, but were settled shortly after *Kimel* (2000) was decided. The Court dismissed the writs of *certiorari,* leaving the question of state immunity in ADA litigation for resolution at a later time *(Florida Department of Corrections v. Dickson* 2000; *Alsbrook* 2000).

The prevailing view among the circuits during the late 1990s was that Congress had validly abrogated state immunity in the ADA. Specifically, the Ninth Circuit in *Clark v. California* (1997) and *Dare v. California Department of Motor Vehicles* (1999), the Seventh Circuit in *Crawford v. Indiana Department of Corrections* (1997), and the Fifth Circuit in *Coolbaugh v. Louisiana* (1998) held that the states were not shielded from liability in Title II suits. Similarly, the Eleventh Circuit in *Kimel* (1998), the Second Circuit in *Muller v. Costello* (1999), the First Circuit in *Torres v. Puerto Rico Tourism Company* (1999), and the Tenth Circuit in *Martin v. Kansas* (1999) all rejected the states' immunity defenses in employment discrimination cases.[20]

Only three circuits reached a contrary conclusion. In *Alsbrook* (1999), the Eighth Circuit had ruled that the Title II plaintiff was barred from seeking damages in his employment discrimination claim against the state because Congress was not authorized to abrogate state immunity. Late in 2000, a three-judge panel of the Sixth Circuit also held in *Popovich v. Cuyahoga County Court of Common Pleas* (2000a) that the Eleventh Amendment barred Title II damage suits against states.

The Fourth Circuit was internally divided, initially dismissing a suit against the Maryland Corrections Department on the grounds that the ADA did not apply to state prisons *(Amos* 1997). The Supreme Court vacated and remanded *(Amos* 1998). Upon remand, a divided panel of the Fourth Circuit held that Congress had the constitutional authority to enact a law applying the ADA to state prisons and that the state lacked Eleventh Amendment immunity *(Amos* 1999). Subsequently, the circuit granted the state's petition for a rehearing en banc and vacated the 1999 ruling; before the rehearing, however, the parties settled and the case was dismissed *(Amos* 2000). In *Brown v. North Carolina* (1999), another three-judge panel of the Fourth Circuit dismissed the plaintiffs' suit to recover a five dollar fee for parking placards, holding that the regulation prohibiting public entities from charging fees to recover their costs exceeded the scope of Congress's remedial power under section 5.[21]

With the exception of *Popovich,* however, these cases were decided before the Supreme Court announced its decision in *Kimel* in 2000; after *Kimel,* the circuits began to reverse course. In *Erickson v. Board of Governors of State Colleges & Universities for Northeastern Illinois University* (2000), the Seventh Circuit stated that in light of *Kimel,* it must reconsider its prior decision in *Craw-*

ford. It then ruled that Congress had no authority to hold states accountable for damages in Title I suits.[22] In *Neinast v. Texas* (2000, 280n29), the Fifth Circuit suggested that *Kimel* may cause it to reconsider its holding in *Coolbaugh*. Of all the circuits ruling in ADA suits after *Kimel,* only the Second Circuit acknowledged *Kimel* and adhered to its position that the Eleventh Amendment did not bar an ADA damage suit against a state. In *Kilcullen v. New York State Department of Labor* (2000), another Second Circuit decision, the court flatly rejected the state's immunity defense and refused to dismiss the plaintiff's claim of employment discrimination.[23]

State Sovereign Immunity and Title I

By 2000, it was inevitable that a state would challenge Congress's authority to abrogate state immunity in ADA suits and the Supreme Court would respond either by extending *Kimel* or by calling a halt to further expansion of the new federalism jurisprudence. The opportunity for the Court to determine the course of ADA litigation presented itself in Patricia Garrett's suit against the University of Alabama Hospital.

Garrett, a former director of obstetrical and neonatal services, claimed she had been demoted to a position at a lower salary after she returned from a four-month medical leave. She filed suit in 1997 under the ADA and the Rehabilitation Act. Milton Ash, an officer with the Alabama Department of Youth Services, joined her suit, complaining that his employer failed to accommodate his chronic asthma by not enforcing its no-smoking policy.

The state moved for summary judgment, citing its Eleventh Amendment immunity. District Court Judge William Acker acknowledged that most circuits favored the plaintiffs' position, but he found the contrary view of the Ohio district court judge in *Nihiser v. Ohio Environmental Protection Agency* (1997) more persuasive because it was consistent with the limitations *City of Boerne* had placed on Congress's section 5 authority. Acker agreed that Congress intended to abrogate the state's Eleventh Amendment immunity in the ADA and the Rehabilitation Act but found that it had exceeded its authority in authorizing private suits under these statutes. Adopting the reasoning of the Ohio district judge in *Nihiser,* he stated that "Congress cannot stretch Section 5 and the Equal Protection Clause of the Fourteenth Amendment" to require states to provide "special treatment" for people with disabilities under the rubric of accommodating them (*Garrett v. Board of Trustees of the University of Alabama* 1998, 1410).

The Eleventh Circuit reversed. In an opinion handed down before the high court had announced its decision in *Kimel* (2000), the appellate court held that states may be sued under the ADA as well as under the Rehabilitation Act (*Garrett v. Board of Trustees of the University of Alabama* 1999). The circuit court simply cited its ruling in *Kimel* (1998), noting that the trial court had dismissed Garrett and Ash's suit before the circuit court ruling in *Kimel*.

An impressive group of amici urged the Supreme Court to affirm the circuit court, including former President H. W. Bush; numerous disability rights organizations, such as the AAPD, the NOD, the NCD, the National Multiple Sclerosis Society, and the National Federation for the Blind, to name a few; groups of law professors, historians, and scholars; current and former members of Congress; and an array of traditional civil rights advocacy groups such as the American Civil Liberties Union, Lambda Legal Defense and Education Fund, the National Asian Pacific American Legal Consortium, and the National Women's Law Center.

The plaintiffs distinguished the ADEA from the ADA, stressing that the latter explicitly revoked Eleventh Amendment immunity; moreover, the legislative history of the ADA showed there had been extensive congressional hearings with express findings of pervasive unconstitutional action against persons with disabilities by state and local governments. They contended that the ADA was the "reasonably prophylactic [section 5] legislation" (*Kimel* 2000, 88) that satisfied the standards set in *City of Boerne* ("Brief for Respondents," in *Board of Trustees of the University of Alabama v. Garrett*).

The state maintained that the ADA was not properly enacted under section 5 for two reasons: first, Congress had presented insufficient evidence of unconstitutional state action; and second, by prohibiting conduct that satisfied the constitutional standard of minimal scrutiny, Congress had created new rights and had substantively altered the guarantees of the Fourteenth Amendment ("Brief for Petitioners," in *Board of Trustees of the University of Alabama v. Garrett*). Only three amicus curiae briefs were submitted to support the state's position: a brief joined by seven states (Hawaii, Arkansas, Ohio, Idaho, Nebraska, Nevada, and Tennessee), and one each from the Pacific Legal Foundation and the Association of State Correctional Administrators.

Providing the Court with another opportunity to weigh state sovereignty against Congress's authority to enforce civil rights laws, *Garrett* was argued on October 11, 2000, and announced on February 21, 2001. However, although it settled some of the uncertainty in Title I litigation, it provided no resolution for the conflict among the circuits in Title II cases.

In his opinion for the 5–4 majority, Rehnquist acknowledged that the plain text of the ADA abrogated state immunity, but he questioned whether Congress had exceeded its authority under section 5 in doing so. In determining the parameters of Congress's authority to abrogate state immunity, the Court applied the "congruence and proportionality" test from *City of Boerne*. Echoing *Kimel*, it examined constitutional limits on state policies toward people with disabilities, that is, the extent to which the Court's interpretation of the equal protection clause prohibited laws based on disabilities.

The case turned in part on whether people with disabilities represented a class of individuals meriting heightened scrutiny. The Court reiterated its holding in *Cleburne* (1985) that the Constitution permitted states latitude in enacting laws based on disability, merely requiring them to act rationally.[24] Based on this minimal scrutiny standard, the Court found that, as in *Kimel*, Congress had not provided sufficient evidence that states had acted unlawfully with respect to people with disabilities. Applying the *City of Boerne* test, the Court found because the remedy was not "congruent and proportional" to state misconduct, Congress lacked the power to abrogate state immunity.

Rehnquist emphasized that states were not required to offer "special accommodations" to persons with disabilities. As long as they acted reasonably, they did not have to make exceptional arrangements for employees with disabilities. They "could quite hard headedly—and perhaps hard-heartedly—hold to job-qualification requirements which do not make allowances for the disabled" (*Board of Trustees of the University of Alabama v. Garrett* 2001, 367–68). After identifying the limits of permissible state conduct, the Court next considered whether plaintiffs had shown that states had exceeded the limits and subjected persons with disabilities to unlawful employment discrimination. Hartley (2001, 52) contends that among section 5 laws, "the ADA's legislative record makes an overwhelming case demonstrating a pattern of invidious discrimination . . . [including] societal discrimination against persons with disabilities generally and a pattern of unconstitutional state and local disability-based discrimination in particular." Nevertheless, despite extensive documentation of discrimination as well as Congress's general finding of pervasive discrimination against people with disabilities, the Court held that there was insufficient evidence to show that states had exhibited the kind of irrational behavior in the employment context that justified Congress's inclusion of a damage remedy. The pattern of discriminatory employer conduct identified in hearings before the Senate and House committees pertained to private employers, Rehnquist said, not government entities—or, at least, not states. He characterized Breyer's evidence of discriminatory acts by states as "unexamined, anecdotal accounts of adverse, disparate treatment by state officials," rather than "legislative findings" (*Board of Trustees of the University of Alabama v. Garrett* 2001, 370). Additionally, he noted, other remedies, including state antidiscrimination laws, were available to redress claims of discrimination by state employees.[25]

Conceding that public policymaking was within Congress's domain, the Court nevertheless concluded that the remedy of authorizing employees to sue states in damage actions was not "congruent and proportional" to any unconstitutional state action as established under the rationality standard articulated in *Cleburne*. It contrasted the evidence of unconstitutional discrimination against people with disabilities with the evidence of unconstitutional discrimination against racial minorities in voting that Congress had amassed to justify passage of the Voting Rights Act under section 2 of the Fifteenth Amendment, the equivalent of section 5 of the Fourteenth Amendment. The difference between the two was "stark," said the Court (*Board of Trustees of the University of Alabama v. Garrett* 2001, 374).

Breyer's dissent challenged the majority's finding of insufficient evidence of discriminatory state action against people with disabilities; in a lengthy appendix, he documented scores of examples of state discrimination against people with disabilities. He also noted the incongruity of imposing judicial restraint doctrines on the exercise of congressional authority under section 5 and equated the Court's present-day judicial activism with its now discredited pre–New Deal activism. Finally, he questioned the logic of a jurisprudence that applied lenient standards to statutes that burdened people with disabilities, but strict standards to statutes aimed at removing burdens on them.

Hartley (2001, 57) argues that "*Garrett* left unanswered the most interesting and important issue[s] the case presented." He asks why Congress cannot abrogate state immunity under its section 5 authority when there is sufficient evidence of unconstitutional discrimination on the basis of disability by state and local governments, when it is convinced that a solution to the existing pattern of discrimination is the integration of people with disabilities into society, and when it believes that integration can best be accomplished by a societywide effort, including the government workforce.

State Sovereign Immunity and Title II

Although the litigants had asked the Supreme Court to address the state's immunity under both Titles I and II, the Court expressly declined to discuss the availability of a Title II damage remedy, noting that Title II has "somewhat different remedial provisions from Title I" (*Board of Trustees of the University of Alabama v. Garrett* 2001, 360n1). Additionally, the Court refused to decide whether Title II encompassed claims of employment discrimination against state and local governments, a question left unanswered in the act.[26] In a footnote, Rehnquist emphasized that the Court's holding did not excuse states from their obligation to comply with the ADA, nor did it disturb the *Young* doctrine, which allowed individuals to sue states for injunctive relief; moreover, the federal government remained empowered to sue states for money damages (*Board of Trustees of the University of Alabama v. Garrett* 2001, 374n9).

Despite these assurances, the disability rights community feared that *Garrett* might lead to a virtual repeal of Title II—at least as applied to states—if the lower courts expanded on the high court's reasoning and extended the principle of state sovereign immunity governing Title I suits to Title II suits.[27] At a minimum, there was uncertainty about the effectiveness of litigation to achieve compliance as the circuits began to reassess their earlier Title II rulings in light of *Garrett.*

Although *Garrett* only conferred immunity on states in Title I suits, a number of circuits extended it to Title II, either by overruling their prior decisions, or, if they were considering the state's immunity defense for the first time, applying *Garrett* to bar Title II claims. Circuits such as the Eighth and Sixth merely reaffirmed the positions they had taken before *Garrett.*

The Fifth Circuit initially held in *Shaboon v. Duncan* (2001) that it was bound by its earlier ruling on state immunity under Title II in *Coolbaugh* (1998). However, although it denied the state's sovereign immunity claim and remanded the case to the court below because the parties had not briefed the effects of *Garrett* on Title II, the appeals court encouraged the state to pursue its argument on remand.

When the circuit later revisited the issue of immunity in *Reickenbacker v. Louisiana Department of Safety* (2001), it noted that *Coolbaugh,* which involved a Title II claim for immunity, had been interpreted to deny immunity to states in Title I suits as well. Thus, to the extent that *Coolbaugh* had barred state immunity in Title I suits, it was overruled by *Garrett.* Additionally, *Reickenbacker* (2001, 981) held that, considering both *Kimel* and *Garrett,* "the Supreme Court has effectively overruled *Coolbaugh.*" Starting afresh, the court applied the "congruence and proportionality" test of *City of Boerne* to Title II and concluded that the accommodations necessitated by the act exceeded the constitutional requirements of the Fourteenth Amendment.

The Tenth Circuit assessed the state's immunity defense in *Thompson v. Colorado* (2001), a class action suit challenging a state fee for "handicapped" parking placards. The court reviewed its decision in *Martin* (1999), indicating that it was unclear whether that had been intended to apply to the entire act or merely to Title I. But there was no need to ferret out the answer, it said, because *Garrett* had established that the abrogation analysis should be applied to each title independently. In doing so, the court held that Congress exceeded its authority in abrogating the state's immunity under Title II because it had failed to identify a pattern of unconstitutional discrimination against people with disabilities by states. Because Title II suffered from the same defect as Title I, that is, it was not "congruent and proportional" to identified constitutional violations, the abrogation was invalid.

When the Ninth Circuit addressed the issue of state immunity in *Wroncy v. Oregon Department of Transportation* (2001, 2–3), shortly after the high court had announced *Garrett,* it determined that because *Garrett* only addressed Title I, it was not required to reconsider its rulings on Title II in *Clark* (1997) and *Dare* (1999). However, in *Demshki v. Monteith* (2001), the Ninth Circuit applied the Supreme Court's reasoning in *Garrett* to a Title V (retaliation) claim against the state and dismissed the plaintiff's suit. The court believed there was insufficient evidence that the states had committed unconstitutional retaliatory actions against employees complaining of discrimination, and therefore immunity was warranted. And last, in *Hason v. Medical Board of California* (2002a), the appellate court reiterated its commitment to permitting Title II litigants to sue states for money damages by explicitly holding that *Garrett* did not overrule *Clark* (1997) and *Dare* (1999).

Prior to *Garrett,* the law of the Eighth Circuit had already established that states were protected from Title II damage suits (*Alsbrook* 1999). In *Randolph* (2001), the circuit court cited *Alsbrook* and *Garrett* and upheld the lower court's dismissal of the plaintiff's Title II claim for damages against the Missouri Department of Corrections.

One of the few cases following *Garrett* to reach a contrary conclusion about immunity was *Kiman* (2002), in which the First Circuit reversed a lower court ruling in favor of the state prison system. The appellate court explained that Title II implicated a number of constitutional protections; the right involved in this case was a prisoner's Eighth Amendment right to be free from "cruel and unusual punishment" in his conditions of confinement. Because there was an identified pattern of unconstitutional behavior in this area, the damage remedy satisfied the "congruent and proportional" test.

The Sixth and Second Circuits reacted to *Garrett* in interesting, and different, ways. The leading Sixth Circuit case, *Popovich* (2002), concluded that only certain Title II claims were barred by Eleventh Amendment immunity.[28] The plaintiff in this case had won a jury verdict of $400,000 in a suit against a state court for failing to provide him with hearing assistance during a child custody case. When the state later asserted a sovereign immunity defense, the appeals court explained that the plaintiff's case consisted of three claims: "an equal protection-type claim of discrimination, a due process-type claim of unreasonable exclusion from participation in the custody proceeding, and a claim of retaliation for filing an administrative complaint for failing to accommodate his disability" (*Popovich* 2002, 811).

The court noted that *Garrett* offered states immunity when the plaintiff's claim was based on a law arising under congressional authority to enforce the equal protection clause. But, it reasoned, the Eleventh Amendment does not confer immunity on actions derived from Congress's power to enforce the due process clause of the Fourteenth Amendment. Congress has broader powers to regulate state conduct under the due process clause because its authority under the equal protection clause is limited to preventing or remedying irrational state actions. Similarly, in *Carten v. Kent State University* (2002), another Sixth Circuit panel dismissed a case brought by a student dismissed from a library science program. The court held that the state was protected by the Eleventh Amendment because the plaintiff's Title II claim was based on equal protection only and had not alleged procedural irregularities. Citing *Popovich* and *Garrett,* the court dismissed the case.

In *Garcia* (2001), its much-cited opinion, the Second Circuit engaged in an extensive analysis, comparing the commands of Title II and the Fourteenth Amendment to determine if the statute accorded with Congress's section 5 authority to prohibit unconstitutional state discrimination on the basis of disability. The court concluded that Title II as a whole does not abrogate state immunity, but the state cannot claim immunity if the plaintiff can prove it was motivated by "animus" or discriminatory intent. Allowing a damage remedy for intentional discrimination in Title II satisfied the test of "congruence and proportionality" because it comported with Congress's authority to proscribe intentional acts of discrimination under the Fourteenth Amendment. But because the plaintiff in *Garcia* was unable to show that the medical school administrators at the state university were motivated by discriminatory intent, the court dismissed his suit.

State Immunity under the Rehabilitation Act

States may waive their immunity either by agreeing to subject themselves to suit or by voluntarily participating in a federal spending program that clearly indicates that the funds are conditioned on a waiver of immunity. As the validity of Congress's abrogation of immunity in Title II suits was increasingly challenged, the question of state immunity under section 504 of the 1973 Rehabilitation Act assumed even greater importance. If states were immune from damage remedies in both section 504 and Title II, the prohibition against state discrimination on the basis of disability would be greatly attenuated.

Most Title II actions against state entities included claims based on the Rehabilitation Act, with states asserting that the Eleventh Amendment also conferred immunity on them in section 504 suits. However, although section 504 suits are subject to the same constraints under the Fourteenth Amendment as Title II suits, section 504 is also grounded in Congress's spending authority (Paradis 2003, 412–13).

When the Eleventh Circuit reconsidered *Garrett* on remand, it affirmed the lower court's original grant of summary judgment to the state agencies on both the ADA and Rehabilitation Act claims (*Garrett v. Board of Trustees of the University of Alabama* 2001a).[29] However, shortly thereafter, the circuit court granted a rehearing to consider the plaintiffs' (Garrett and Ash) argument that the state waived its Eleventh Amendment immunity in section 504 suits by accepting federal funds (*Garrett v. Board of Trustees of the University of Alabama* 2001b). It vacated its earlier ruling and remanded the case to the district court with instructions to consider the issue of Eleventh Amendment immunity under section 504. In 2003, after the state won its motion for summary judgment in the lower court, the appeals court reversed, agreeing with the plaintiffs that the state had waived immunity in section 504 suits (*Garrett v. Board of Trustees of the University of Alabama* 2003).

Ultimately most circuits agreed that states waived immunity in section 504 suits by accepting federal dollars for programs related to people with disabilities.[30] The Eighth Circuit case of *Jim C. v. United States* (2000) is one of the most frequently cited cases on state waivers of immunity in section 504. The appellate court had consolidated two lower court decisions, *Bradley v. Arkansas Department of Education* (1997) and *Jim C. v. Atkins School District* (1998), in which the district courts had denied the state's motions to dismiss on Eleventh Amendment grounds, ruling that the IDEA and section 504, respectively, were valid exercises of Congress's section 5 powers.

On appeal, the three-judge panel in *Bradley v. Arkansas Department of Education* (1999) sought to determine whether Congress had successfully abrogated the state's immunity in section 504 and IDEA actions and the separate question of whether the state had waived its immunity.[31] The panel held that Congress's abrogation of state immunity in section 504 satisfied the *Seminole Tribe* test because Congress clearly indicated its intent to do so by enacting the Civil Rights Remedies Equalization Act of 1986 (section 2000d-7). This 1986 law revoked sovereign immunity in suits brought to enforce specified civil rights laws, including section 504.[32] The court then addressed the second part of the *Seminole Tribe* test, whether Congress's abrogation of state immunity was a valid exercise of its power under section 5 of the Fourteenth Amendment and whether section 504 is a "congruent and proportional" remedy for state misconduct. It concluded that Congress had not sufficiently identified the constitutional misconduct it sought to remedy in enacting either section 504 or section 2000d-7.[33] Moreover, it said, *Alsbrook* (1999) compelled its ruling because of the similarity between section 504 and the ADA.

The plaintiffs also argued that, abrogation aside, the state had waived its immunity by accepting section 504 funds. The panel disagreed, noting that section 504 was an invalid exercise of Congress's spending power because its conditions were "overly broad" and "amounted to impermissible coercion" (*Bradley* 1999, 756). States were not given a "meaningful choice" about accepting federal funding because they were "forced to renounce all federal funding, including funding wholly unrelated" to the goals of the Rehabilitation Act, if they were unwilling to adhere to the conditions in section 504 (*Bradley* 1999, 757). The case was remanded to the lower court with instructions to dismiss the section 504 claim in *Jim C.*

Sitting en banc in *Jim C.* (2000), the Eighth Circuit vacated the panel's ruling on the spending power issue and considered whether the state had waived its immunity by accepting federal section 504 funds.[34] The court began by explaining that states are not required to reject all federal funding in order to avoid complying with section 504. Rejecting the view that the statute was coercive, the court held that the state Department of Education could have avoided complying with the conditions of section 504 simply by refusing federal funds for education. The amount of money flowing to the state earmarked for education, approximately $250 million or 12 percent of its yearly education budget, would likely make that choice "politically painful," the court said, but it did not compel the state's choice (*Jim C.* 2000, 1082). By accepting federal funds, the state had waived its immunity in section 504 suits against its Department of Education. The court noted that although the waiver applied to all state education programs, not simply those related to section 504, it did not extend to all state programs.[35]

The Ninth Circuit agreed with the other circuits that states waived immunity in suits brought under the Rehabilitation Act. In *Dare* (1999) and *Clark* (1997), it had ruled that Congress was within its authority under section 5 of the Fourteenth Amendment to abrogate state immunity in section 504 as well as in Title II. Several years later, in *Douglas v. California Department of Youth Authority* (2001), the appeals court held that it was unnecessary to decide the issue of Congress's section 5 authority. It agreed with the Eighth Circuit that Congress had the authority under the spending clause to condition the receipt of federal funds on the state waiver of immunity and that the state had waived its immunity by accepting section 504 funds.

The Supreme Court and Title II

After *Garrett,* it was inevitable that the Supreme Court would be presented with a case that raised the question of state immunity in Title II. It appeared that the cloud of uncertainty hovering over Title II would be lifted when the Supreme Court agreed to review a Ninth Circuit ruling.

Dr. Michael Hason first applied for a license to practice medicine in California in 1995; three years later, the state medical board rejected his application, citing his history of depression. He sued, charging several state officials and the medical board with violating Title II by refusing to accommodate his disability. He claimed the board should have granted him an interim license while requiring him to undergo psychotherapy or other treatment. Indeed, by the time the board had announced its decision, he had already received treatment.[36]

In April 2000, the trial court dismissed his suit on grounds of sovereign immunity, and a three-judge panel of the Ninth Circuit reversed. The panel held that because *Garrett* had not addressed immunity in Title II suits, it had not overruled *Dare* (1999) and *Clark* (1997). With four judges dissenting, the appeals court denied a rehearing en banc. The dissenters contended that the circuit court had given insufficient consideration to the Supreme Court's approach to the immunity question in *Garrett* and was "all but invit[ing] a grant of certiorari and reversal for putting us out of step with the Supreme Court *and creating a split with every other circuit to have considered the issue*"

(*Hason v. Medical Board of California* 2002b, 1167; emphasis in the original). The state appealed to the high court, arguing that the suit was barred by the Eleventh Amendment. The Court granted *certiorari* to consider whether the Eleventh Amendment protected the medical board from suit (*Medical Board of California v. Hason* 2002).[37]

As in *Garrett,* there were numerous amici briefs: disability rights groups, past and present members of Congress, and eleven state governments all urged the Court to affirm the lower court. Only one brief representing the views of eight states was submitted on behalf of California. Oral argument was scheduled for March 25, 2003. On March 7, although the parties had not reached a settlement, Attorney General William Lockyer petitioned the Court to withdraw the case, and it was removed from the argument calendar (*Medical Board of California v. Hason* 2003). Both Lockyer and Governor Gray Davis had written to the board a few weeks earlier, asking it to drop the appeal to serve the "greater public interest." When the board agreed, the attorney general's petition followed.[38]

The Court's next opportunity to determine the issue of state immunity in Title II actions was presented in a Sixth Circuit opinion handed down early in 2003; as in *Dickson, Garrett,* and *Hason,* the United States intervened to defend the constitutionality of the Title II damage remedy.

The two principal parties in the case were George Lane and Beverly Jones, who filed suit on August 10, 1998, to challenge inaccessible court facilities. In 1996, Lane had been summoned to appear in the Polk County Courthouse for arraignment on two misdemeanor charges arising from a car accident in which he was accused of reckless driving.[39] He arrived at the courthouse in a wheelchair, and with no elevator in the building was forced to crawl up two flights of stairs to attend his hearing on the second floor. Later, returning for his trial, he refused to crawl up the stairs again or permit court officers to carry him, fearing they would purposely drop him. He refused the judge's offer to hold the hearing on a ground floor, saying he wanted to be treated equally. He was arrested for failure to appear at his hearing. During subsequent hearings, the judge was upstairs, Lane was downstairs, with his attorney running up and down the stairs between the two. The criminal case was eventually stayed while an elevator was constructed in the courthouse.[40] Lane filed suit, claiming discrimination under Title II and seeking $100,000 in damages.

Jones was a certified court reporter with paraplegia who used a wheelchair. Her requests for accommodations in four county courthouses were ignored, and on one occasion a judge was forced to carry her into the courthouse restroom. She filed suit, asking for $250,000 in damages, alleging that she was unable to pursue her livelihood because of inaccessible courthouses and had to suffer the humiliation of being carried to work.

A three-judge panel of the Sixth Circuit issued a per curiam opinion, reiterating the earlier holding in *Popovich* (2002). It held that the Eleventh Amendment does not insulate states from damage remedies in Title II suits that are based on the due process clause of the Fourteenth Amendment (*Lane v. Tennessee* 2002). The panel subsequently granted the state a rehearing and issued an amended opinion, rejecting the state's arguments that the plaintiffs' claims were not based on due process violations (*Lane v. Tennessee* 2003). It stressed that Congress was well aware that physical barriers denied people with disabilities their due process right of access to the courts and had recognized the need for corrective legislation. Moreover, the court ruled, there was evidence that Congress believed the states' refusal to accommodate the needs of people with disabilities may have stemmed "from unconstitutional animus and impermissible stereotypes" (*Lane v. Tennessee* 2003, 683). It concluded that the district court had correctly denied the state's motion to dismiss and remanded the case to the court below to further develop the factual record on the alleged violations.

The Supreme Court granted *certiorari* to decide whether Title II exceeds Congress's authority under section 5 and does not effectively abrogate the state's immunity for damages (*Tennessee v. Lane* 2003). In agreeing to decide this case, the Court had raised expectations of those seeking to limit sovereign immunity and those seeking to expand it. The brief submitted on behalf of Lane and Jones addressed the importance of the "core principles" of access to state courthouses inherent in Title II. It argued that, in contrast to Title I, "which implicates no fundamental rights and therefore involves conduct that triggers only rational-basis scrutiny . . . Title II affects an array of conduct in which states have heightened constitutional obligations." And as a consequence, Congress would have wider leeway to "craft a remedy than in Title I's employment context" ("Brief for the Private Respondents," in *Tennessee v. Lane*).

The state's brief began by acknowledging the significance of the ADA. It conceded its duty to comply with the law or face a private action for injunctive relief as well as suit by the federal government. But it argued that Title II, like the rest of the ADA, was primarily "equal protection" legislation and that there was no evidence that congressional action had been necessary to remedy state constitutional equal protection violations. Turning to the charge of due process violations, the brief insisted that "the legislative record [also] fails to support the Sixth Circuit's claim that Title II was enacted to remedy wide-spread and persisting due process violations by the States." Other than a mention of "voting" and a vague reference to "public services," Congress evidenced no concern about "a systematic pattern of fundamental rights violations by the States" ("Brief of Petitioner," in *Tennessee v. Lane*).

As is customary in significant ADA cases, there was a plethora of amicus curiae briefs—almost all supporting Lane and Jones—urging the Court to affirm the court of appeals ruling. Briefs were filed by numerous disability rights groups, including NOD, AAPD, ADA Watch, the Bazelon Center, and Easter Seals; by traditional civil rights groups such as People for the American Way Foundation, the NAACP, Lawyers' Committee for Civil Rights Under Law, and the Anti-Defamation League; and by NAPAS, the ABA, and the governments of twelve states.

Only one brief, submitted jointly by seven states, supported the state's position. Amici for the state urged the Supreme Court to limit the scope of its investigation to Congress's regulation of access to public buildings rather than to the overall validity of Title II as section 5 legislation ("Brief of *Amici Curiae* Alabama, Nebraska, Nevada, North Dakota, South Dakota, Oklahoma, Utah, and Wyoming," in *Tennessee v. Lane*). Oral arguments were heard on January 13, 2004. Before the argument began, a group of seven disability rights activists, some in wheelchairs, signaled their support of the plaintiffs by crawling up the steps to the Court plaza. "We wanted to show our solidarity, to do what he was forced to do," said Jim Ward, head of ADA Watch and the National Coalition for Disability Rights. When threatened with arrest, they left. According to Ward, they had "accomplished what [they] had set out to do" (*Legal Times,* January 26, 2004).

During oral arguments, the attorney for Lane and Jones contended that the absence of an elevator infringed on Lane's right to defend himself in his criminal trial. "We are talking about a quintessential element of the 14th Amendment; the right to due process and to participate in civic life" (*Disability Compliance Bulletin,* February 6, 2004). According to the state solicitor general, however, "there is no indication Congress thought courtroom access was a matter of particular concern" (*Recorder,* January 14, 2004).

The justices explored the degree to which states were responsible for accessibility in specific state facilities and what kind of accommodations they were required to provide. Justice Scalia noted that being carried up stairs was "less dignified," but he queried whether states should be subject to suit because a courthouse lacked an elevator (*Legal Times,* January 19, 2004). He also questioned whether an inaccessible state-owned hockey rink would violate an individual's fundamental right.

Responding to questions from Justices Kennedy and O'Connor about how narrowly or broadly the Court could rule in the case, the deputy solicitor general indicated that he was there to defend the whole statute, but he seemed to suggest that the Court might limit its ruling to the issue of state accountability for inaccessible courtrooms if it chose to. In enacting Title II, he said, Congress had ample evidence of such courtrooms and was "clearly . . . reacting to a real problem" (*Legal Intelligencer,* January 14, 2004). Silverstein (2000) believes that the ADA had satisfied the standards of the *City of Boerne* test: "there was a "history of discrimination by the states," he said, "and a comprehensive need to address these issues." Nevertheless, most of the disability rights advocates feared that the Court would extend the *Garrett* principle of state immunity to Title II.

The Supreme Court handed down its decision in *Tennessee v. Lane* on May 17, 2004. Although the ruling addressed the immediate question of whether Title II allowed damages in the claims made by Lane and Jones, the Court left a number of questions unanswered. In deciding the case, the Court had a number of options: it could affirm the lower court on the narrow ground that damages were available in Title II suits for due process violations (or even more narrowly, when physical access to the courts is denied); or, it could adhere to the distinction *Garrett* drew between Titles I and II and permit plaintiffs to recover damages when states violated Title II.[41] The Court could also have expanded the new federalism jurisprudence by barring damages in all Title II actions against states, and perhaps have even declared Title II unconstitutional as it applied to states.

In a 5–4 decision, with Stevens announcing the opinion for himself, O'Connor, Souter, Ginsburg, and Breyer, the majority held that the Eleventh Amendment did not shield states from damage suits in Title II actions involving the fundamental right of access to courts. The Court began by dismissing the state's argument that Congress had not intended to abrogate state immunity in Title II actions; the record was clear that it had. The Court then reviewed the familiar case law arising out of its new federalism jurisprudence and applied the "congruence and proportionality" test in *City of Boerne* to determine whether Congress had the authority to do so. Reiterating that *Garrett* had distinguished between Title I and Title II, Stevens also distinguished between the statute's effect on "irrational disability discrimination," that is, equal protection violations and its enforcement of "other basic constitutional guarantees, infringements of which are subject to more searching judicial review" (*Tennessee v. Lane* 2004, 1988).

In addition to physical access to courtrooms, Stevens identified other fundamental rights related to the courts, such as the right to be present during trial and the right to trial by jury. The appropriateness of the Title II damage remedy, he noted, depended on the ills it was intended to cure. Citing a long history of discrimination in voting rights, involuntary commitment to mental institutions, and zoning, Stevens concluded that Title II was intended to address problems of "pervasive unequal treatment of the administration of state services and programs, including systematic deprivations of fundamental rights" (*Tennessee v. Lane* 2004, 1989). And, he continued, when enacting Title II, Congress had ample evidence of unconstitutional conduct by states and other government and nongovernment actors in the distribution of public services. Because such evidence differed from the evidence of employment discrimination, which the *Garrett* plaintiffs had used to justify Title I, Congress had been warranted in enacting Title II to remedy discriminatory access to courthouses. Moreover, he added, the legislature had chosen a restrained approach that merely required public entities to reasonably modify exiting structures without imposing "undue burdens" upon them. The state could have complied with the law simply by relocating its courtrooms to accessible locations. Thus, the Court held "that Title II, as it applies to the class of cases implicating the fundamental right of access to the courts, constitutes a valid exercise of Congress' §5 authority to enforce the guarantees of the Fourteenth Amendment" (*Tennessee v. Lane* 2004, 1994).

Although the media portrayed this ruling as a major victory for the disability community, the extent of the victory is uncertain. Despite language in the opinion suggesting that sovereign immunity will not shield states from damage remedies when Title II plaintiffs allege violations of due process or other fundamental rights, the ruling itself was limited to the fundamental right of access to courtrooms, leaving the matter of access to other public buildings and services open to question and subject to further litigation (*Western Massachusetts Law Tribune*, July 2004; *Legal Times*, July 5, 2004).[42]

7 Conclusion

One of the challenges of the disability rights movement was to transform the status of people with disabilities, a group characterized by Congress in 1990 as "politically powerless." The ADA was intended to send a clear message to society that discrimination on the basis of disability was unacceptable. In setting forth the purpose of the act, Congress stated that its intent was to "provide clear, strong, consistent, enforceable standards addressing discrimination against individuals with disabilities [and] to ensure that the Federal government plays a central role in enforcing the standards established in this Act." However, despite the strong civil rights rhetoric in the legislative history and statutory text, disability rights remain an imperfectly realized goal, at best because of a lack of understanding of the needs of people with disabilities, at worst because of a refusal to accommodate those needs. Although most advocates readily acknowledge the changes the law has engendered in societal attitudes and behavior toward people with disabilities, a good number believe these accomplishments have come about despite the courts, rather than because of the courts.

As a civil rights statute, the ADA borrows heavily from the enforcement mechanisms and remedial schemes of prior civil rights laws, but it is sui generis in a number of ways. First, unlike the traditional civil rights laws, the ADA only permits people with disabilities to file suit, requiring the courts to make an initial determination about whether the plaintiffs are members of the statutorily protected class. This is known as the "definition of disability" stage, which has been the subject of much dispute, raising concerns within the disability community that the courts are blocking the courthouse entrance to people with disabilities by raising the bar higher than Congress intended. Second, unlike the civil rights laws of the 1960 and 1970s, the ADA explicitly allows cost and reasonableness to be interposed as defenses in litigation. Consequently, the rights guaranteed in the law are balanced against an unspecified monetary and social cost so that discrimination is permissible if the price for relief is too great. Additionally, unlike the traditional civil rights laws, the ADA is based on a principle of structural equality so that equal opportunity is not achieved by treating all persons equally. In contrast to discrimination on the basis of race, sex, or age, where, for the most part, one can escape liability simply by ceasing to engage in the prohibited conduct, providing a remedy for inequality on the basis of disability requires positive, that is, affirmative, action.

The judiciary was given primary responsibility for establishing the parameters of disability rights policy in both the public and private sector. Disability rights advocates turned to the courts, hoping they would follow the oft-stated approach to civil rights laws of effectuating the remedial purposes of the statute. But in the decade of litigation following the enactment of the ADA, many members of the disability community have grown disappointed in the judicial implementation of the law. They believe that, largely as a result of the interpretation of the statute by federal court judges—in contradiction to Congress's intent—the ADA has failed to achieve the goals they envisioned.

It is clear that ADA litigation has not served the disability community as well as disability rights advocates had hoped. The cases show that the Supreme Court's interpretation of the act has constricted the parameters of disability rights and excluded large numbers of claimants from the reach of the law, primarily in the employment context. The majority of disability rights advocates interviewed for this study echo the view that the courts' interpretation of the law has not been faithful to the legislative intent; most cited the employment cases to support their beliefs.

Silverstein (2000) says that the judiciary's interpretation was not anticipated and he was "very distressed about the treatment [of the ADA] by the courts." As another respondent put it, "in places [where] we thought we had it figured out so the courts couldn't screw it up, they did." Osolinik (2001) says the courts "have substituted their judgments for Congress's" and have not been "deferential enough to Congress." Similarly, Mayerson (2001) criticizes the courts for their narrow view of disability, for adopting a "medical model" and insisting that a plaintiff be "totally disabled" to fit within the parameters of the law.

Breslin (2001) explains it this way:

in order to meet the ADA definition of disability, an individual must show his or her impairment substantially limits a major life activity. At the same time, that person must show that he or she is qualified for the job with or without accommodation. These tests are counterintuitive. The first showing also tends to disregard the impact of purely prejudicial acts that do not relate to someone's actual capacity to perform specific job functions. The courts want the focus of the case to be on the plaintiff and not on the conduct of the employer.

There were far fewer cases outside the employment context, and, in general, the courts were more favorably disposed to plaintiffs in nonemployment cases. However, even the rulings decided in the plaintiffs' favor, were, for the most part, decided on narrow grounds, with qualifications that would allow future defendants to win in the courts below. Additionally, the Court instructed the lower courts to carefully consider defendants' affirmative defenses, such as the cost and reasonableness of an accommodation or the threat of potential harm that the plaintiff might cause.

More broadly, this study also shows that there has been a marked shift in civil rights decisionmaking. The ADA litigation over the last decade demonstrates that the Supreme Court strayed from its policy of interpreting civil rights laws broadly to further their remedial purposes. Instead, in recent years, the Court has adopted a textualist approach in which it closely adheres to the statutory language and only inquires into the legislative history when it believes it is necessary for deciding the case. Moreover, textualism is less concerned with the administrative regulations and guidelines that have typically played an important role in statutory interpretation.

Reflecting the Court's penchant for the use of textualism, the ADA decisions—especially in cases from 1999 to 2002—illustrate that language usage, rules of grammar, and sentence structure have become more important variables in determining the outcome of the case than the intent of the framers and the motivation behind the law. Against this backdrop of a shifting standard of statutory interpretation, ADA plaintiffs discovered to their dismay that the text was key and that Congress's intent that the act be broadly interpreted did not prevail.

The high court's method of decisionmaking was mirrored in the constrained interpretations of the law by the courts below. Predictions that ADA litigants would arouse the courts' sympathy, resulting in victories by nonmeritorious claimants, have not been substantiated. Indeed, this study has shown that the opposite has been true, at least in the first decade of litigation. Consistent with the findings reported in other studies of ADA litigation, the results of this investigation indicate that the defendants' success depended heavily on procedural rulings, with plaintiffs frequently unable to overcome the jurisdictional barriers erected by the courts.

The analysis of judicial implementation of Titles II and III shows that through strict interpretation of the rules of pleading, especially the standing requirements, narrow applications of the definitions of disability, constrained interpretations of the statutory language, and refusals to waive the mootness doctrine in claims for injunctive relief—despite evidence that the discriminatory conduct would continue to "evade review"—the courts often elevated procedure over substance in adjudicating the civil rights claims of ADA litigants. In a variety of ways, the courts placed numerous obstacles in the way of plaintiffs seeking their day in court. Indeed, Decker (2000) believes the primary obstacle to effective enforcement of the law has been that "courts stop plaintiffs from getting in the courthouse door." As a consequence of these roadblocks, the courts dismissed a significant number of cases without addressing the merits of the plaintiffs' claims, allowing seemingly clear incidences of discrimination to go unchecked because plaintiffs were refused the opportunity to make their case for discrimination.

The data reported here show that although there are differences in their rate of success, most ADA defendants prevail in the federal courts, especially at the appellate level. This is significant from a public policy perspective because, with few prospects of further appellate review, this is typically the judiciary's final decision. Ironically, despite the rhetoric about the federal courts' reluctance to interfere with state sovereignty and the fiscal autonomy of subnational governments, Title II defendants were the least successful of the ADA defendants. The defendants in the Title III cases, though they have a very impressive litigation record, were not quite as successful as the defendants in employment discrimination cases because the latter were more effective at capitalizing on the catch-22 of ADA litigation. Indeed, the most successful defendants in the Titles II and III actions were those who were able to mirror the arguments of Title I defendants and persuade the courts that the plaintiff did not meet the definition of disability or was not qualified for a position. Perhaps as well, as one respondent commented, litigants suing under Titles II and III were more likely to be perceived as disabled, in contrast to plaintiffs in Title I actions.

Based on their experiences, most respondents expressed greater satisfaction with the results of Title II litigation than Titles I and III. Laski (2002), for example, differentiated between litigating against public entities, which "has had a great impact," and litigating against businesses, which "has been less effective." In employment cases, especially, he said, "the overall picture is still pretty bad." Similarly, Thomas-Akhtar (2001) agreed that, although the threat of litigation was effective in some cases, she believed it was less so with "giant corporations" because of the financial drain of litigating against them.

Disability rights litigants also unwittingly became enmeshed in the battle raging in the courts over the sovereign immunity doctrine and state liability for damage suits. It may be that one of the greatest threats to the ADA will arise from the state sovereign immunity doctrine. Despite the Court's recent ruling in *Tennessee v. Lane* (2004), the impact of the new federalism jurisprudence is not yet known and will likely remain unknown for some time. In upholding Congress's authority to abrogate state immunity in damage suits alleging inaccessible courts, the Court left open the question of whether damage claims based on due process, or fundamental rights more generally, or on equal protection, fell within the constraints of sovereign immunity. Without the prospect of damage awards in such cases, there will be less incentive to sue states for Title II violations.

Moreover, as a consequence of the new federalism jurisprudence, defendants have also been encouraged to dispute the constitutionality of other laws, such as section 504. Although it appears unlikely, some respondents gloomily suggested that the Court's new federalism jurisprudence may prompt defendants to challenge the traditional civil rights laws. Thinking of the worst case scenario, Dart (2001) warned that all civil rights would be jeopardized if Congress were unable to impose the ADA on the states. "What about other civil rights?" he asked.

Thus, as demonstrated in this study, the judiciary's constricted interpretation of the law is the single most important reason why ADA litigants fared so badly: the courts have simply been unwilling to impose the social and financial costs of compliance on business defendants in Title I and Title III cases, and, to a lesser degree, on public entities in Title II actions.

However, Congress—another significant actor in the disability policy-making process—must share responsibility for the statute's failure to live up to its promises. During the passage of the bill, there was overwhelming support for the principle of ending discrimination on the basis of disability. Yet, at the same time, a substantial number of the members of Congress expressed alarm about the cost of compliance for business and industry; the debates centered on small business owners who, at least in Title III cases, represented only a small minority of the defendants. Members of Congress also feared that the rights language of the statute would lead to expensive and unnecessary litigation and far-reaching judicial interpretation of the law. The final version of the bill reflected these contradictory impulses by extending civil rights guarantees to a newly protected class while simultaneously safeguarding the interests of Congress's business constituency by inserting affirmative defenses in the law such as the cost of the accommodation or modification.

Despite the evident commitment of a large number of congressional supporters, the law contains vague and ill-defined provisions that allow the courts a great deal of discretion in implementation. The framers of the law, both in and out of Congress, believed the legislative history and statutory language adequately expressed Congress's intent that the law should be broadly interpreted. Disability rights advocates note that the text of the act is consistent with other civil rights laws and that, as in all civil rights laws, legislative compromises (often resulting in less precise language) may be necessary to gain majority support for a bill.[1]

Colker (2004) has gone even further to argue that there was a clear understanding among members of Congress, and indeed the White House, that the ADA was "an unabashedly liberal piece of legislation that broadly protected the disability community." Moreover, she contends that the law was written in "much more detail" than its predecessor civil rights statutes (2–3). In her view, the legislative history of the act shows that Congress made its intent plain in all important aspects and that the Court has refused to credit this history, instead relying on the text to resolve the legal disputes arising under the act.

In part also, the ADA has been a victim of unfortunate timing. As a number of advocates have noted, today's Congress is not the Congress of the early 1990s that enacted the ADA. There is a long history of congressional reversal of Supreme Court decisions in civil rights cases affecting disability rights when Congress determined that the courts were not following legislative intent and were frustrating the aims of the legislation: the 1986 Handicapped Children's Protection Act, reversing *Smith* (1984); the Civil Rights Restoration Act, reversing *Grove City* (1984); the Civil Rights Remedies Equalization Act, reversing *Atascadero* (1985); the Air Carrier Access Act, reversing *Paralyzed Veterans* (1986); and the EAHCA amendments, reversing *Dellmuth* (1990). Notwithstanding this legislative record, and despite voluminous evidence that the Court has consistently failed to carry out the remedial purposes of the law, Congress has done nothing to require the courts to reverse course. One attempt, a law mandating equality in insurance benefits, failed to pass. Moreover, on two occasions, Congress even considered reining in disability rights by applying UMRA to the ADA and by passage of the ADA Notification Act.

What about the litigants and the disability community? Although the lack of success among ADA plaintiffs is chiefly attributable to judicial interpretation, the litigants themselves, and by extension the disability community, must also shoulder some of the responsibility for the legal defeats. The disability rights advocates had presented a united front in educating the public about the need for the legislation and in lobbying government officials for passage of the law. A number of respondents noted that this unity had been crucial in passing a strong civil rights act. But, as some also ruefully observed, July 26, 1990—the date the ADA became law—may have been the high point of the cohesiveness of the disability rights movement.

Debbie Fletter (2002), co-founder of Wired on Wheels (an Internet-based rating system of business accessibility), comments that "the ADA pulled everyone in the disability community together and, while there are powerful local actions, it hasn't been that way since at the national level." Over the next decade, the coalition began to splinter at the same time that disability rights advocates were forced to deal with media backlash and intransigence from the business community, as well as a judiciary that, as some respondents said, "just didn't get it." Also, as Max Lapertosa (2002), staff attorney at Chicago's Access Living, notes, "the nonmeritorious cases have led to the perception among people and among the courts that too many people are 'trying to get away with things.'" Similarly, Fletter (2002) believes that the current assaults on the ADA reflect a misunderstanding of the law in the media and an emphasis on lawyers rather than civil rights violations against people with disabilities.

The Effectiveness of Litigation

The disability rights advocates interviewed for this study all agree that the ADA has been most successful in transforming inaccessible sidewalks, buildings, and transportation systems. Wright (2000) comments that physical accessibility has been the most successful, the most "concrete"; it has been "totally different in the last decade," she says. The rulings confirm that plaintiffs with mobility impairments are, as a whole, the most successful ADA litigants in Title II and Title III cases. It is not surprising that plaintiffs prevail more frequently in claims involving physical barriers because these are at the heart of the disability rights movement. Congress intended the ADA to play an important role in removing obstacles to mobility, and the rulings show that courts are sympathetic to plaintiffs in such cases in both the public and private sector. Moreover, the impact of this litigation has been more widely felt than the number of rulings suggests because the relief ordered by the courts is usually widespread, affecting large numbers of people with disabilities.

When asked about the role of the courts in implementing the law and the effectiveness of litigation more broadly, the disability advocates express reservations about the courts while affirming the value of litigation as a strategy to achieve compliance. As one respondent puts it, "I wouldn't list the courts as champions of the ADA"; Decker (2000) called the courts a "mixed bag." But although the respondents differ somewhat in their assessment of public and private sector compliance with the act (most believe the public sector has a higher rate of compliance) and with their degree of satisfaction with the courts, they all believe that litigation and the threat of litigation have helped to achieve compliance with the ADA. One respondent summarizes the views of many by calling litigation "a vital tool in the disability rights agenda."

Breslin (2001) notes that "the promise of litigation drives compliance." Another respondent bluntly says, "without litigation, there would be no compliance." "Lawsuits get attention from businesses," says one respondent; "litigation is an important part of the civil rights process." Another comments that although it is "unfortunate, . . . the threat of litigation is about 80 percent" of what makes the law work. Silverstein (2000) agrees that it is unfortunate that litigation plays such a significant role; "unfortunate," he said, "because there should be more voluntary compliance."

Most advocates stressed that without the possibility of litigation, ADA enforcement would have been less effective. Eichner (2002) believes litigation has been "critically important." Without it, he stresses, we "would have been much worse off." Similarly, Hanson (2001), noting that his office does not file lawsuits, describes litigation as a "major part of any civil rights law," adding, "you need that component, without a doubt." Henderson (2001) describes litigation as a "tool," adding that even when settlement agreements are reached, one needs litigation to start the process. Osolinik (2001) says litigation and the threat of litigation are important so that entities would know they "would be called to account if they didn't comply." Mayerson (2001) says she "truly believed litigation always brings things from the back burner to the front burner—and the threat of litigation is the same."

Moving beyond the issue of compliance, Lapertosa (2002) observes that litigation can serve as an organizing tool by the disability rights community as well as raise public awareness of the need for accessible public accommodations.

Although all ultimately endorse it, some respondents have more mixed feelings about the effectiveness of litigation. Rosen (2000) expresses some concern about the "the litigation strategy," commenting that it "was not working well," with defendants winning 92 percent of Title I cases.[2] Herman (2002) is also cautious, saying litigation helped to force compliance, "but also produced a backlash." On the other hand, he says, without the threat of litigation from the DOJ, "wheelchairs would still be at the screen (way up front)." The threat of litigation, he continues, "gets people to the table," where the possibility of a settlement exists. Kenneth Walden (2001), senior attorney and civil rights team leader at Access Living in Chicago, seems to express the views of a number of advocates by commenting that "sometimes litigation is the only way to get things done, [although] you want to avoid it if you can."

Summing up his perception of the role of litigation and the courts in enforcing the ADA, Andrew Imparato (2001), president and chief executive officer of the AAPD, one of the most effective and diverse disability rights organizations, says litigation has been useful, but there has been "no *Brown vs. Board of Education* for the disability community." In this same vein, commenting on ADA litigation generally, one respondent notes that, unlike the planned litigation of the NAACP, ADA cases were unplanned, without a legal infrastructure to select the best cases, allowing some attorneys to bring "bad" cases to the Supreme Court. Another comments that the strongest cases were more likely to be settled, leaving the weaker ones to go to trial. And Dickson (2001) remarks that when the earlier civil rights laws were passed, a legal team and a nonprofit structure were already in place to initiate legal challenges.

The scholarly literature, the statements of the ADA's congressional sponsors, the disability community, and the perceptions of disability rights advocates interviewed for this study all attest to the fact that the Americans with Disabilities Act was intended to be a potent weapon in society's battle against discrimination on the basis of disability. However, the weight of the evidence, including the data presented in this study, points to the federal judiciary's constrained interpretation of the law as the most important element in disabling it.

Chapter 1 | Introduction

1. Ironically, this statement appeared in a ruling that limited the reach of the ADA.

2. This represented 19.3 percent of the 257 million people aged five and over in the civilian uninstitutionalized population in the United States. These data were derived from answers to questions 16 and 17 on the census long-form questionnaire. Because of the more restricted wording of the questions, the number of people with disabilities reported here differs slightly from the 53 million people reported in the *Survey of Income and Program Participation* last conducted by the Census Bureau in 1997. Another source of information from the Census Bureau about people with disabilities comes from the Current Population Survey (CPS), which counts people who are out of work because of a disability. Every March since 1980, a supplemental question is asked: "Does anyone in this household have a health problem or disability which prevents them from working or limits the kind or amount of work they can do?"

3. Congress explicitly stated that its intention was to put the ADA on a plane with earlier federal antidiscrimination laws by basing the statute on the Fourteenth Amendment and the Interstate Commerce Clause (Percy 1993).

4. State protection and advocacy agencies sprang up as a result of the Developmental Disabilities Assistance and Bill of Rights Act of 1975 to represent people with mental disabilities. After the enactment of the ADA, they turned their attention to all kinds of disabilities.

5. A survey of 1,330 people in forty-eight states conducted by the United Cerebral Palsy Association and released in 1996 showed that 84 percent of the respondents said the ADA had changed their communities, 87 percent reported that local businesses were more accessible, and 79 percent stated that public facilities were more accessible (*Washington Post*, July 26, 1996).

Chapter 2 | Disability Rights as Civil Rights

1. It is difficult to offer a precise definition of the phrase "people with disabilities" as there are many types of disabilities with varying degrees of severity. Likewise, it is difficult to get a precise count of the number of people with disabilities, as there are no commonly agreed upon referents for what constitutes a disability. Members of the disability community have coined the term, "temporarily able-bodied (TAB)," to indicate that most people are likely to have a disability at some time in their lives. In 1977, the White House Conference on Handicapped Individuals estimated that 35 million people had a mental or physical disability (Percy 1989, 3). Pfeiffer (1993, 729) discusses various measures used in estimating the number of people with disabilities in the United States, with the results ranging from 20 to 50 million.

2. In *Securities and Exchange Commission v. Zandford* (2002) and *National Railroad Passenger Corporation v. Morgan* (2002), the high court acknowledged its role in furthering a statute's remedial purpose.

3. In *Chevron, Inc. v. Natural Resources Defense Council* (1984), the Court emphasized that courts must attempt to discern congressional intent through analysis of the text and legislative history and, in case of doubt, defer to reasonable agency interpretations of the statute under review (Gores 2000; Howard and Segal 2002).

4. Gores (2000) explicitly contrasts "textualism" with "intentionalism." Howard and Segal (2002) assess the impact of text and intent separately as part of their analysis of the effects of originalist arguments and ideology on judicial voting behavior, but they do not explore possible conflicts between the two; see Whittington (1999).

5. Parmet (2003) argues that the drafters of the ADA should have been more aware of the justices' growing preference for textualism and not have simply assumed as they did that the courts would interpret the law according to legislative history and administrative interpretation.

6. Classic studies of implementation include Lowi (1972); Pressman and Wildavsky (1973); Van Meter and Van Horn (1975) and Mazmanian and Sabatier (1983). For the most part, however, these do not discuss judicial implementation.

7. Russell (2000, 13) argues, however, that despite their efforts disability rights advocates have been unsuccessful in "substitut[ing] a minority/social model of disability over the dominant medical/clinical model."

8. Katzman (1986) and Scotch (2001) provide useful analyses of the 1973 act.

9. The term "handicap" is not part of the common parlance today because the disability community believes it has negative connotations. It will be used in this text only in a direct quotes or when necessary to reflect historical accuracy. Burgdorf (1997, 411n1) and Batavia (1993, 736–37) discuss the terminology of "handicap" and "disability."

10. The guidelines went into effect in 1982 (West 1993, 11).

11. Five years later, litigants unsuccessfully attempted to rely on the committee reports issued during passage of the 1974 act as the authoritative interpretation of the

1973 act, which had not been accompanied by a committee report (Katzman 1986, 170).

12. The 1978 law was the Rehabilitation, Comprehensive Services and Developmental Disabilities Act of 1978. This law also broadened section 504 to bring the executive branch of the federal government within its reach. Additionally, Congress established a program of Comprehensive Services for Independent Living in Title VII of the Rehabilitation Act.

13. Section 508 was originally part of the Rehabilitation Act of 1986; the 1998 version strengthened it, in part by adding enforceable standards (McLawhorn 2001, 64).

14. The committee report for the 1974 Rehabilitation Act Amendments directed HEW to produce implementing regulations by the end of 1974 (Katzman 1986, 53).

15. Each federal agency is responsible for drafting its own section 504 regulations for programs channeled through it.

16. In *Cherry v. Mathews* (1976), the district court for the District of Columbia held that, despite its omission in the law, Congress had intended regulations to be issued and ordered HEW to fulfill this task.

17. Scotch (2001, 87–88) indicates that another major cause of Mathews's and Califano's concern was that the law would offer civil rights protection to drug addicts and alcoholics.

18. Heumann was a transplanted New Yorker, who, in 1970 at the age of twenty-two, founded a New York–based disability rights group called Disabled in Action. She later became President Clinton's assistant secretary for education.

19. There was no finding of unconstitutionality by the *PARC* court, merely a finding that the plaintiffs had raised a valid constitutional claim.

20. Salomone (1986, 150) points out that states learned that if they must comply with section 504 to receive federal funds, it made sense to comply with the similar provisions of the EAHCA to obtain additional sources of funding.

21. Two disability rights cases revolved around the question of Eleventh Amendment immunity: *Atascadero State Hospital v. Scanlon* (1985), which held that states were immune from section 504 suits, was reversed by Congress in the Civil Rights Remedies Equalization Act of 1986; *Dellmuth v. Muth* (1989) found states immune from suit under the EAHCA but was reversed when Congress amended the EAHCA in 1990 to specify that states were liable, notwithstanding immunity conferred by the Eleventh Amendment. The Eleventh Amendment is discussed in chapter 5.

22. Southeastern also contended that the statute did not provide a private right of action, that is, a right to sue. Davis argued that even absent a private right of action in section 504, she could sue under 42 U.S.C. §1983, a federal remedy. The Court did not address this issue because Davis lost the suit on the merits; see Mezey (1983) for discussion of 42 U.S.C. §1983 and private rights of action in federal statutes.

23. Congress incorporated the "undue burden" language into the ADA.

24. It was five years before the high court decided another section 504 case. In *Consolidated Rail Corporation v. Darrone* (1984), the Court held that section 504 applied to

recipients of federal funding even if the primary objective of the aid was not to provide employment.

25. The CCD was a consortium of disability organizations based in Washington DC; the prime mover within the organization was the Association for Retarded Citizens, headed by Paul Marchand. The DDA also required states to establish protection and advocacy agencies.

26. In *Cedar Rapids Community School District v. Garret F.* (1999), the Court applied the *Tatro* test and ordered the school to provide a child with the nursing services, that is, the "related services" necessary to enable him to attend school.

27. The case arose from a suit brought by the parents of child with cerebral palsy and other physical and mental disabilities who had been attending a private day school for almost a year, with his tuition paid by the school district. The school district informed his parents that he was no longer their responsibility and that they must look to the state mental health agency to fund his education. The parents argued that the district policy conflicted with the federal law guaranteeing their son a free appropriate public education. After a lengthy process, the Smiths won relief. The Court held that the EAHCA was the exclusive remedy for parents suing to protest special education arrangements for their child. And because the EAHCA did not explicitly authorize attorneys' fees to prevailing parties, no fees could be awarded.

28. Kemp, whose parents helped found the Muscular Dystrophy Association (MDA), suffered from a muscle-debilitating disease with symptoms similar to muscular dystrophy. In 1981, Kemp criticized the MDA which, through Jerry Lewis's annual telethons, helped raise millions of dollars for research. In his view, the MDA and its telethons sanctioned pity and stimulated prejudice against people with disabilities (Shapiro 1994, chap. 1).

29. Bush frequently consulted Kemp on disability issues and, in 1989, appointed him to chair the EEOC, which he had been serving as commissioner since 1987.

30. The Independent Living Movement had its roots in the 1950s, but gained momentum during the 1960s and 1970s as independent living centers were organized around the country. The Berkeley Center, incorporated in 1972, was the most well known. The centers were guided by a rights mentality, intent on allowing people with disabilities to increase self-determination in decisionmaking and avoid dependency on others, especially people without disabilities (Shapiro 1994, chap. 2).

31. The NCH dates back to 1972 when Congress included an Office for the Handicapped in one of the early versions of the Rehabilitation Act. After the bill was vetoed by Nixon, the idea for such an office was shelved, but it was revived in 1977 at the White House Conference on Handicapped Individuals, and the agency was created shortly thereafter (Young 1997, 50). The NCH has fifteen members appointed by the president and confirmed by the Senate.

32. The work of the task force, which heard testimony from over seven thousand people and submitted almost a dozen interim reports to Congress, culminated in a final report in 1990 (NCD 2002, 5).

33. The NCH, established in 1978 within the Department of Education, was transformed into an independent agency in 1984 in the Rehabilitation Act Amendments. In April 1996, the NCD, under the leadership of Dart and Bristo, held a National Summit on Disability Policy in Dallas attended by three hundred people. At the end of the April conference, the NCD (1996, 4–5) released a report, entitled *Achieving Independence: The Challenge for the 21st Century*. It acknowledged the progress that had been made, but was critical of the current state of public policy, saying it did not "yet promote the goals of ADA—equality of opportunity, full participation, independent living, and economic self-sufficiency." Among other things, the report called for more effective enforcement of existing laws and increased empowerment of people with disabilities in making decisions that affected their lives.

34. Cook (1991) and Burgdorf (1991) both argued that section 504 was inadequate to remedy discrimination in public services.

35. Weicker's bill would have allowed plaintiffs to prevail in court, despite the absence of proof of intentional discrimination (O'Brien 2001, 169). A number of respondents commented that they had been convinced that the 1988 version of the bill would not pass.

36. 42 U.S.C. §12201. Congress directed the DOJ to pattern Title II regulations after the section 504 regulations.

37. Craig was elected to the Senate in 1990.

38. The legislative compromise is discussed in chapter 4.

39. Although the amendment stated that the employer must make a reasonable accommodation to place the employee in an alternative job for which the worker is qualified, many doubted that this was adequate protection (*Congressional Record* 1990, S7440–41). In *School Board of Nassau County v. Arline* (1987), the Supreme Court ruled that a school board violated section 504 by firing an elementary school teacher because she had recurring incidences of tuberculosis. Ruling that the language and legislative intent of the act dictated that a person with a contagious disease could be considered "handicapped" within the meaning of the law, the Court cited the 1974 Rehabilitation Act Amendments, which had added the "regarded as" prong for precisely this reason. Congress had intended to protect individuals who may suffer discrimination because of societal fear or prejudice of their impairment. Because the lower court had not determined whether the plaintiff was "otherwise qualified" for the job, the Court remanded the case to allow it to decide whether she posed risks to others and whether she could perform the work required.

40. Of the eighty-one differences between the Senate and House versions, seventy-nine were easily resolved, with most decided in favor of the House version.

41. Dart (1993, xxiii) noted that the lopsided vote was "misleading" in that there was "massive opposition" to the law from business groups, such as the Chamber of Commerce and the NFIB, as well as the public transportation industry.

42. Dart lived to see the ADA in operation for a little over a decade; he died of respiratory failure in his home on June 22, 2002 (*Washington Post,* June 23, 2002).

43. The 1991 law modified or reversed six civil rights rulings in the Court's 1988–1989 term. It imposed no limits on damages for back pay or expenses, such as medical bills; compensatory damages (for pain and suffering) and punitive damages were dictated by the size of the business, ranging from $50,000 for employers with fifteen to one hundred workers to $300,000 for a company with more than five hundred employees (*Congressional Quarterly,* October 26, 1991, 3124–26; *New York Times,* October 26, 1991).

44. A mental or physical impairment refers to a wide array of disorders and conditions.

45. In *Arline* (1987), the Supreme Court had defined "handicapped individual" very broadly to include individuals who were discriminated against because of *any* impairment (Feldblum 2000a, 92). Arline's record of impairment arose from her hospitalization from tuberculosis. The Court held that the "regarded as" prong stemmed from Congress's belief that "society's accumulated myths and fears about disability and disease are as handicapping as are the physical limitations that flow from actual impairment" (*Arline* 1987, 284).

46. Feldblum (2000a, 154) reports that this number was first suggested by a staff member and supported by several disability rights advocates, but that "its implications for the definition of disability were never considered by them."

Chapter 3 | Disability Rights and the Workplace

1. Congress substituted "qualified" for the section 504 term "otherwise qualified." The law originally covered only employers with at least twenty-five employees; on July 26, 1994, the threshold was lowered to its current status of fifteen employees.

2. Moss and Malin (1998) maintain that economic models assessing the utility of the ADA are embedded with assumptions and urge researchers from a variety of fields to address the question of whether the ADA has a harmful or beneficial effect on employment.

3. See 29 C.F.R. Part 1630 generally for regulations relating to employment. The ADA regulations departed slightly from the section 504 regulations by defining terms such as "substantially limits," "reasonable accommodation," and "essential functions" (Switzer 2003, 117).

4. The number for total charges reflects the number of individual charge filings; because individuals often file charges alleging multiple types of discrimination, the number of total charges in a fiscal year will be less than the total number of types of discrimination within the EEOC mandate. The federal fiscal year begins October 1 and ends on September 30, leaving only about two months during which charges could have been filed during FY1992.

5. The EEOC was established by section 705 of the 1964 Civil Rights Act; it is responsible for enforcing the nation's employment discrimination laws, namely, Title VII, the ADA, the Age Discrimination in Employment Act, the Equal Pay Act, and sec-

tion 501 of the 1973 Rehabilitation Act. The local field offices of the EEOC often have relationships with the state or local agencies (see Moss 2000 for a discussion of the EEOC charging process).

6. State and local government employees prefer to sue under Title II rather than Title I to avoid filing charges with the EEOC; the circuits remain split over whether Title II covers suits for employment discrimination. The principal case for the view that it does is *Bledsoe v. Palm Beach County Soil and Water Conservation District* (1998); the leading case for the opposing position is *Zimmerman v. Oregon Department of Justice* (1999) (McDonald 2003).

7. This does not include cases filed under more than one antidiscrimination statute, such as the ADA and the Age Discrimination in Employment Act. Beginning in FY2002, suits to enforce administrative settlements were included in the data. FY1993 was the first full year the EEOC enforced Title I.

8. The 1991 Civil Rights Act expanded the availability of Title VII remedies, allowing limited money damages to victims of intentional discrimination based on sex, religion, or disability, including punitive damages in certain circumstances, in addition to back pay; plaintiffs can demand jury trials when seeking such damages (Hagood 1999). There are no limits on damages for back pay or past expenses, such as medical bills, but damages for pain and suffering and punitive damages are dictated by the size of the business, ranging from $50,000 for employers with fifteen to one hundred workers to $300,000 for a company with more than five hundred employees. See *Congressional Quarterly*, October 26, 1991, 3124–26; *New York Times*, October 26, 1991.

9. Malloy (2001, 609) argues that the courts rely too heavily on Title VII case law, which, she believes, indicates their inability to understand the essential differences between the goals of the two statutes and the needs of the groups protected by these laws. In her view, the principal difference is that "the reasonable accommodation requirement is based upon a more complex conception of equality than the simple notion that the disabled and non-disabled should be treated the same."

10. A disparate treatment claim requires a plaintiff in a protected class, in this case, a person with a disability, to show that an employment policy or practice was motivated by an intent to discriminate based on the disability. Courts use a three-step process to adjudicate such charges; with each side alternately presenting evidence, plaintiffs retain the burden of proof at all times. Plaintiffs must initially demonstrate four facts to establish a prima facie case of discrimination: that they are members of a protected class; that they are qualified for the job; that they applied for and were rejected for the job; and that the prospective employer continued to seek employees with their qualifications. Employers try to refute the prima facie case by presenting a legitimate, nondiscriminatory reason for the decision. Plaintiffs must then persuade the court that the proffered reason was a pretext for a discriminatory motive.

A disparate impact case does not require proof of a discriminatory motive. It involves an employment practice or policy that is facially neutral, but has the *effect* of harming persons in a protected class and is not justified by a business necessity.

11. Discussing her experience as an employer of people with disabilities, Bristo (2002) stresses that accommodations do not require great expenditures. Karlan and Rutherglen (1996, 30n95) cite a study of accommodations at Sears Roebuck & Company, showing "that the average cost per reasonable accommodation for employees with disabilities was $121.42, and that 301 of 432 (69%) of accommodations required no cost at all" (see Ulgen 2003).

12. Some have equated the requirement of reasonable accommodations with affirmative action; others disagree (Weber 1998).

13. O'Brien cites *City of Cleburne v. Cleburne Living Center* (1985) to justify her theory of the Court's view of disability rights.

14. Successful SSDI claimants must be unable to perform any "substantial gainful work . . . in the national economy," including their prior jobs.

15. Eligibility for benefits is determined by application of a grid, which consists of categories of types of impairments and does not involve individual consideration of the claimant's ability to work with an accommodation.

16. The EEOC regulations themselves do not speak to the issue of mitigation, but the appendix to 29 C.F.R. Part 1630, called the "Interpretive Guidance," is clearly contrary to the Court's posture in these cases (Parmet 2003).

17. Their vision met the FAA standard for flying commuter planes.

18. Flores (2001, 933) argues that because the airline rejected the plaintiffs on the basis of their uncorrected vision, the courts should have evaluated them on this basis as well (see Russotto 2001).

19. The DOT and DOJ were given responsibility for issuing the regulations to implement Titles II and III; additionally, the act authorized the Architectural and Transportation Barriers Compliance Board to issue minimum accessibility guidelines.

20. An individual is considered disabled if an impairment creates a substantial limitation in a major life activity such as reproduction, seeing, hearing, or walking. If no other major life activity is involved, the courts assess whether the impairment substantially limits the individual's capacity to engage in work, meaning the inability to perform a range or class of jobs, not simply one specific job (Kimberlin and Headley 2000, 589).

21. The reference is to footnote 4 in *United States v. Carolene Products* (1938).

22. O'Connor had countered this argument in the majority opinion, stressing that the key question is not whether there was a prosthesis, but whether the individual with a prosthesis was substantially limited in a major life activity as required by the law.

23. There was some confusion because Murphy might have been able to obtain a temporary DOT health certificate, but this issue was not before the Court.

24. The significant part of the ruling in favor of the employer was unanimous; Stevens and Breyer did not join the majority in the part (Part II) that discussed the lower court errors.

25. 45 C.F.R. 84.3(j)(2)(ii), a Rehabilitation Act regulation, provides a nonexclusive

list of major life activities, including "caring for one's self, performing manual tasks, walking, seeing, hearing, speaking, breathing, learning, and working."

26. As in *Sutton*, O'Connor noted that no agency had responsibility for defining the term, "disability," but the EEOC had done so and the parties accepted its authority. Therefore, O'Connor assumed without deciding that the regulations were reasonable, but did not speak to the degree of deference they were due by a reviewing court.

27. In *Colmenares v. Braemer Country Club, Inc.* (2003), the California Supreme Court held that the plaintiff's disability should have been assessed under the standard of the California law known as the Fair Housing and Employment Act, even though the standard was not clarified until a 2001 amendment. Under California law, an employee is considered disabled if an impairment "limits a major life activity," in contrast to the ADA's requirement of a substantial limitation.

28. In the first five years after passage of the ADA, the number of people reported to have disabilities increased by 5 percent (Rich, Erb, and Rich 2002, 6).

29. The FAA was enacted in 1925 and reenacted in 1947 to strengthen judicial enforcement of arbitration agreements. The preference for arbitration in the FAA was circumvented by such acts as Title VII, as amended by the 1991 Civil Rights Act, which allow the EEOC to seek relief for victims who may be barred from suing on their own by arbitration clauses (Graves 2002; see Byrnes and Pollman 2003).

30. The Equal Employment Opportunity Act of 1972 authorized the EEOC to file suit on its own behalf.

31. 29 C.F.R. §1630.15(b)(2) provides that "the term 'qualification standard' may include a requirement than an individual shall not pose a direct threat to the health and safety of the individual or others in the workplace."

32. The company relied on the principle established in *Chevron* (1984), in which the Court held that when Congress is silent on an issue, reasonable agency regulations are entitled to judicial deference.

33. Hernandez raised his disparate impact claim for the first time in response to the defendant's motion for summary judgment.

34. Hughes Missile Systems was acquired by the Raytheon Company.

35. Although the ruling was indeterminate, *Clackamas* is considered a victory for the employer.

36. The cases were reported in the *Mental and Physical Disability Law Reporter,* which includes decisions discovered through online computer searches as well as those obtained through media outlets. The data initially included over 1,200 cases, which were reduced to 760 so that the success of the parties could be included as a variable.

37. The 475 employment cases in her analysis constituted 76 percent of the total of the 620 ADA cases decided at the circuit court level; the 145 nonemployment cases included 122 Title II and 23 Title III actions. The ABA database of district court cases consisted of all final trial outcomes at the state and federal level, with more than 90 percent decided in the federal courts. Unlike the appellate court data, the ABA data-

base is limited to Title I cases against private employers, omitting claims against public entities (Colker 1999, 109n45). Colker also assessed trial court outcomes in the appellate court cases she reviewed and found that of the 475 cases included in her study, the defendant won in 448 cases (94 percent). Her findings revealed that the "results for both appealed and unappealed trial court outcomes were virtually identical—around 93%" (109).

38. Colker's review of prior research on the outcome of ADA claims compiled by the editors of the *National Disability Law Reporter* and the *Disability Compliance Bulletin*, as well as statistics gathered by the EEOC, all disclosed a similarly high success rate for ADA defendants in employment discrimination cases (100n9).

39. Colker's (2001, 250) study of employment discrimination rulings in the circuit courts found only 5 appeals by defendants (out of 720 cases), "suggest[ing] that a winnowing out process has occurred before the appellate process begins." She believes this can be explained by the fact that defendants generally pay their attorneys by the hour and have "more financial incentive to pursue only strong cases." In contrast, the plaintiffs' lawyers may feel it is worthwhile to pursue a case on appeal after expending the time and effort to bring a case to trial. Moreover, if the attorney is being paid on a contingency fee, the plaintiff has a strong incentive to appeal.

40. The Court addressed this issue in *Cleveland* (1999).

41. Willborn (2000, 106) cites studies showing that for the first twenty years that Title VII was in effect, the ratio of hiring to discharge cases was about three to one; in 1986, the number of discharge cases began to climb, and starting in 1990, the ratio was three to one in the opposite direction.

42. Weber (1998, 133) also reports that most complaints to the EEOC are filed by those who are currently (or were recently) employed.

Chapter 4 | Disability Rights and Public Entities

1. 42 U.S.C. §12131. Part A of Title II (§§12131–134) refers to public services generally; Part B governs public transportation services (§§12141–165).

2. 28 C.F.R. §35.150(a); see 28 C.F.R. Part 35, appendix A for Title II regulations generally.

3. Rosen made it clear in his interview that he was speaking in his individual, not his official, capacity.

4. St. George (1995) also observes that if state and local governments reformed their outdated and inefficient taxing structure, they would be better able to manage their responsibilities.

5. In 1993, despite bipartisan support and much fanfare, a bill to restrict unfunded mandates failed to clear either house (Conlan, Riggle, and Schwartz 1995). Having read the handwriting on the wall, public interest groups were highly critical of what they perceived as Congress's attempt to weaken the nation's commitment to environmental protection and civil rights (Kriz 1995).

6. 2 U.S.C. §1503. This section also explicitly excludes federal law or regulations advancing national security or treaty obligations, requiring compliance with federal accounting or auditing procedures, providing emergency assistance requested by the state, relating to Title II of the Social Security Act (the old-age, survivor, and disability insurance programs), or emergency legislation as designated by the president or Congress.

7. Bristo (2002) describes how the disability rights community and other civil rights organizations lobbied Congress to shelter the ADA from the reach of the UMRA, fearing that Title II would be targeted by state and local governments.

8. 2 U.S.C. §658. An example of participation in a voluntary federal program is when federal funds are used to encourage states to enact motorcycle helmet laws (*Congressional Quarterly*, April 15, 1995, 1087–89).

9. 2 U.S.C. §1532. The UMRA provides that a member may raise a point of order with respect to any new legislation put forward without a CBO cost estimate or with a cost estimate exceeding $50 million (or private sector spending of more than $100 million) unless the mandate is fully funded. There must be a separate vote to waive the point of order and consider the legislation, thereby placing members on record in favor of the mandate. The act does not apply to existing mandates, but reauthorization is subject to a point of order if significant additional spending or reduced federal funding is involved. Federal agencies must prepare cost benefit analyses before promulgating regulations and consult with state and local government officials during the regulatory process (*Congressional Quarterly*, April 15, 1995, 1087–89; see Troy 1997).

10. Although Title VI is silent on whether individuals have a right to sue under the act, the Supreme Court has long held that plaintiffs have a private cause of action under Title VI. However, more recently, in *Alexander v. Sandoval* (2001), the Court held that litigants do not have a private cause of action under Title VI for claims of disparate impact. In *Ability Center of Greater Toledo v. City of Sandusky* (2001b), the district court rejected the city's argument that *Sandoval* precluded a private right of action against the city for violation of curb-cut regulations, a disparate impact claim. But in *Love v. Delta Air Lines* (2002), the Eleventh Circuit reversed the lower court ruling in the plaintiff's favor on whether a person with disabilities has a private right of action under the 1986 ACAA. Citing *Sandoval* and the limitations it placed on its inquiry into congressional intent, the circuit court concluded that the plaintiff did not have a cause of action.

11. Because municipalities are immune from punitive damages in suits brought under 42 U.S.C. §1983, this claim was dismissed.

12. The state cited *Gregory v. Ashcroft* (1991, 460), in which the high court had reiterated that a statute altering the balance of power between the federal government and the states must clearly indicate Congress's intent to override the states' "substantial sovereign powers."

13. The circuit court relied on a previous Fourth Circuit ruling in *Torcasio v. Murray* (1995, 1344), in which the court held that despite the broad language of the ADA,

because of its implications for the federal balance it was unwilling to extend the reach of the law to state prisons, "absent a far clearer expression of congressional intent." In contrast, in *Crawford v. Indiana Department of Corrections* (1997), the Seventh Circuit found that Title II applied to prison systems.

14. Although the state also argued that the ADA was beyond the constitutional exercise of Congress's authority under both the commerce clause and section 5 of the Fourteenth Amendment to regulate state prisons, because the lower courts had not reached this constitutional issue, the Supreme Court simply limited its ruling to whether Congress had intended the ADA to apply to state prisons.

15. L. C. filed suit in 1995; E. W. intervened in the case a year later.

16. As of 1981, the Medicaid program reimburses states for providing community-based services to individuals with mental retardation and chronic mental illness if they can show that the cost is less than institutional care; states, however, are often reluctant to take advantage of these "waivers" (Karger 1999, 1229–30).

17. L. C. had been placed in a community-based treatment program in February 1996 at the time of the trial; the judge ordered that she be given the necessary services to enable her to remain there. E. W. was placed there after the lower court's ruling. By the time case reached the Supreme Court, the two women were living in community settings, but the Supreme Court refused to dismiss the case as moot.

18. The district court subsequently determined on remand that the cost of the community-based care given to the women was not unreasonable in light of the state's total expenditure for mental health (*Olmstead v. L.C.* 1999, 596n7).

19. The high court vacated the Eleventh Circuit ruling in part and remanded the case to the district court to examine the state's fundamental alteration defense in light of the Court's formulation.

20. The "American Rule," in which individuals pay their own attorneys' fees, governs most lawsuits in the United States. To encourage litigation by "private attorneys general," Congress explicitly authorized fee-shifting in statutes such as the 1964 Civil Rights Act, the Voting Rights Act amendments of 1975, the FHAA, and the ADA (Curry 2001, 728). One hundred federal laws, encompassing the majority of environmental and civil rights laws, have fee-shifting provisions (*New York Times*, May 30, 2001).

21. Winter (2002) speculates that "there would probably be many fewer cases filed under Title II and III in light of *Buckhannon* because plaintiffs could not recover fees in the event of a settlement that did not involve an 'adjudication.' In some cases," he adds, "the effect of *Buckhannon* may decrease the number of settlements because there would be less incentive for plaintiffs to settle if they could not recover attorneys fees unless they obtained favorable judgment or verdict."

22. As stated in *Newport v. Facts Concerts, Inc.* (1981), local governments are immune from punitive damage awards in cases brought under 42 U.S.C. §1983; suits against state officials in their official capacities are considered suits against the state, and state governments are therefore immune from damages under the Eleventh

Amendment (Harrington 2000). Title II suits can only be brought against government entities, not individuals.

23. The 1991 Civil Rights Act exempts units of government, but allows limited punitive damages to be assessed against private employers in discrimination suits.

24. Horvath (2004) discusses the use of the *Young* doctrine in employment discrimination suits against states.

25. The rulings were accessed through a Lexis-Nexis computer search with "Title II and ADA or Americans w/3 disabilit!" as the search terms in the "District Court" and "Circuit Court" libraries. The data in the next two chapters include all opinions published in bound reports or reported to Lexis-Nexis. Although there has been concern in the past that published opinions systematically differ from nonpublished opinions, this concern has lessened because since 1990, courts are increasingly reporting their opinions to electronic databases such as Lexis-Nexis, thus reducing the discrepancy between published and nonpublished opinions (Colker 2001, 246–47).

26. The Ninth Circuit does not permit employment discrimination claims under Title II.

27. Computer-based word searches typically yield cases outside the scope of the inquiry and these were initially excluded from the data. Rulings on ancillary matters such as statutes of limitations, discovery motions, attorneys' fees, class certifications, and settlement agreements were also excluded. Cases that were dismissed because the suit was brought against an improper party (such as the federal government or a private individual) were also eliminated. The rulings were coded by date, court level, type of defendant, prevailing party, and type of claim.

28. Following Rule 12(b)(6) of the Federal Rules of Civil Procedure, courts may dismiss a plaintiff's claim "for failure . . . to state a claim upon which relief can be granted." Rule 56(c) of the Federal Rules of Civil Procedure permit courts to grant summary judgments if "there is no genuine issue of material fact and . . . the moving party is entitled to judgment as a matter of law." The burden is on the party making the motion to demonstrate the absence of any genuine issue of material fact; the burden then shifts to the other side to demonstrate that a genuine issue of material fact remains to be tried.

29. Colker's (2001, 246) study included 720 appellate decisions in employment discrimination cases, 540 (75 percent) were appeals of summary judgments that favored defendants, and 88 (12.2 percent) were appeals of dismissals. There were only two cases in which the defendants appealed a summary judgment for the plaintiff.

30. According to Colker (2001, 247–48), this is the most common method of measuring success at the circuit court level. In her study of appellate decisions, the plaintiff was considered successful if the court reversed a lower court victory for the defendant and remanded the case for further adjudication. Although she acknowledged that the plaintiff may still lose in the court below, she believes this approach is more accurate because the plaintiff has actually won in the circuit court and, in her view, this coding

scheme is most common among scholars. Another approach is to consider the plaintiffs successful only if the appellate court affirms a district court ruling in their favor.

31. Even when the suits had initially named local and state government agencies as defendants, these rulings applied to only one of the defendants, typically because the other had settled with the plaintiffs.

32. These associations were considered public entities by the courts because they determined the rules of competition for public schools.

33. The types of claims are presented in alphabetical order.

34. In *Hamilton v. City College of the City University of New York* (2001), the district court joined with the other New York district courts in holding that the senior colleges of the City University of New York are entitled to Eleventh Amendment immunity under the "Arm of the State" theory.

35. Public facilities must comply with one of two sets of technical accessibility standards: the Uniform Federal Accessibility Standards (UFAS) promulgated under section 504 or the ADA Accessibility Guidelines (ADAAG) for Buildings and Facilities accompanying Title III. Although Congress did not order the use of ADAAG in Title II cases, most courts and the DOJ refer to these guidelines when assessing compliance under Title II in the case of barrier removal or new construction (Harrington 2000, 441–42; see Wood 1998).

36. The suit had originally named both state and city as defendants; the state had settled, leaving the court to adjudicate only the city's liability.

37. Under most circumstances, a third party to a dispute does not have standing to sue.

38. These cases were combined into one category because the line between prisons and other law enforcement agencies tended to blur at times.

39. Prior to 1998, prison authorities had a success rate of 62 percent in the appellate courts; after 1998, the success rate had risen to 80 percent. Similarly, before 1998, they prevailed in only 28 percent of the district court decisions; after 1998, their success rate was 47 percent.

40. A year later, the lower court decision was reversed on appeal in *Kiman v. New Hampshire Department of Corrections* (2002).

41. Recognizing the myriad physical, mental, and emotional problems confronting people with AIDS and HIV, DASIS had been established to assist them in receiving government benefits, including Medicaid, food stamps, or Social Security, as well as services such as emergency shelters, transportation, and food assistance. In addition to charging the agency with assisting its clientele in negotiating through an often opaque bureaucratic structure, the law under which DASIS was created included intensive case management, expedited review of applications, and lower case manager-to-client ratios.

42. Although the state was also held liable for failing to supervise the city's administration of public services, the primary defendant was the city and these rulings were

coded as suits against a local government defendant. After much procedural wrangling over the next few years, the Second Circuit upheld the lower court (*Henrietta D. v. Bloomberg* 2003).

43. As in Title VII cases, although the burden of production shifts, the burden of persuasion, that is, proof, remains with the plaintiff at all times.

44. Prior to 1999, when *Olmstead* was decided, the defendants prevailed in 25 percent of the appellate cases and 38 percent of the district court rulings. The defendants' success rate increased to 50 percent in the six district court rulings after the Supreme Court ruled in the case.

45. Because the season had ended and the students had graduated by the time these cases reached the courts, the courts declared parts of them moot.

46. The plaintiffs also named the Democratic and Republican Parties as defendants; after the city impleaded the secretary of state, the plaintiffs added him as a defendant also. When the other parties settled, the secretary of state remained the sole defendant.

Chapter 5 | Disability Rights and Public Accommodations

1. Stowe (2000, 327–28) acknowledges that the broader interpretation of the phrase, "place of public accommodation," is inconsistent with the prevailing view of the term as used in Title II of the 1964 Civil Rights Act. But, he says, the courts' reasoning is circular; they cite *Welsh v. Boy Scouts of America* (1993), a Title II case which relied on an interpretation of Title III to conclude that the Boy Scouts did not constitute a public accommodation for purposes of Title II. Stowe argues that the circuit court in *Welsh* did not engage in extensive analysis of Title III and did not have the benefit of more recent Title III case law. In his view, courts should not give undue emphasis to *Welsh* and should adopt the broader interpretation in Title II cases.

2. A "commercial facility" is a catch-all category that includes a wide range of non-residential establishments that affect commerce and are not included within the twelve types of public accommodations (Moore 1992, 1158–59).

3. The law took effect for businesses with more than twenty-five employees on January 26, 1992, and six months later for businesses with fewer than twenty-five employees; no businesses are exempt from Title III.

4. The DOJ may sue in "practice and pattern" cases or if the discrimination "raises an issue of general importance." In such cases, the court may award an injured party monetary relief, excluding punitive damages, as well as assess civil penalties against the defendant; in determining a civil penalty, the court may consider whether there was a "good faith" effort to comply with the act. Percy (2000) presents data on settlement agreements in suits initiated by the DOJ.

5. In some cases, the FHAA mandates the attorney general to file suit against offenders.

6. 42 U.S.C. §12181(9). In determining the meaning of the term, "readily achievable," the courts are instructed to consider the cost of the alteration as well as factors such as the type, size, and financial resources of the business.

7. Because the cost of making new or altered construction accessible is very low, the ADA requires owners to conform, for the most part, to DOJ guidelines issued in July 1991, unless they are able to prove it is "structurally impracticable" to meet the guidelines, a rarely successful defense.

8. Section 2000a–3(c) of Title II of the 1964 Civil Rights Act requires a plaintiff to notify the appropriate state or local agency thirty days before filing suit against the owner of the public accommodation. Although there has been some confusion over whether Title II plaintiffs must exhaust administrative remedies, in addition to giving notice, before filing suit, most courts have not required it. With respect to Title III, as the court explained in *Stan v. Wal-Mart Stores, Inc.* (2000), the ADA did not explicitly incorporate section 2000a–3(c); it only incorporated 42 U.S.C. §2000a–3(a), the provision limiting the remedy to injunctive relief. The courts are split on whether a Title III plaintiff must notify state agencies or exhaust administrative remedies (Milani 2001).

9. HR3590 also states that, for complaints filed without the requisite notice, the court could "sanction" the attorneys. And in cases where the plaintiff ultimately satisfied the law with the passage of ninety days and the requisite notice, the court could not award the attorneys' fees and litigation expenses or costs normally allowed under section 505 of the ADA.

10. The attorneys claimed the fees were for approximately two thousand hours of work (Kelly 2002, 376–77).

11. Title III suits may be filed in conjunction with state laws (such as the Unruh Civil Rights Act of California or the California Disabled Persons Act). Colker (2000b) reports that plaintiffs may be able to collect money damages under state tort claims when they are injured by a property owner's failure to make the premises accessible.

12. Although she had been HIV-positive for nine years, she was asymptomatic (*Abbott v. Bragdon* 1995).

13. She was not infertile, but the court held that the statute does not require an individual to be entirely unable to perform a major life activity.

14. 42 U.S.C. §12182(b)(3) provides that a place of public accommodation may refuse service to anyone who constitutes a "direct threat" to the health and safety of others, an affirmative defense under the law. A "direct threat" is "a significant risk to the health or safety of others that cannot be eliminated by a modification of policies, practices, or procedures or by the provision of auxiliary aids or services."

15. The Court rejected the argument that to qualify as a "major life activity," the activity had to have a "public, economic, or a daily dimension" (*Bragdon v. Abbott* 1998, 638).

16. Although it had agreed with the conclusions of the district court judge, the appellate court had rejected some of the affidavits upon which the judge had relied.

17. Martin's victory in the lower court had allowed him to use a golf cart in the

1998 U.S. Open because the USGA voluntarily agreed to honor the magistrate's decision in Martin's favor even though it was not the defendant in that case (*Martin v. PGA Tour, Inc.* 1998). When Olinger also asked to use a golf cart in the 1998 U.S. Open and his request was denied, he won a temporary restraining order from a district court judge that enabled him to use a cart in the early round of the tournament. It was a short-lived victory, however, as he did not advance beyond this round. He subsequently lost at trial.

18. The PGA also argued unsuccessfully that, as a private club, it was exempt from Title III.

19. Martin could not bring a Title I claim against the PGA because he was an independent contractor, not an employee. In *Menkowitz v. Pottstown Memorial Medical Center* (1998), the circuit court ruled that a doctor who had had his staff privileges revoked was not an employee of the hospital, but was an "individual" protected by Title III.

20. Colker's (2000b) study was based on federal court actions, although some of the plaintiffs in these cases asked the federal court judge to exercise pendent jurisdiction over a state law claim such as negligence or, when available, a state disability law, to allow for the possibility of a compensatory or punitive damage award.

21. Colker (2000b) also examined verdicts in Title III cases and saw nothing in these data to disturb her conclusions.

22. Following the method used in the Title II cases, the rulings were accessed though a Lexis-Nexis computer search with "Title III and ADA or Americans w/3 disabilit!" as the search terms in the "District Court" and "Circuit Court" libraries. The unrelated cases were eliminated, as were rulings on settlement agreements and ancillary matters, such as statutes of limitations, discovery motions, attorneys' fees, and class certification. The opinions were coded by date, court level, type of defendant, prevailing party, and type of claim.

23. In addition to the constitutional prerequisites for standing, there are prudential dictates that may, under some circumstances, be waived by the courts; constitutional requirements may not be waived.

24. In *Lyons*, the Court distinguished between the plaintiff's claim for damages and his claim for injunctive relief. Noting that the police officers' use of a "chokehold" on the plaintiff might support damages, the Court dismissed his claim for injunctive relief against the city. It held he had no standing because there was "no real or immediate threat" of future harm, that is, it was only speculative that he would be subjected to the same treatment by the police even if the practice continued.

25. Although this was a Title II suit, the requirements of standing for injunctive relief apply generally.

26. The United States appeared on behalf of the plaintiffs in three of the six cases in which the defendants prevailed.

27. Promulgated by the DOJ, ADAAG is codified at 28 C.F.R. Part 36, Appendix A; the standards also apply in Title II cases involving construction and accessibility. The ADA mandated that the U.S. Architectural and Transportation Barriers Compliance

Board (Access Board) issue interim guidelines for Title III; federal agencies, including the DOJ, would then issue their own guidelines, consistent with the Access Board guidelines. The Access Board had been established to ensure compliance with the Architectural Barriers Act of 1968, which regulated access to government buildings. When Congress ordered the Access Board to develop advisory guidelines for Titles II and III of the ADA, the result was ADAAG, which was subsequently adopted by the DOJ as its own regulation (see *Caruso v. Blockbuster-Sony Music Entertainment Centre* 1997).

28. In an earlier ruling in the same action, *Independent Living Resources v. Oregon Arena Corporation* (1997), the court ruled on the defendant's motion to dismiss as well as motions for summary judgment from each side, and various other motions. The plaintiffs' complaint cited almost one hundred ADA violations; some, such as the placement of a mobile trash cart, seem fairly trivial.

29. The arena was also ordered to discontinue its practice of "infilling" wheelchair spaces with conventional seats.

30. The store was also ordered to remove existing barriers of movable (not fixed) displays to the extent that it was "readily achievable."

31. The court questioned why the plaintiff had sued the parent company when she only sought injunctive relief rather than damages. The reason, perhaps, according to the court, was that she may have wanted the court to consider the resources of the parent company in determining whether the structural changes were "readily achievable."

32. In *Colorado Cross Disability Coalition v. Williams* (2001), the Tenth Circuit held that once the plaintiff presented evidence that removing a barrier was "readily achievable," the defense bore the burden of proving it was not.

33. The court determined that because the Bistro's restroom alteration would cost $19,251 and its net annual income was $11,246.73, it was not "readily achievable." But because a ramp might cost $1,347, less than 10 percent of the income, the court held that it could not conclude that it was "not readily achievable." Similarly, the ramp into a neighboring wine shop, which would cost $1,985, also less than 10 percent of the net income of $14,319.91, was considered "readily achievable."

34. The four requirements for a preliminary injunction are: a substantial likelihood that the plaintiff will succeed on the merits; that the plaintiff will suffer irreparable harm if the injunction is not granted; that the balance of hardships are in the plaintiff's favor; and that the public interest will be advanced if an injunction is granted.

35. In two Ninth Circuit cases, *Scott v. Western State University College of Law* (1997) and *Norris v. Seattle University School of Law* (1997) the appellate court briefly affirmed the lower court rulings, without hearing oral argument. In *Scott,* the court held that the plaintiff did not claim he had a disability until five months after he was dismissed from the law school and, in *Norris,* the court ruled that the plaintiff had presented no evidence of a disability.

36. The district court had granted the plaintiff a preliminary injunction, allowing him to return to school while the matter was further adjudicated.

37. Private testing services such as the Educational Testing Service (ETS) were

charged with either refusing to allow more time for tests or "flagging" tests in which students with disabilities were accommodated in some way. According to the terms of a settlement agreement in 2002, ETS agreed to cease "flagging" such tests after September 2003 (*New York Times,* July 28, 2002). Although the tests were no longer flagged as a result of the settlement, ETS began to reject an increasing number of requests for accommodations, requiring applicants to have a diagnosis and a plan for accommodations filed at the school at least four months before taking the test; it also often asked for more extensive documentation of a disability (*New York Times,* November 8, 2003). More recently, a suit brought to require accommodations in graduation tests for Alaska high school students reached a settlement when the state agreed to allow a variety of accommodations in high school exit examinations (*New York Times,* August 3, 2004).

38. Denials of preliminary injunctions are accorded a great deal of deference by appellate courts.

39. The court suggested several theories to help the plaintiff prove the defendant was his employer within the meaning of Title I.

40. The court ruled that she lacked standing to sue her employer under Title I because she was not a "qualified individual with a disability" (Shuman 2000/2001, 562). Her Title III claim against her employer also failed because Title III does not regulate conditions of employment. The lower court also dismissed her claim under the Employee Retirement Security Income Act (ERISA).

41. The MHPA, originally proposed as part of the Health Insurance Portability and Accountability Act of 1996, was defeated because of its broad mandate requiring parity between mental and physical disabilities. Enacted in September 1996 and effective in January 1998, a scaled-down version of the MHPA was included as part of the appropriations bill for the Veterans Affairs and Housing and Urban Development Departments. As enacted, the law was a relatively modest attempt at eradicating disparities in insurance coverage. It had no effect on differences in lengths of stay, copayments, or deductibles. Moreover, the act did not apply to companies with fewer than fifty employees and was inapplicable if it increased the cost of insurance by more than 1 percent; it also contained a sunset provision that expired on September 30, 2001. A more comprehensive measure aimed at eliminating disparities between mental and physical disabilities in insurance coverage was introduced in the 107th Congress. The Mental Health Equitable Treatment Act was approved in committee, but no final action was taken. A similar bill was introduced in the 106th Congress, but it was never reported out of committee (see Gold 1997/1998; Nelson 2001; Harrison 2002).

Chapter 6 | Disability Rights and State Sovereignty

1. The Court's commitment to federalism principles was apparent in *National League of Cities v. Usery* (1976), in which the majority relied in part on the Tenth Amendment to hold that Congress lacked the power to extend federal minimum wage

laws to police officers, firefighters, and other key state employees. *National League of Cities* was overruled by *Garcia v. San Antonio Metropolitan Transit Authority* (1985).

2. The Court also restricted Congress's authority to enact laws under the interstate commerce clause (Article I, §8) in *United States v. Lopez* (1995)—striking the Gun-Free School Zones Act of 1990—and *United States v. Morrison* (2000)—striking a portion of the Violence Against Women Act of 1994.

3. The suit must name the state official rather than the state or a state agency, but courts do not seem to enforce this rule very rigorously.

4. Under *Young*, because actions for prospective relief against state officials in their official capacities are not considered suits against the states, the officials are considered "persons" for purposes of section 1983 suits. Lawsuits seeking money damages that name state officials in their official capacities, but are construed as suits against the state, are barred by the Eleventh Amendment because the damages are likely to come out of state funds (*Scheuer v. Rhodes* 1974). The Eleventh Amendment does not bar suits against state officials in their individual capacities for damages, but in such cases public officials are entitled to qualified immunity if they can show that their conduct does "not violate clearly established statutory or constitutional rights of which a reasonable person would have known" (*Harlow v. Fitzgerald* 1982, 818). However, a number of courts have held that Title II only allows suits against public entities. Because public officials do not have personal liability under Title II, they can only be sued in their official capacities, not their individual capacities, making qualified immunity irrelevant (see *Walker v. Snyder* 2000).

5. In *Idaho v. Coeur d'Alene Tribe of Idaho* (1997), Justice Kennedy argued that the lower courts must carefully consider the state's interests before allowing suits to proceed under *Young* and advocated a balancing approach to determine the circumstances under which the exception should apply. He noted that *Young* was most important where there was no state forum for the federal claim and the federal interest in enforcing the law outweighed the state's interest in its sovereignty. In his view, federal courts should dismiss claims against states when there are special concerns about state sovereignty. In *Verizon Maryland Inc. v. Public Service Commission of Maryland* (2002), the Court reaffirmed the *Young* doctrine, explicitly rejecting the balancing test Kennedy proposed in *Coeur d'Alene Tribe of Idaho* (Silver 2003). It held that the suit was within the *Young* exception because it was for an "'ongoing violation of federal law [that] seeks relief properly characterized as prospective'" (*Verizon* 2002, 645, quoting *Coeur d'Alene Tribe of Idaho* 1997, 296).

6. In *Atascadero* (1985, 242–43), a suit under the Rehabilitation Act of 1973, the Court announced the "clear statement rule," requiring Congress to make "its intention [to abrogate state immunity] unmistakably clear in the language of the statute." And again in *Dellmuth* (1989, 228), a case involving a claim under the EAHCA, the Court stressed that the evidence of congressional intent must be "unequivocal."

7. The issue in *Seminole Tribe* was Congress's power to "regulate commerce with the Indian tribes," known as the "Indian commerce clause" (Article I, §8).

8. The "proportionality" requirement was not novel, although Hamilton and Schoenbrod (1999) note that Congress had not been required to adhere to it strictly in earlier civil rights cases.

9. In articulating the "congruence and proportionality" standard in *City of Boerne,* the Court relied on *Katzenbach v. Morgan* (1966, 651) to determine whether an act was consistent with Congress's section 5 authority. In *Morgan,* the Court had created a three-part test that asked (1) whether the statute enforced the Fourteenth Amendment; (2) whether it was "plainly adapted to that end"; and (3) whether it was consonant with the "letter and spirit" of the Constitution.

10. The Court cited *South Carolina v. Katzenbach* (1966) and *Morgan* (1966), in which it approved of Congress's remedial authority to enact the Voting Rights Act because it had documented systematic evidence of racial discrimination in voting as well as other evidence of the need for remedial legislation.

11. Post and Siegel (2000) argue that the Court views Congress's efforts to enact legislation under section 5 through a separation of powers lens in which the Court is determined to prevent Congress from infringing on its role as the final arbiter of the meaning of the Constitution. Prior to *City of Boerne,* some viewed section 5 as akin to the "necessary and proper clause" of Article I, granting Congress broad remedial powers (see Levy 2000).

12. Most plaintiffs in employment discrimination cases seek money damages in addition to, or instead of, reinstatement in their jobs, in part because attorneys have fewer incentives to represent them without the availability of damages.

13. The latest available census figures, as of March 2002, report that there are 5,072,130 state government employees (U.S. Bureau of the Census 2002).

14. The constitutionality of the ADEA as applied to state and local governments was upheld in *EEOC v. Wyoming* (1983), in which the Court ruled that the 1974 amendments were a valid exercise of Congress's power to regulate commerce and did not run afoul of the Tenth Amendment. The Court had not inquired into Congress's section 5 authority, but when *Seminole Tribe* denied Congress the power to abrogate state immunity under Article I, it was required to revisit the issue.

15. The 1974 amendments were in part a reaction to *Employees v. Department of Public Health and Welfare* (1973), in which the Court held that the 1966 amendments to the FLSA, which included state workers in the wages and hours limits set by the FLSA, had not abrogated the state's immunity from suit in federal court.

16. The Florida cases were *Kimel v. Florida Board of Regents* (1996) and *Dickson v. Florida Department of Corrections* (1996); the Alabama case was *MacPherson v. University of Montevallo* (1996).

17. In contrast, the panel held that the ADA explicitly abrogated state immunity. One judge on the panel argued that both the ADEA and the ADA abrogated state immunity; the other maintained that states were immune from damage liability under both statutes.

18. The circuits were divided over whether the ADEA satisfied the *Seminole Tribe* test, most disagreeing with the Eleventh Circuit (Durham 1999).

19. The Supreme Court did not consider the ADA claim in *Kimel.*

20. It was unclear whether *Muller* and *Martin* were brought under Title I or Title II.

21. 28 C.F.R. §35.130(f) provides that "a public entity may not place a surcharge on a particular individual with a disability . . . to cover the costs of measures, such as the provision of auxiliary aids or program accessibility that are required to provide that individual or group with the nondiscriminatory treatment required by the Act or this part." Because the court decided the case solely on the basis of the constitutionality of the regulation, it found it unnecessary to rule on the statute (*Brown* 1999, 708n*).

22. Shortly thereafter, two Seventh Circuit panels independently held in *Stevens v. Illinois Department of Transportation* (2000), a Title I action, and *Walker v. Snyder* (2000), brought under Title II, that *Erickson* controlled and the cases must be dismissed.

23. Shortly after *Kilcullen,* another panel of the Second Circuit reached the same conclusion in *Jackan v. New York State Department of Labor* (2000).

24. Although *Cleburne* dealt with people with mental disabilities, *Garrett* indicated that a classification based on any type of disability merits minimal scrutiny.

25. Okin (2001, 687–88) argues that few state laws are as comprehensive as the ADA and federal agencies lack the resources to deal with the large number of employment discrimination charges.

26. Although some circuits allowed plaintiffs to file employment discrimination claims against states under Title II, most did not, thus foreclosing the possibility of circumventing *Garrett* by suing under Title II.

27. The Eleventh Amendment is limited to states, but local government units may also claim immunity under the "Arm of the State" theory, a matter governed by state law and judicial interpretation. Shortly after the high court's ruling in *Garrett,* the Chicago Transit Authority (CTA) attempted to assert immunity in *Access Living v. Chicago Transit Authority* (2001a). Under the law of the Seventh Circuit, the judge explained, there are several factors determining whether a municipal corporation or other political subdivision of the state is considered an Arm of the State: the extent to which it serves the state as a whole or is regionally based, the extent to which it is financially autonomous, and the extent to which it has the authority to raise its own funds. His one-page order unequivocally stated that the Eleventh Amendment did not insulate the CTA from damage liability. Similarly, in *Cash v. Granville County Board of Education* (2001) and *Parker v. Anne Arundel County* (2001), the Fourth Circuit rejected the arguments of a school district and county fire department, respectively, that they were entitled to Eleventh Amendment immunity as an Arm of the State. Hartley (2001, 59–60) argues that it is difficult for courts to decide whether a local unit is an Arm of the State or a political subdivision of the state because the distinctions are unclear.

28. A three-judge panel in *Popovich* (2000a) held that states are shielded from Title II damage suits by the Eleventh Amendment. Subsequently in *Popovich* (2000b), the

circuit court vacated this ruling and granted a rehearing en banc, ordering it held in abeyance until the Supreme Court decided *Garrett*.

29. Another plaintiff, Joseph Stevenson, was added to the suit; his action was against the Alabama Department of Corrections.

30. The other appellate courts cases were: *Clark* (1997); *Sandoval* (1999); *Litman v. George Mason University* (1999); *Stanley v. Litscher* (2000); *Pederson v. Louisiana State University* (2000), *Nihiser* (2001); and *Koslow v. Pennsylvania Department of Corrections* (2002). The Second Circuit, however, held in *Garcia* (2001) that although Congress could condition federal funding on a state's waiver of immunity, the state had not knowingly waived its immunity by accepting funds under the Rehabilitation Act. The appellate court reasoned that New York had accepted the money before the Supreme Court's decision in *Seminole Tribe* and had assumed that Congress had authority to abrogate state immunity under the commerce clause. The state could not have known it was waiving immunity by receiving the federal funds because it had not known that it had immunity.

31. In an earlier ruling, *Little Rock School District v. Mauney* (1999), the Eighth Circuit had held that the IDEA abrogated state immunity because it satisfied the standards demanded by the Supreme Court in *Seminole Tribe* and *City of Boerne*. But after *Mauney* had been decided, the Supreme Court handed down its decisions in *Alden* (1999), *Florida Prepaid Postsecondary Education Expense Board v. College Savings Bank* (1999), and *College Savings Bank v. Florida Prepaid Postsecondary Education Expense Board* (1999) and the Eighth decided *Alsbrook* (1999). Therefore, in *Bradley* (1999) the Eighth Circuit ruled that *Mauney* had been superseded. Applying the "congruence and proportionality" test, the appellate court concluded that Congress had not satisfactorily identified the misconduct it sought to correct in the IDEA. Moreover, despite extensive congressional findings that public school systems were not meeting the needs of children with disabilities, the court found that Congress had not sufficiently demonstrated that the states caused these failures; "*Florida Prepaid*," the court emphasized, specified "that Congress [must] find that the states themselves are transgressing the constitution" (*Bradley* 1999, 752). The court also found that the IDEA imposed a stringent standard of conduct on states, far stricter than the constitutional standard that permits states to differentiate among persons with disabilities as long as there are rational grounds for doing so. Holding that the prior ruling in *Mauney* was no longer valid, the Eighth Circuit found that Congress exceeded its authority in abrogating state immunity in the IDEA. However, because the waiver portion of *Mauney* was still controlling, the panel had agreed with the prevailing view of the circuits that the state had waived its Eleventh Amendment immunity by accepting federal IDEA funds (McConville 2001).

32. 42 U.S.C. §2000d–7(a)(1), adopted as part of the Rehabilitation Act Amendments of 1986, deprives states of Eleventh Amendment immunity in federal suits brought to redress violations of section 504, Title IX of the Education Amendments of 1972, the Age Discrimination Act of 1975, Title VI of the 1964 Civil Rights Act, "or the

provisions of any other Federal statute prohibiting discrimination by recipients of Federal financial assistance." The Supreme Court has acknowledged that section 504 entails an "unambiguous waiver of the State's Eleventh Amendment immunity" (*Lane v. Pena* 1996, 200). The Court recognized in *Pena* that section 2000d–7 was a direct response to its decision in *Atascadero* (1985), which held that Congress must clearly indicate its intent that federal funding is conditioned on a waiver of immunity. The Eleventh Circuit held in *Sandoval v. Hagan* (1999, 493) that section 2000d–7 demonstrated an "unmistakable intent to condition federal funds on a state's waiver of sovereign immunity" and that states waived immunity if they accepted federal funds after 1986, when the law was enacted. Although the Supreme Court had reversed the appeals court's ruling that Title VI of the 1964 Civil Rights Act created an implied right of action to enforce the regulations, it left its interpretation of section 2000d–7 undisturbed (*Sandoval* 2001).

33. The court acknowledged that section 2000d–7 was a response to *Atascadero,* but it held that although Congress had made it clear that it was intended to override *Atascadero,* it had not made it clear why it thought it necessary to do so.

34. The constitutionality of restrictions in statutes enacted under Congress's spending power arose in *South Dakota v. Dole* (1987), a case challenging Congress's condition for the receipt of highway funds on the state raising the drinking age. First, the spending must be for the general welfare; second, the condition must be clearly stated; third, there must be a relationship between the condition and the purpose of the spending; and fourth, the condition must be constitutional, that is, it must not be coercive (Levy 2000, 1654).

35. The court also held that the abrogation provision of section 2000d–7 was a valid exercise of Congress's spending power and the state waived its immunity by continuing to accept federal funding after 1986.

36. Hason eventually filed a successful petition for his license and, in January 2003, was awaiting word on his medical competence ("Petitioner's Brief," in *Medical Board of California v. Hason*).

37. The state urged the high court to restrict the inquiry to whether Congress had the authority to abrogate Eleventh Amendment immunity in suits challenging decisions of state professional and vocational licensing agencies ("Petitioner's Brief," in *Medical Board of California v. Hason*).

38. It appeared that Lockyer might have been motivated by political reasons. He was positioned to run for governor in 2006 and may have wanted to avoid alienating disability rights groups by pursuing the litigation (*Washington Post,* April 11, 2003).

39. Lane was no stranger to law enforcement authorities; he had been arrested thirty times for various offenses, including drunken driving, drugs, and traffic offenses (*Chattanooga Times Free Press,* January 10, 2004).

40. Lane ultimately pleaded guilty to driving with a revoked license (*Legal Times,* January 12, 2004).

41. In another case involving a federal law aimed at employment discrimination, *Nevada Department of Human Resources v. Hibbs* (2003), the Supreme Court was asked to decide if the Eleventh Amendment granted states immunity from a suit brought under the 1993 Family and Medical Leave Act (FMLA). The FMLA, enacted under Congress's authority under the interstate commerce clause and the Fourteenth Amendment, requires employers to allow workers up to twelve weeks of unpaid leave because of their own health problems or to care for an ailing family member; workers can sue their employers, including states, for damages for violating the act. Encouraged by the high court's decisions in the age and disability discrimination suits, states soon began to argue they were immune from damages in FMLA suits.

William Hibbs was fired in 1997 after taking time off to care for his wife. He sued, charging that the state violated the FMLA and the state claimed immunity. Following the principles established in *Seminole Tribe*, the high court confirmed that Congress had clearly intended that the FMLA abrogate state immunity. Applying the *City of Boerne* standard, the Court reiterated that in revoking state immunity, Congress must demonstrate a "congruence and proportionality" between the injury to be remedied and the law. The Court determined that the FMLA was aimed at addressing the pervasive problem of sex discrimination in the workplace; Congress was concerned that women's family responsibilities for their children or parents had a detrimental effect on their employment. The Court distinguished the FMLA from the ADA and the ADEA because Congress was reacting to a long history of state laws restricting women's opportunities in the workplace. Moreover, it had found significant evidence that states were continuing to discriminate on the basis of sex, especially in the administration of workers' leave benefits. Policies, such as restricting parental leaves to women, were based on a stereotype that caring for the family is the woman's responsibility. In establishing a gender-neutral leave policy, the FMLA aimed at eradicating the stereotype and reducing the employer's incentive to hire only men. The Court concluded that state discrimination justified the law abrogating state immunity.

42. The uncertain status of damage liability in Title II largely stems from the uncertainty of O'Connor's vote in the next new federalism case. While abandoning the dissenters—Scalia, Thomas, Rehnquist, and Kennedy—in this case, her votes in previous new federalism cases suggest that she is unlikely to be amenable to the argument that individual rights should supersede the state's sovereign immunity.

Chapter 7 | Conclusion

1. A number of respondents pointed out that assigning specified dollar amounts or percentages to assess the reasonableness of an accommodation or modification would actually serve to limit expenditures.

2. Rosen makes it clear he is speaking in his individual, not his official, capacity.

REFERENCES

Cases

Abbott v. Bragdon, 912 F. Supp. 580 (D. Me. 1995).

Abbott v. Bragdon, 107 F.3d 934 (1st Cir. 1997).

Abbott v. Bragdon, 163 F.3d 87 (1st Cir. 1999).

Ability Center of Greater Toledo v. City of Sandusky, 133 F. Supp.2d 589 (N.D. Ohio 2001) (2001a).

Ability Center of Greater Toledo v. City of Sandusky, 181 F. Supp.2d 797 (N.D. Ohio 2001) (2001b).

Access Living v. Chicago Transit Authority, No. 00 C 770 (N.D. Ill. March 12, 2001) (2001a).

Access Living v. Chicago Transit Authority, 2001 U.S. Dist. LEXIS 6041 (N.D. Ill. 2001) (2001b).

Access Now v. South Florida Stadium Corporation, 161 F. Supp.2d 1357 (S.D. Fla. 2001).

Adam v. Linn-Benton Housing Authority, 147 F. Supp.2d 1044 (D. Or. 2001).

Aikins v. St. Helena Hospital, 843 F. Supp. 1329 (N.D. Cal. 1994).

Albertsons, Inc. v. Kirkingburg, 527 U.S. 555 (1999).

Alden v. Maine, 527 U.S. 706 (1999).

Alexander v. Choate, 469 U.S. 287 (1985).

Alexander v. Sandoval, 532 U.S. 275 (2001).

Alford v. Bistro Restaurant, 2000 U.S. Dist. LEXIS 20730 (D. Or. 2000).

Alsbrook v. City of Maumelle, 184 F.3d 999 (8th Cir. 1999).

Alsbrook v. City of Maumelle, 529 U.S. 1001 (2000).

Alvarez v. Fountainhead, Inc., 55 F. Supp.2d 1048 (N.D. Cal. 1999).

Amir v. St. Louis University, 184 F.3d 1017 (8th Cir. 1999).

Amos v. Maryland Department of Public Safety & Correctional Services, 126 F.3d 589 (4th Cir. 1997).

Amos v. Maryland Department of Public Safety & Correctional Services, 524 U.S. 935 (1998).

Amos v. Maryland Department of Public Safety & Correctional Services, 178 F.3d 212 (4th Cir. 1999).

Amos v. Maryland Department of Public Safety & Correctional Services, 205 F.3d 687 (4th Cir. 2000).

Atascadero State Hospital v. Scanlon, 473 U.S. 234 (1985).

Atia v. New York City Housing Authority, 2001 U.S. Dist. LEXIS 22864 (E.D.N.Y. 2001).

Axelrod v. Phillips Academy, Andover, 46 F. Supp.2d 72 (D. Mass. 1999).

Babicz v. School Board of Broward County, 135 F.3d 1420 (11th Cir. 1998).

Ballard v. Kinkaid School, 147 F. Supp.2d 603 (D. Tex. 2000).

Barber v. Guay, 910 F. Supp. 970 (D. Me. 1995).

Barnes v. Gorman, 536 U.S. 181 (2002).

Bartlett v. New York State Board of Law Examiners, 970 F. Supp. 1094 (S.D.N.Y. 1997).

Bartlett v. New York State Board of Law Examiners, 156 F.3d 321 (2d Cir. 1998).

Bartlett v. New York State Board of Law Examiners, 2001 U.S. Dist. LEXIS 11926 (S.D.N.Y. 2001).

Beno v. Shalala, 853 F. Supp. 1195 (E.D. Cal. 1993).

Bercovitch v. Baldwin School, 964 F. Supp. 597 (D.P.R. 1997).

Blake v. Southcoast Health System, Inc., 145 F. Supp.2d 126 (D. Mass. 2001).

Bledsoe v. Palm Beach County Soil and Water Conservation District, 133 F.3d 816 (11th Cir. 1998).

Board of Education of the Henrik Hudson Central School District v. Rowley, 458 U.S. 176 (1982).

Board of Trustees of the University of Alabama v. Garrett, 531 U.S. 356 (2001).

Bradley v. Arkansas Department of Education, No. LR-C-96-1004 (E.D. Ark. November 21, 1997).

Bradley v. Arkansas Department of Education, 189 F.3d 745 (8th Cir. 1999).

Bragdon v. Abbott, 524 U.S. 624 (1998).

Brown v. Board of Education, 347 U.S. 483 (1954).

Brown v. North Carolina, 166 F.3d 698 (4th Cir. 1999).

Buckhannon Board and Care Home v. West Virginia Department of Health and Human Resources, 532 U.S. 598 (2001).

Carparts Distribution Center v. Automotive Wholesaler's Association of New England, 37 F.3d 12 (1st Cir. 1994).

Carten v. Kent State University, 282 F.3d 391 (6th Cir. 2002).

Caruso v. Blockbuster-Sony Music Entertainment Centre, 968 F. Supp. 210 (D.N.J. 1997).

Cash v. Granville County Board of Education, No. 00-1496 (4th Cir. March 1, 2001).

Cedar Rapids Community School District v. Garret F., 526 U.S. 66 (1999).

Cherry v. Mathews, 419 F. Supp. 922 (D.D.C. 1976).

Chevron, Inc. v. Natural Resources Defense Council, 467 U.S. 837 (1984).

Chevron U.S.A. Inc. v. Echazabal, 536 U.S. 73 (2002).

Chisholm v. Georgia, 5 U.S. (2 Dall.) 419 (1793).

City of Boerne v. Flores, 521 U.S. 507 (1997).

City of Cleburne v. Cleburne Living Center, 473 U.S. 432 (1985).

City of Los Angeles v. Lyons, 461 U.S. 95 (1983).

Clackamas Gastroenterology Associates, P.C. v. Wells, 538 U.S. 440 (2003).

Clark v. California, 123 F.2d 1267 (9th Cir. 1997).

Clark v. Woods, 2001 U.S. Dist. LEXIS 2384 (N.D. Tex. 2001).

Cleveland v. Policy Management Systems, 120 F.3d 513 (5th Cir. 1997).

Cleveland v. Policy Management Systems, 526 U.S. 795 (1999).

College Savings Bank v Florida Prepaid Postsecondary Education Expense Board, 527 U.S. 666 (1999).

Colmenares v. Braemer Country Club, Inc., 29 Cal.4th 1019 (Cal. 2003).

Colorado Cross Disability Coalition v. Williams, 264 F.3d 999 (10th Cir. 2001).

Consolidated Rail Corporation v. Darrone, 465 U.S. 624 (1984).

Coolbaugh v. Louisiana, 136 F.3d 430 (5th Cir. 1998).

County Centre v. Doe, 242 F.3d 437 (3d Cir. 2001).

Crawford v. Indiana Department of Corrections, 115 F.3d 481 (7th Cir. 1997).

Crowder v. Hawaii, 81 F.3d 1480 (9th Cir. 1996).

Dadian v. Village of Wilmette, 269 F.3d 831 (7th Cir. 2001).

Dare v. California Department of Motor Vehicles, 191 F.3d 1167 (9th Cir. 1999).

Davis v. Southeastern Community College, 574 F.2d 1158 (4th Cir. 1978).

Davis v. University of North Carolina at Wilmington, 263 F.3d 95 (4th Cir. 2001).

Dellmuth v. Muth, 491 U.S. 223 (1989).

Demshki v. Monteith, 2001 U.S. App. LEXIS 14802 (9th Cir. 2001).

Department of Transportation v. Paralyzed Veterans of America, 477 U.S. 597 (1986).

Dickson v. Florida Department of Corrections, No. 5:9cv207-RH (N.D. Fla. Nov. 5, 1996).

Doe v. Frommer, 148 F.3d 73 (2d Cir. 1998).

Doe v. Mutual of Omaha, 179 F.3d 557 (7th Cir. 1999).

Douglas v. California Department of Youth Authority, 271 F.3d 812 (9th Cir. 2001).

Echazabal v. Chevron U.S.A. Inc., 226 F.3d 1063 (9th Cir. 2000).

EEOC v. Waffle House, Inc., 1998 U.S. Dist. LEXIS 23245 (D.S.C. 1998).

EEOC v. Waffle House, Inc., 193 F.3d 805 (4th Cir. 1999).

EEOC v. Waffle House, Inc., 534 U.S. 279 (2002).

EEOC v. Wyoming, 460 U.S. 226 (1983).

El Kouni v. Trustees of Boston University, 169 F. Supp.2d 1 (D. Mass. 2001).

Ellit v. U.S.A. Hockey, 922 F. Supp. 217 (E.D. Mo. 1996).

Employees v. Department of Public Health and Welfare, 411 U.S. 279 (1973).

Employment Division, Department of Human Resources of Oregon v. Smith, 494 U.S. 872 (1990).

Erickson v. Board of Governors of State Colleges & Universities for Northeastern Illinois University, 207 F.3d 945 (7th Cir. 2000).

Ex Parte Young, 209 U.S. 123 (1908).

Ferguson v. City of Phoenix, 157 F.3d 668 (9th Cir. 1998).

Fitzpatrick v. Bitzer, 427 U.S. 445 (1976).

Florida Department of Corrections v. Dickson, 528 U.S. 1184 (2000).

Florida Prepaid Postsecondary Education Expense Board v. College Savings Bank, 527 U.S. 627 (1999).

Ford v. Schering-Plough Corporation, 145 F.3d 601 (3d Cir. 1998).

Franklin v. Gwinnet, 503 U.S. 60 (1992).

Ganden v. National Collegiate Athletic Association, 1996 U.S. Dist. LEXIS 17368 (N.D. Ill. 1996).

Garcia v. San Antonio Metropolitan Transit Authority, 469 U.S. 528 (1985).

Garcia v. State University of New York Health Sciences Center, 280 F.3d 98 (2d Cir. 2001).

Gardiner v. Mercyhurst College, 942 F. Supp. 1050 (W.D. Pa. 1995).

Garrett v. Board of Trustees of the University of Alabama, 989 F. Supp. 1409 (N.D. Ala. 1998).

Garrett v. Board of Trustees of the University of Alabama, 193 F.3d 1214 (11th Cir. 1999).

Garrett v. Board of Trustees of the University of Alabama, 261 F.3d 1242 (11th Cir. 2001) (2001a).

Garrett v. Board of Trustees of the University of Alabama, 276 F.3d 1227 (11th Cir. 2001) (2001b).

Garrett v. Board of Trustees of the University of Alabama, 344 F.3d 1288 (11th Cir. 2003).

Gonzales v. National Board of Medical Examiners, 225 F.3d 620 (6th Cir. 2000).

Gorman v. Bartch, 152 F.3d 907 (8th Cir. 1998).

Gorman v. Easley, 257 F.3d 738 (8th Cir. 2001).

Gregory v. Ashcroft, 501 U.S. 452 (1991).

Grove City College v. Bell, 465 U.S. 555 (1984).

Guardians Association v. Civil Service Commission of New York, 463 U.S. 582 (1983).

Hainze v. Richards, 207 F.3d 795 (5th Cir. 2000).

Hamilton v. City College of the City University of New York, 173 F. Supp.2d 181 (S.D.N.Y. 2001).

Hans v. Louisiana, 134 U.S. 1 (1890).

Harlow v. Fitzgerald, 457 U.S. 800 (1982).

Harris v. Oregon Health Sciences University, 1999 U.S. Dist. LEXIS 16231 (D. Or. 1999).

Hason v. Medical Board of California, 279 F.3d 1167 (9th Cir. 2002) (2002a).

Hason v. Medical Board of California, 294 F.3d 1166 (9th Cir. 2002) (2002b).

Hedgepath v. Tennessee Department of Safety, 215 F.3d 608 (6th Cir. 2000).

Helen L. v. DiDario, 46 F.3d 325 (3d Cir. 1995).

Henrietta D. v. Bloomberg, 331 F.3d 261 (2d Cir. 2003).

Henrietta D. v. Guiliani, 119 F. Supp.2d 181 (E.D.N.Y. 2000).

Hernandez v. Hughes Missile System Company, 298 F.3d 1030 (9th Cir. 2002).

Herschaft v. New York Board of Elections, 2001 U.S. Dist. LEXIS 11801 (E.D.N.Y. 2001).

Hexom v. Oregon Department of Transportation, 177 F.3d 1134 (9th Cir. 1999).

Idaho v. Coeur d'Alene Tribe of Idaho, 521 U.S. 261 (1997).

Independent Living Resource v. Oregon Arena Corporation, 982 F. Supp. 698 (D. Or. 1997).

Independent Living Resources v. Oregon Arena Corporation, 1 F. Supp.2d 1159 (D. Or. 1998).

Innovative Health Systems, Inc. v. City of White Plains, 117 F.3d 37 (2d Cir. 1997).

International Union, United Auto Workers v. Johnson Controls, 499 U.S. 187 (1991).

Irving Independent School District v. Talro, 468 U.S. 883 (1984).

Jackan v. New York State Department of Labor, 205 F.3d 562 (2d Cir. 2000).

Jim C. v. Atkins School District, No. LR-C-96-748 (E.D. Ark. February 23, 1998).

Jim C. v. United States, 235 F.3d 1079 (8th Cir. 2000).

Katzenbach v. Morgan, 384 U.S. 641 (1966).

Kessler Institute for Rehabilitation, Inc. v. Mayor and Council of Borough of Essex Falls, 876 F. Supp. 641 (D.N.J. 1995).

Kilcullen v. New York State Department of Labor, 205 F.3d 77 (2d Cir. 2000).

Kiman v. New Hampshire Department of Corrections, 2001 U.S. Dist. LEXIS 21894 (D.N.H. 2001).

Kiman v. New Hampshire Department of Corrections, 301 F.3d 13 (1st Cir. 2002).

Kimel v. Florida Board of Regents, 1996 U.S. Dist. LEXIS 7995 (N.D. Fla. 1996).

Kimel v. Florida Board of Regents, 139 F.3d 1426 (11th Cir. 1998).

Kimel v. Florida Board of Regents, 528 U.S. 62 (2000).

Kinney v. Yerusalim, 9 F.3d 1067 (3d Cir. 1993).

Koslow v. Pennsylvania Department of Corrections, 302 F.3d 161 (3d Cir. 2002).

Lane v. Pena, 518 U.S. 187 (1996).

Lane v. Tennessee, 2002 U.S. App. LEXIS 14482 (6th Cir. 2002).

Lane v. Tennessee, 315 F.3d 680 (6th Cir. 2003).

L.C. v. Olmstead, 1997 U.S. Dist. LEXIS 3540 (N.D. Ga. 1997).

L.C. v. Olmstead, 138 F.3d 893 (11th Cir. 1998).

Leiken v. Squaw Valley Ski Corporation, 1994 U.S. Dist. LEXIS 21281 (E.D. Cal. 1994).

Levy v. Mote, 104 F. Supp.2d 538 (D. Md. 2000).

Lewis v. Truitt, 960 F. Supp. 175 (S.D. Ind. 1997).

Lieber v. Macy's West, Inc., 80 F. Supp.2d 1065 (N.D. Cal. 1999).

Lightbourn v. County of El Paso, 904 F. Supp. 1429 (W.D. Tex. 1995).

Lightbourn v. County of El Paso, 118 F.3d 421 (5th Cir. 2001).

Litman v. George Mason University, 186 F.3d 544 (4th Cir. 1999).

Little Rock School District v. Mauney, 183 F.3d 816 (8th Cir. 1999).

Love v. Delta Air Lines, 310 F.3d 1347 (11th Cir. 2002).

Lujan v. Defenders of Wildlife, 504 U.S. 555 (1992).

MacPherson v. University of Montevallo, 938 F. Supp. 785 (N.D. Ala. 1996).

Martin v. Kansas, 190 F.3d 1120 (10th Cir. 1999).

Martin v. PGA Tour, Inc., 994 F. Supp. 1242 (D. Or. 1998).

Martin v. PGA Tour, Inc. 204 F.3d 994 (9th Cir. 2000).

Matthews v. National Collegiate Athletic Association, 179 F. Supp.2d 1209 (E.D. Wash. 2001).

McDonnell Douglas v. Green, 411 U.S. 792 (1973).

McPherson v. Michigan High School Athletic Association, 119 F.3d 453 (6th Cir. 1997).

Medical Board of California v. Hason, 537 U.S. 1028 (2002).

Medical Board of California v. Hason, 538 U.S. 901 (2003).

Menkowitz v. Pottstown Memorial Medical Center, 154 F.3d 113 (3d Cir. 1998).

Mills v. Board of Education, 348 F. Supp. 866 (D.D.C. 1972).

Muller v. Costello, 187 F.3d 298 (2d Cir. 1999).

Murphy v. United Parcel Service, 946 F. Supp. 872 (D. Kan 1996).

Murphy v. United Parcel Service, 1998 U.S. App. LEXIS 4439 (10th Cir. 1998).

Murphy v. United Parcel Service, 527 U.S. 516 (1999).

National League of Cities v. Usery, 426 U.S. 833 (1976).

National Railroad Passenger Corporation v. Morgan, 536 U.S. 101 (2002).

Neff v. American Dairy Queen, 58 F.3d 1063 (5th Cir. 1995).

Neinast v. Texas, 217 F.3d 275 (5th Cir. 2000).

Nevada Department of Human Resources v. Hibbs, 538 U.S. 721 (2003).

Newport v. Facts Concerts, Inc., 453 U.S. 247 (1981).

New York State Board of Law Examiners v. Bartlett, 527 U.S. 1031 (1999).

Nihiser v. Ohio Environmental Protection Agency, 979 F. Supp. 1168 (S.D. Ohio 1997).

Nihiser v. Ohio Environmental Protection Agency, 269 F.3d 626 (6th Cir. 2001).

Norris v. Seattle University School of Law, 1997 U.S. App. LEXIS 8666 (9th Cir. 1997).

Olinger v. United States Golf Association, 205 F.3d 1001 (7th Cir. 2000).

Olmstead v. L.C., 527 U.S. 581 (1999).

O'Shea v. Littleton, 414 U.S. 488 (1974).

Pallozzi v. Allstate Life Insurance Company, 198 F.3d 28 (2d Cir. 1999).

Panzer v. New York State Board of Law Examiners, 849 F. Supp. 284 (S.D.N.Y. 1994).

Parker v. Anne Arundel County, 2001 U.S. Dist. LEXIS 3462 (D. Md. 2001).

Parker v. Metropolitan Life Insurance Company, 875 F. Supp. 1321 (W.D. Tenn. 1995).

Parker v. Metropolitan Life Insurance Company, 99 F.3d 181 (6th Cir. 1996).

Parker v. Metropolitan Life Insurance Company, 121 F.3d 1006 (6th Cir. 1997).

Pathways Psychosocial v. Town of Leonardtown, Maryland, 133 F. Supp.2d 772 (D. Md. 2001).

Pederson v. Louisiana State University, 213 F.3d 858 (5th Cir. 2000).

Pennhurst State School and Hospital v. Halderman, 451 U.S. 1 (1981).

Pennsylvania Association for Retarded Children v. Pennsylvania, 334 F. Supp. 1257 (E.D. Pa 1971).

Pennsylvania Department of Corrections v. Yeskey, 524 U.S. 206 (1998).

Pennsylvania v. Union Gas Company, 491 U.S. 1 (1989).

PGA Tour, Inc. v. Martin, 532 U.S. 661 (2001).

Plumley v. Landmark Chevrolet, Inc., 122 F.3d 308 (5th Cir. 1997).

Pona v. Cecil Whittaker's Inc., 155 F.3d 1034 (8th Cir. 1998).

Popovich v. Cuyahoga County Court of Common Pleas, 227 F.3d 627 (6th Cir. 2000) (2000a).

Popovich v. Cuyahoga County Court of Common Pleas, 2000 U.S. App. LEXIS 33978 (6th Cir. 2000) (2000b).

Popovich v. Cuyahoga County Court of Common Pleas, 276 F.3d 808 (6th Cir. 2002).

Pottgen v. The Missouri High School Activities Association, 40 F.3d 926 (8th Cir. 1994).

Proctor v. Prince George's Hospital Center, 1998 U.S. Dist. LEXIS 21830 (D. Md. 1998).

Randolph v. Rogers, 170 F.3d 850 (8th Cir. 1999).

Randolph v. Rogers, 2001 U.S. App. LEXIS 12138 (8th Cir. 2001).

Raytheon Company v. Hernandez, 540 U.S. 44 (2003).

Regents of University of Michigan v. Ewing, 474 U.S. 214 (1985).

Reickenbacker v. Louisiana Department of Safety, 274 F.3d 974 (5th Cir. 2001).

Sandison v. Michigan High School Athletic Association, 64 F.3d 1026 (6th Cir. 1995).

Sandoval v. Hagan, 197 F.3d 484 (11th Cir. 1999).

Scheuer v. Rhodes, 416 U.S. 232 (1974).

School Board of Nassau County v. Arline, 480 U.S. 273 (1987).

Scott v. Western State University College of Law, 1997 U.S. App. LEXIS 9089 (9th Cir. 1997).

Securities and Exchange Commission v. Zandford, 535 U.S. 813 (2002).

Seminole Tribe of Florida v. Florida, 517 U.S. 441 (1996).

Shaboon v. Duncan, 252 F.3d 722 (5th Cir. 2001).

Shirey v. City of Alexandria School Board, 2000 U.S. App. LEXIS 21236 (4th Cir. 2000).

Shultz v. Hemet Pony League, 943 F. Supp. 1222 (C.D. Cal. 1996).

Smith v. Robinson, 468 U.S. 992 (1984).

South Carolina v. Katzenbach, 383 U.S. 301 (1966).

South Dakota v. Dole, 483 U.S. 203 (1987).

Southeastern Community College v. Davis, 442 U.S. 397 (1979).

Stanley v. Litscher, 213 F.3d 340 (7th Cir. 2000).

Stan v. Wal-Mart Stores, Inc., 111 F. Supp.2d 119 (N.D.N.Y. 2000).

Stevens v. Illinois Department of Transportation, 210 F.3d 732 (7th Cir. 2000).

Stoutenborough v. National Football League, 59 F.3d 580 (6th Cir. 1995).

Sutton v. United Air Lines, 1996 U.S. Dist. LEXIS 15106 (D. Colo. 1996).

Sutton v. United Air Lines, 130 F.3d 893 (10th Cir. 1997).

Sutton v. United Air Lines, 527 U.S. 471 (1999).

Tcherepnin v. Knight, 389 U.S. 332 (1967).

Tennessee v. Lane, 539 U.S. 941 (2003).

Tennessee v. Lane, 541 U.S. 509 (2004).

Thompson v. Colorado, 278 F.3d 1020 (10th Cir. 2001).

Torcasio v. Murray, 57 F.3d 1340 (4th Cir. 1995).

Torres v. AT&T Broadband, 158 F. Supp.2d 1035 (N.D. Cal. 2001).

Torres v. Puerto Rico Tourism Company, 175 F.3d 1 (1st Cir. 1999).

Toschia Falls v. Prince George's Hospital Center, 1999 U.S. Dist. LEXIS 22551 (D. Md. 1999).

Toyota Motor Manufacturing v. Williams, 584 U.S. 184 (2002).

Turner v. Safley, 482 U.S. 78 (1987).

Tyler v. The Kansas Lottery, 14 F. Supp.2d 1220 (D. Kan. 1998).

U.S. Airways, Inc. v. Barnett, 535 U.S. 391 (2002).

United States of America v. Days Inn of America, 1998 U.S. Dist. LEXIS 21945 (E.D. Cal. 1998).

United States v. Carolene Products, 304 U.S. 144 (1938).

United States v. Lopez, 514 U.S. 549 (1995).

United States v. Morrison, 529 U.S. 598 (2000).

Verizon Maryland Inc. v. Public Service Commission of Maryland, 535 U.S. 635 (2002).

Walker v. Snyder, 2000 U.S. App. LEXIS 16037 (7th Cir. 2000).

Welsh v. Boy Scouts of America, 993 F.2d 1267 (7th Cir. 1993).

Weyer v. Twentieth Century Fox Film Corporation, 198 F.3d 1104 (9th Cir. 2000).

Williams v. Toyota Motor Manufacturing, 224 F.3d 840 (6th Cir. 2000).

Williams v. Wasserman, 164 F. Supp.2d 591 (D. Md. 2001).

Wisconsin Correctional Service v. City of Milwaukee, 173 F. Supp.2d 284 (E.D. Wis. 2001).

Wright v. Universal Maritime Service, 525 U.S. 70 (1998).

Wroncy v. Oregon Department of Transportation, 2001 U.S. App. LEXIS 8761 (9th Cir. 2001).

Yeskey v. Pennsylvania Department of Corrections, 118 F.3d 168 (3d Cir. 1997).

Zimmerman v. Oregon Department of Justice, 170 F.3d 1169 (9th Cir. 1999).

Zukle v. Regents of the University of California, 166 F.3d 1041 (9th Cir. 1999).

Works Cited

Abel, Cabrelle. 2001. "To Allow to Sue, or Not Allow to Sue: *Zimmerman v. Oregon Department of Justice* Decides Title II of the Americans with Disabilities Act Does Not Apply to Employment Discrimination." *Seattle University Law Review* 24:969–87.

Abraham, Henry J., and Barbara A. Perry. 2003. *Freedom and the Court: Civil Rights and Liberties in the United States.* 2d ed. Lawrence: University of Kansas Press.

Allbright, Amy. 2001. "2000 Employment Decisions under the ADA Title I—Survey Update." *Mental and Physical Disability Law Reporter* 25:508–10.

———. 2002. "2001 Employment Decisions under the ADA Title I—Survey Update." *Mental and Physical Disability Law Reporter* 26:394–97.

———. 2003. "2002 Employment Decisions under the ADA Title I—Survey Update." *Mental and Physical Disability Law Reporter* 27:387–89.

Anderson, Ann M. 2000. "Whose Malice Counts? *Kolstad* and the Limits of Vicarious Liability for Title VII Punitive Damages." *North Carolina Law Review* 78:799–830.

Annas, Katherine R. 2003. "*Toyota Motor Manufacturing, Kentucky, Inc. v. Williams:* Part of an Emerging Trend of Supreme Court Cases Narrowing the Scope of the ADA." *North Carolina Law Review* 81:835–52.

Batavia, Andrew I. 1993. "Relating Disability Policy to Broader Public Policy: Understanding the Concept of Handicap." *Policy Studies Journal* 21:735–39.

Batavia, Andrew I., and Kay Schriner. 2001. "The Americans with Disabilities Act as Engine of Social Change: Models of Disability and the Potential of a Civil Rights Approach." *Policy Studies Journal* 29:690–702.

Bauer, Louise. 1993. "Trying to Comply with the ADA." *State Legislatures* 19:40–46.

Befort, Stephen F., and Holly Lindquist Thomas. 1999. "The ADA in Turmoil: Judicial Dissonance, the Supreme Court's Response, and the Future of Disability Discrimination Law." *Oregon Law Review* 78:27–104.

Berkowitz, Edward D. 1987. *Disabled Policy: America's Programs for the Handicapped.* Cambridge: Cambridge University Press.

Bishop, Peter C., and Augustus J. Jones. 1993. "Implementing the Americans with Disabilities Act of 1990: Assessing the Variables of Success." *Public Administration Review* 53:121–28.

Blanck, Peter David. 2000a. "The Economics of the Employment Provisions of the Americans with Disabilities Act." In *Employment, Disability, and the Americans with Disabilities Act: Issues in Law, Public Policy, and Research*, edited by Peter David Blanck, 201–27. Evanston, IL: Northwestern University Press.

Blanck, Peter David, ed. 2000b. *Employment, Disability, and the Americans with Disabilities Act: Issues in Law, Public Policy, and Research.* Evanston, IL: Northwestern University Press.

Breslin, Mary Lou. 2001. Interview with the author, August 31.

"Brief of *Amici Curiae* Alabama, Nebraska, Nevada, North Dakota, South Dakota, Oklahoma, Utah, and Wyoming in Support of Petitioner in *Tennessee v. Lane*." 2002. No. 02-1667 (2002 U.S. Briefs 1667). web.lexis nexis.com/universe/document.

"Brief of *Amicus Curiae* of the National Council on Disability in Support of Respondents in *Olmstead v. L.C.*" 1998. No. 98-536 (1998 U.S. Briefs 536). web.lexis-nexis.com/universe/document.

"Brief of Petitioner in *Tennessee v. Lane*." 2002. No. 02-1667 (2002 U.S. Briefs 1667). web.lexis-nexis.com/universe/document.

"Brief for Petitioners in *Board of Trustees of the University of Alabama v. Garrett*." 1999. No. 99-1240 (1999 U.S. Briefs 1240). web.lexis-nexis.com/universe/document.

"Brief for Petitioners in *Pennsylvania Department of Corrections v. Yeskey*." 1997. No. 97-634 (1997 U.S. Briefs 634). web.lexis-nexis.com/universe/document.

"Brief for the Private Respondents in *Tennessee v. Lane*." 2002. No. 02-1667 (2002 U.S. Briefs 1667). web.lexis-nexis.com/universe/document.

"Brief for Respondents in *Board of Trustees of the University of Alabama v. Garrett*." 1999. No. 99-1240 (1999 U.S. Briefs 1240). web.lexis-nexis.com/universe/document.

Bristo, Marca. 2002. Interview with the author, April 10.

Brown, Jennifer Gozdowski. 2003 "Mitigating Measures and the ADA after *Sutton:* Can Employers Limit Our Liability to Care for Ourselves in the Workplace?" *Journal of Small and Emerging Business Law* 7:113–44.

Buhai, Sande, and Nina Golden. 2000. "Adding Insult to Injury: Discriminatory Intent as a Prerequisite to Damages under the ADA." *Rutgers Law Review* 52:1121–59.

Bullock, Charles S., and Charles U. Lamb. 1984. *Implementation of Civil Rights Policy.* Monterey, CA: Brooks/Cole.

Burgdorf, Robert L., Jr. 1991. "The Americans with Disabilities Act: Analysis and Implications of a Second Generation Civil Rights Statute." *Harvard Civil Rights–Civil Liberties Law Review* 26:413–522.

———. 1997. "'Substantially Limited' Protection from Disability Discrimination: The Special Treatment Model and Misconstructions of the Definition of Disability." *Villanova Law Review* 42:409–585.

Burke, Thomas. 1997. "On the Rights Track: The Americans with Disabilities Act." In *Comparative Disadvantages? Social Regulations and the Global Economy,* edited by Pietro S. Nivola, 242–318. Washington, DC: Brookings Institution.

———. 2002. *Lawyers, Lawsuits, and Legal Rights: The Battle over Litigation in American Society.* Berkeley and Los Angeles: University of California Press.

Burris, Scott, and Kathryn Moss. 2000. "A Road Map for ADA Title I Research." In *Employment, Disability, and the Americans with Disabilities Act: Issues in Law, Public Policy, and Research,* ed. Peter David Blanck, 19–50. Evanston, IL: Northwestern University Press.

Bush, George H. W. 1990a. "Remarks on Signing the Americans with Disabilities Act of 1990." *Presidential Records.* July 26. http://bushlibrary.tamu.edu/papers/1990/90072600.html (accessed March 24, 2003).

———.1990b. "Statement on Signing the Americans with Disabilities Act of 1990." *Presidential Records.* July 26. http://bushlibrary.tamu.edu/papers/1990/90072601.html (accessed March 24, 2003).

Bush, George W. 2001. "Remarks by the President in Announcement of New Freedom Initiative." *Presidential News and Speeches.* http://www.whitehouse.gov/news/releases20010201-3.html (accessed June 2, 2003).

Byrnes, Jaime Dodge, and Elizabeth Pollman. 2003. "Arbitration, Consent and Contractual Theory: The Implications of *EEOC v. Waffle House.*" *Harvard Negotiation Law Review* 8:289–312.

Canon, Bradley C., and Charles A. Johnson. 1999. *Judicial Policies: Implementation and Impact.* 2d ed. Washington, DC: Congressional Quarterly Press.

Cerreto, Mary C. 2001. "Olmstead: The *Brown v. Board of Education* for Disability Rights: Promises, Limits, and Issues." *Loyola Journal of Public Interest Law* 3:47–78.

Clegg, Roger. 1999. "The Costly Compassion of the ADA." *The Public Interest* 136:100–112.

Clinton, Bill. 1999. "Remarks on Signing the Ticket to Work and Work Incentives Improvement Act of 1999." *Weekly Compilation of Presidential Documents.* December 20. http://frwebgate5.access.gpo.gov/cgi-bin/waisgate.cgi?WAISdocID=583416348786+1+2+0& WAISaction=retrieve (accessed June 2, 2003).

Cole, Melissa. 2003. "In/Ensuring Disability." *Tulane Law Review* 77:839–84.

Colker, Ruth. 1999. "The Americans with Disabilities Act." *Harvard Civil Rights–Civil Liberties Law Review* 34:99–162.

———. 2000a. "ADA Title III: A Fragile Compromise." *Berkeley Journal of Employment and Labor Law* 21:377–412.

———. 2000b. "The Section Five Quagmire." *UCLA Law Review* 47:653–702.

———. 2001. "Winning and Losing under the Americans with Disabilities Act." *Ohio State Law Journal* 62:239–78.

———. 2002. "The Americans with Disabilities Act: The Death of Section 504." *University of Michigan Journal of Law Reform* 35:219–34.

———. 2004. "The ADA's Journey through Congress." *Wake Forest Law Review* 39: 1–48.

Colker, Ruth, and James L. Brudney. 2001. "Dissing Congress." *Michigan Law Review* 100:80–144.

Condrey, Stephen, and Jeffrey Brudney. 1998. "The Americans with Disabilities Act of 1990." *American Review of Public Administration* 28:26–42.

Congressional Record. 1988. 100th Cong., 2d sess. Vol. 134.

———. 1989. 101st Cong., 1st sess. Vol. 135.

———. 1990. 101st Cong., 2d sess. Vol. 136.

———. 1995. 104th Cong., 1st sess. Vol. 141.

Conlan, Timothy J., James D. Riggle, and Donna E. Schwartz. 1995. "Deregulating Federalism: The Politics of Mandate Reform in the 104th Congress." *Publius* 25:23–40.

Cook, Timothy. 1991. "The Americans with Disabilities Act: The Move to Integration." *Temple Law Review* 64:393–469.

Cooper, Brett E. 2000. "Ageism, the ADEA, and the Ageless Debate over Statutory Interpretation." *St. John's Law Review* 74:175–207.

Craig, Larry. 1999. "The Americans with Disabilities Act: Prologue, Promise, Product, and Performance." *Idaho Law Review* 35:205–25.

Cross, Frank B., and Emerson H. Tiller. 2000. "The Three Faces of Federalism: An Empirical Assessment of Supreme Court Federalism Jurisprudence." *Southern California Law Review* 73: 741–71.

Curry, Caroline L. 2001. "Attorney's Fees-'Prevailing Party' and Rejection of the Catalyst Theory." *Arkansas Law Review* 54:727–38.

Dart, Justin W., Jr. 1993. "The ADA: A Promise to Be Kept." In *Implementing the Americans with Disabilities Act: Rights and Responsibilities of All Americans,* edited by Lawrence O. Gostin and Henry A. Beyer, xxi–xxvii. Baltimore: Paul H. Brookes.

———. 2001. Interview with the author, July 27.

Decker, Curtis. 2000. Interview with the author, July 14.

Dickson, James. 2001. Interview with the author, April 24.

Diller, Matthew. 2000. "Judicial Backlash, the ADA, and the Civil Rights Model." *Berkeley Journal of Employment and Labor Law* 21:19–52.

Durham, Lisa M. 1999. "Protection from Age Discrimination for State Employees: Abrogation of Eleventh Amendment Sovereign Immunity in the Age Discrimination in Employment Act." *Georgia Law Review* 33:541–601.

Edmonds, Curtis D. 2002. "Snakes and Ladders: Expanding the Definition of 'Major Life Activity' in the Americans with Disabilities Act." *Texas Tech Law Review* 33: 321–76.

Eichner, Stan. 2002. Interview with the author, September 20.

Ely, John Hart. 1980. *Democracy and Distrust: A Theory of Judicial Review*. Cambridge: Harvard University Press.

Equal Employment Opportunity Commission. 2003a. "Charge Statistics FY 1992 through FY 2002." http://eeoc.gov/stats/charges.html (accessed May 21, 2003).

———. 2003b. "EEOC Litigation Statistics, FY 1992 through FY 2002." http://eeoc.gov /stats/ litigation.html (accessed May 21, 2003).

Eskridge, William N., Jr. 1990. "The New Textualism." *UCLA Law Review* 37: 621–90.

Farber, Daniel. 2000. "Pledging a New Allegiance: An Essay on Sovereignty and the New Federalism." *Notre Dame Law Review* 75: 1133–45.

Feldblum, Chai R. 1993. "Antidiscrimination Requirements of the ADA." In *Implementing the Americans with Disabilities Act: Rights and Responsibilities of All Americans,* edited by Lawrence O. Gostin and Henry A. Beyer, 35–54. Baltimore: Paul H. Brookes.

——— 2000a. "Definition of Disability under Federal Anti-Discrimination Law: What Happened? Why? And What Can We Do about It?" *Berkeley Journal of Employment and Labor Law* 21:91–165.

———. 2000b. Interview with the author, September 7.

Fleischer, Doris Zames, and Frieda Zames. 1998. "Disability Rights." *Social Policy* 28:52–55.

———. 2001. *The Disability Rights Movement: From Charity to Confrontation*. Philadelphia: Temple University Press.

Fletter, Debbie. 2002. Interview with the author, November 5.

Flores, Stephanie C. 2001. "Reading the ADA with 20/20 Vision: Anti-Discrimination Protection for Individuals with Corrective Disabilities after *Sutton v. United Air Lines, Inc." Whittier Law Review* 22:909–35.

Garbus, Martin. 2002. *Courting Disaster: The Supreme Court and the Unmaking of American Law*. New York: Times Books.

Gold, Maggie D. 1997/1998. "Must Insurers Treat All Illnesses Equally? Mental vs. Physical Illness: Congressional and Administrative Failure to End Limitations to and Exclusions from Coverage for Mental Illness in Employer-Provided Health Benefits under the Mental Health Parity Act and the Americans with Disabilities Act." *Connecticut Insurance Law Journal* 4:767–806.

Gores, H. Drewry. 2000. "*Sutton v. United Air Lines, Inc.*: Textualism, Intentionalism, the *Chevron* Doctrine and Judicial Policy-Making." *Northern Kentucky Law Review* 27:853–81.

Gostin, Lawrence O., and Henry A. Beyer, eds. 1993. *Implementing the Americans with Disabilities Act: Rights and Responsibilities of All Americans.* Baltimore: Paul H. Brookes.

Graves, Adam W. 2002. "Does an Employer's Binding Arbitration Agreement Limit the Enforcement Powers of the EEOC? The Supreme Court Rules That It Does Not." *Journal of Dispute Resolution* (2002): 439–51.

Gregory, Robert J. 2002. "Overcoming Text in an Age of Textualism: Practitioner's Guide to Arguing Cases of Statutory Interpretation." *Akron Law Review* 35:451–88.

Groshong, Joseph. 2003. "Curbing State Discrimination against Disabled Drivers: Why the Disabled Need Not Pay the States to Participate in Disabled Parking Programs." *Seton Hall Law Review* 33:811–43.

Guernsey, Thomas F. 1989. "The Education for All Handicapped Children Act, 42 U.S.C. §1983, and Section 504 of the Rehabilitation Act of 1973: Statutory Interaction Following the Handicapped Children's Protection Act of 1986." *Nebraska Law Review* 68:564–600.

Gullo, Theresa A., and Janet M. Kelly. 1998. "Federal Unfunded Mandate Reform: A First-Year Perspective." *Public Administration Review* 58:379–87.

Hagood, Lewis R. 1999. "Claims of Mental and Emotional Damages in Employment Discrimination Cases." *University of Memphis Law Review* 29:577–600.

Hamilton, Marci, and David Schoenbrod. 1999. "The Reaffirmation of Proportionality Analysis under Section 5 of the Fourteenth Amendment." *Cardozo Law Review* 21:469–92.

Hanson, David. 2001. Interview with the author, June 12.

Harrington, James C. 2000. "The ADA and Section 1983: Walking Hand in Hand." *Review of Litigation* 19:435–64.

Harrison, Beth Mellen. 2002. "Mental Health Parity." *Harvard Journal on Legislation* 39:255–79.

Hartley, Roger. 1998. "The New Federalism and the ADA: State Sovereign Immunity from Private Damage Suits after *Boerne.*" *New York University Review of Law and Social Change* 24:481–546.

———. 2001. "Enforcing Federal Civil Rights against Public Entities after *Garrett.*" *Journal of College and University Law* 28:41–96.

Heinrich, Alan J. 2000. "Symposium on New Directions in Federalism: An Introduction." *Loyola of Los Angeles Law Review* 33:1275–82.

Henderson, Susan. 2001. Interview with the author, August 31.

Herman, Robert. 2002. Interview with the author, April 22.

Hermanek, Amy. 1994. "Title III of the Americans with Disabilities Act: Implementation of Mediation Programs for More Effective Use of the Act." *Law and Inequality* 12:457–81.

Herpers, Laura M. 1997. "State Sovereign Immunity: Myth or Reality after *Seminole Tribe of Florida v. Florida.*" *Catholic University Law Review* 46:1005–55.

Hill, Kevin. D. 1986. "Legal Conflicts in Social Education: How Competing Paradigms in the Education for All Handicapped Children Act Create Litigation." *University of Detroit Law Review* 64:129–67.

Holbrook, Thomas M., and Stephen L. Percy. 1992. "Exploring Variations in State Laws Providing Protections for Persons with Disabilities." *Western Political Quarterly* 25:201–20.

Holzer, Jo. 2001. Interview with the author, June 12.

Horvath, Seth A. 2004. "Disentangling the Eleventh Amendment and the Americans with Disabilities Act: Alternative Remedies for State-Initiated Disability Discrimination under Title I and Title II." *University of Illinois Law Review* (2004): 231–65.

Howard, Robert M., and Jeffrey Segal. 2002. "An Original Look at Originalism." *Law & Society Review* 36:113–37.

Imparato, Andrew. 2001. Interview with the author, July 11.

Jeon, Yongjoo, and Donald P. Haider-Markel. 2001. "Tracing Issue Definition and Policy Change: An Analysis of Disability Issue Images and Policy Response." *Policy Studies Journal* 29:215–31.

Jones, Augustus. 1995. "Federal Court Responses to State and Local Claims of 'Undue Burden' in Complying with the Americans with Disabilities Act." *Publius* 25:41–55.

Karger, Joanne. 1999. "Don't Tread on the ADA": *Olmstead v. L.C. Ex Rel Zimring* and the Future of Community Integration for Individuals with Mental Disabilities." *Boston College Law Review* 40:1225–68.

Karlan, Pamela S., and George Rutherglen. 1996. "Disabilities, Discrimination, and Reasonable Accommodation." *Duke Law Journal* 46:1–72.

Katzman, Robert. 1986. *Institutional Disability*. Washington, DC: Brookings Institution.

Kelly, Michael W. 2002. "Weakening Title III of the Americans with Disabilities Act: The *Buckhannon* Decision and Other Developments Limiting Private Enforcement." *Elder Law Journal* 10:361–91.

Kimberlin, Diane L., and Linda Ottinger Headley. 2000. "ADA Overview and Update: What Has the Supreme Court Done to Disability Law?" *Review of Litigation* 19:579–647.

Kincaid, John. 1999. "The Politics of Unfunded Mandates: Whither Federalism?" Review. *Political Science Quarterly* 114:322–23.

Krieger, Linda Hamilton. 2000. "Foreword—Backlash against the ADA: Interdisciplinary Perspectives and Implications for Social Justice Strategies." *Berkeley Journal of Employment and Labor Law* 21:1–18.

———. 2003. Introduction to *Backlash against the ADA: Reinterpreting Disability Rights*, ed. Linda Hamilton Krieger. Ann Arbor: University of Michigan Press.

Kriz, Margaret. "Cutting the Strings." 1995. *National Journal* 27:167–71.

Laing, Aaron Matthew. 2002. "Failure to Accommodate, Discriminatory Intent, and the *McDonnell Douglas* Framework: Distinguishing the Analyses of Claims Arising under Subparts (A) and (B) of §12112(B)(5) of the ADA." *Washington Law Review* 77:913–49.

Langer, Jesse A. 1999/2000. "Combating Discrimination in Insurance Practices: Title III of the Americans with Disabilities Act." *Connecticut Insurance Law Journal* 6:435–75.

Lapertosa, Max. 2002. Interview with the author, June 19.

Laski, Frank. 2002. Interview with the author, September 5.

Leonard, James. 1999. "A Damaged Remedy: Disability Discrimination Claims against State Entities under the Americans with Disabilities Act after *Seminole* and *Flores*." *Arizona Law Review* 41:651–752.

Lester, Brian. 2003. "The Americans with Disabilities Act and the Exclusion of Inmates from Services in Prisons: A Proposed Analytical Approach Regarding the Appropriate Level of Judicial Scrutiny of a Prisoner's ADA Claim." *North Dakota Law Review* 79:83–109.

Levi, Edward H. 1963. *An Introduction to Legal Reasoning*. Chicago: University of Chicago Press.

Levitan, David, and David Pfeiffer. 1992. "The Americans with Disabilities Act of 1990: A Compliance Overview." *National Civic Review* 81, no. 2:143–54.

Levy, Richard E. 2000. "Federalism: The Next Generation." *Loyola of Los Angeles Law Review* 33:1629–64.

Lowi, Theodore J. 1972. "Four Systems of Policy, Politics, and Choice." *Public Administration Review* 32:298–310.

Malloy, S. Elizabeth Wilborn. 2001. "Something Borrowed, Something Blue: Why Disability Law Claims Are Different." *Connecticut Law Review* 33:603–66.

Martinson, Nicole. 1998. "Inequality between Disabilities: The Different Treatment of Mental versus Physical Disabilities in Long-Term Disability Benefit Plans." *Baylor Law Review* 50:361–80.

Mayerson, Arlene. 1993. "The History of the ADA: A Movement Perspective." In *Implementing the Americans with Disabilities Act: Rights and Responsibilities of All Americans*, edited by Lawrence O. Gostin and Henry A. Beyer, 17–24. Baltimore: Paul H. Brookes.

———. 2001. Interview with the author, August 31.

Mazmanian, Daniel, and Paul Sabatier. 1983. *Implementation and Public Policy*. Glenview: Scott, Foresman.

McConville, Celestine Richards. 2001. "Federal Funding Conditions: Bursting through the *Dole* Loopholes." *Chapman Law Review* 4:163–94.

McDonald, Heather. 2003. "*Garrett* under Title II of the Americans with Disabilities Act: Its Broad Implications to Civil Rights Laws." *DePaul University Law Review* 52:993–1041.

McLawhorn, Latresa. 2001. "Leveling the Accessibility Playing Field: Section 508 of the Rehabilitation Act." *North Carolina Journal of Law and Technology* 3:63–100.

Meier, Kenneth J. 1987. *Politics and the Bureaucracy: Policymaking in the Fourth Branch of Government*. 2d ed. Belmont, CA: Brooks/Cole.

Melnick, Shep. 2003. "Deregulating the States: Federalism in the Rehnquist Court." In

Evolving Federalism: The Intergovernmental Balance of Power in America and Europe, edited by the Maxwell European Union Center, 109–41. Syracuse: Campbell Public Affairs Institute, Maxwell School of Syracuse University.

Mezey, Susan Gluck. 1983. "Judicial Interpretation of Legislative Intent: The Role of the Supreme Court in the Implication of Private Rights of Action." *Rutgers Law Review* 36:53-89.

———. 2000. "The U.S. Supreme Court's Federalism Jurisprudence: *Alden v. Maine* and the Enhancement of State Sovereignty." *Publius* 30:21–38.

Milani, Adam A. 2000. "'Oh Say, Can I See—And Who Do I Sue If I Can't?' Wheelchair Users, Sightlines over Standing Spectators, and Architect Liability under the Americans with Disabilities Act." *Florida Law Review* 3:523–601.

———. 2001. "Go Ahead, Make My 90 Days: Should Plaintiffs Be Required to Provide Notice to Defendants before Filing Suit under Title III of the Americans with Disabilities Act?" *Wisconsin Law Review,* no. 1: 107–86.

———. 2004. "Wheelchair Users Who Lack 'Standing': Another Procedural Threshold Blocking Enforcement of Titles II and III of the ADA." *Wake Forest Law Review* 39:69–132.

Miller, Laura. 2002. Interview with the author, May 29.

Miller, Paul Steven. 2000. "The Evolving ADA." In *Employment, Disability, and the Americans with Disabilities Act: Issues in Law, Public Policy, and Research,* edited by Peter David Blanck, 3–15. Evanston, IL: Northwestern University Press.

Moore, Scott S. 1992. "The Americans with Disability Act Title III—The 'New' Building Code." *Nebraska Law Review* 71:1145–68.

Moss, Kathryn. 2000. "The ADA Employment Discrimination Charge." In *Employment, Disability, and the Americans with Disabilities Act: Issues in Law, Public Policy, and Research,* edited by Peter David Blanck, 118–45. Evanston, IL: Northwestern University Press.

Moss, Scott A., and Daniel A. Malin. 1998. "Public Funding for Disability Accommodations: A Rational Solution to Rational Discrimination and the Disabilities of the ADA." *Harvard Civil Rights-Civil Liberties Law Review* 33:197–236.

Mudrick, Nancy. 1997. "Employment Discrimination Laws for Disability: Utilization and Outcome." *Annals of the American Academy of Political and Social Science* (January): 53–70.

Nagel, Robert F. 2001. *The Implosion of American Federalism.* Oxford: Oxford University Press.

National Association of Protection and Advocacy Systems. 2000. *Olmstead Progress Report: Disability Advocates Assess State Implementation after One Year.* Washington, DC: National Association of Protection and Advocacy Systems, July 25. http://www.protectionandadvocacy.com/progressreportfinal.htm.

National Council on Disability. n.d. *Enshrining the ADA: House-Senate Conference and the Signing.* Washington, DC: National Council on Disability. http://ncd.gov/newsroom/publications/equality_2.html (accessed May 19, 2001).

———. 1996. *Achieving Independence: The Challenge for the 21st Century*. Washington, DC: National Council on Disability. http://www.gov/newsroom/publications/achieving.html (accessed June 3, 2003).

———. 1997. *Equality of Opportunity: The Making of the Americans with Disabilities Act*. Washington, DC: National Council on Disability. http://www.ncd.gov/publications/equality.html (accessed August 28, 2001).

———. 1999. *National Disability Policy: A Progress Report*. Washington, DC: National Council on Disability. http://www.ncd.gov/publications/policy9798.html (accessed October 18, 1999).

———. 2002. "Policy Brief No. 2, a Carefully Constructed Law." *The Americans with Disabilities Act Policy Brief Series: Righting the ADA*. Washington, DC: National Council on Disability. http://www.ncd.gov.newsroom/publications/carefullyconstructedlaw.html (accessed March 26, 2003).

National Council on the Handicapped. 1986. *Toward Independence: An Assessment of Federal Laws and Programs Affecting Citizens with Disabilities—With Legislative Recommendations*. Washington, DC: National Council on the Handicapped. http://www.ncd.gov/newsroom/publications/toward.html (accessed March 26, 2003).

National Organization on Disability/Harris. 2000. *Survey of Americans with Disabilities*. New York: Harris Interactive.

Naum, Barry. 2002. "*EEOC v. Waffle House, Inc.*" *Ohio State Journal on Dispute Resolution* 18:225–35.

Neas, Katy Beh. 2002. Interview with the author, April 22.

Neas, Ralph. 1990. "Solidarity Today, Solidarity Forever." *Worklife* (Washington, DC: President's Committee on Employment of People with Disabilities), 3:7.

Nelson, Keith. 2001. "Legislative and Judicial Solutions for Mental Health Parity: S. 543, Reasonable Accommodation, and an Individualized Remedy under Title I of the ADA." *American University Law Review* 51:91–137.

Nevin, Paul. 2002. "'No Longer Caught in the Middle?' *Barnett* Seniority System Ruling Eliminates Managements' Dilemma with ADA Reasonable Accommodation." *Brandeis Law Journal* 41:199–227.

Noonan, John T., Jr. 2002. *Narrowing the Nation's Power*. Berkeley and Los Angeles: University of California Press.

O'Brien, Ruth. 2001. *Crippled Justice: The History of Modern Disability Policy in the Workplace*. Chicago: University of Chicago Press.

Ogle, Becky. 2001. Interview with the author, November 2.

Okin, Jaclyn A. 2001. "Has the Supreme Court Gone Too Far? An Analysis of *University of Alabama v. Garrett* and Its Impact on People with Disabilities." *American University Journal of Gender, Social Policy, & the Law* 9:663–94.

Osolinik, Carolyn. 2001. Interview with the author, November 1.

Paradis, Laurence. 2003. "Title II of the Americans with Disabilities Act and Section 504 of the Rehabilitation Act: Making Programs, Services, and Activities Accessible to All." *Stanford Law and Policy Review* 14:389–415.

Parmet, Wendy E. 2003. "Plain Meaning and Mitigating Measures: Judicial Construction of the Meaning of Disability." In *Backlash against the ADA: Reinterpreting Disability Rights,* edited by Linda Hamilton Krieger, 122–63. Ann Arbor: University of Michigan Press.

Parry, John. 1998. "Study Finds Employers Win Most ADA Title I Judicial and Administrative Complaints." *Mental and Physical Disability Law Reporter* 22:403–7.

———. 1999. "Trend: Employment Decisions under ADA Title I—Survey Update." *Mental and Physical Disability Law Reporter* 23:294–98.

———. 2000. "1999 Employment Decisions under the ADA Title I—Survey Update." *Mental and Physical Disability Law Reporter* 24:348–50.

Pelka, Fred. 1996. "Bashing the Disabled: The Right-Wing Attack on the ADA." *The Humanist* 56:26–31.

Percy, Stephen L. 1989. *Disability, Civil Rights, and Public Policy.* Tuscaloosa: University of Alabama.

———. 1993. "ADA, Disability Rights, and Evolving Regulatory Federalism." *Publius* 23:87–105.

———. 2000. "Administrative Remedies and Legal Disputes: Evidence on Key Controversies Underlying Implementation of the Americans with Disabilities Act." *Berkeley Journal of Employment and Labor Law* 21:413–36.

———. 2001. "Challenges and Dilemma in Implementing the Americans with Disabilities Act: Lessons from the First Decade." *Policy Studies Journal* 29:633–40.

Perlin, Michael L. 2002. "What's Good Is Bad, What's Bad Is Good, You'll Find Out When You Reach the Top, You're on the Bottom: Are the Americans with Disabilities Act (and *Olmstead v. L.C.*) Anything More Than 'Idiot Wind?'" *University of Michigan Journal of Law Reform* 35:235–61.

"Petitioner's Brief on the Merits in *Medical Board of California v. Hason.*" 2002. No. 02-479 (2002 U.S. Briefs 479). web.lexis-nexis.com/universe/document.

Pfeiffer, David. 1993. "Overview of the Disability Movement: History, Legislative Record, and Political Implications." *Policy Studies Journal* 21:724–34.

———. 1996a. "'We Won't Go Back': The ADA on the Grass Roots Level." *Disability & Society* 11:271–84.

———. 1996b. "A Critical Review of ADA Implementation Studies Which Use Empirical Data." *Disability Studies Quarterly* 16:26–43.

Pfeiffer, David, and Joan Finn. 1995. "Survey Shows State, Territorial, Local Public Officials Implementing ADA." *Mental and Physical Disability Law Reporter* 19:537–40.

———. 1997. "The Americans with Disabilities Act: An Examination of Compliance by State, Territorial and Local Governments in the USA." *Disability & Society* 12:753–73.

Pirius, Rebecca. 2003. "'Seniority Rules': Disabled Employees' Rights under the ADA Give Way to More Senior Employees—*U.S. Airways, Inc. v. Barnett.*" *William Mitchell Law Review* 29:1481–1517.

Popkin, William D. 1999. *Statutes in Court: The History and Theory of Statutory Interpretation*. Durham, NC: Duke University Press.

Posner, Paul L. 1997. "Unfunded Mandates Reform Act." *Publius* 27:53–71.

Post, Robert C., and Reva B. Siegel. 2000. "Equal Protection by Law: Federal Antidiscrimination Legislation after *Morrison* and *Kimel*." *Yale Law Journal* 110:441–526.

Pressman, Jeffrey, and Aaron Wildavsky. 1973. *Implementation*. Berkeley and Los Angeles: University of California Press.

Rich, Robert F., Christopher T. Erb, and Rebecca Rich. 2002. "Critical Legal and Policy Issues for People with Disabilities." *DePaul Journal of Health Care Law* 6.1–53.

Rosen, Jeffrey. 2000. Interview with the author, March 30.

Royer, Christine. 2001. "Paradise Lost? State Employees' Rights in the Wake of 'New Federalism.'" *Akron Law Review* 34:637–88.

Russell, Marta. 2000. "The Political Economy of Disablement." *Dollars & Sense* 231:13–15.

Russotto, Sarina Maria. 2001. "Effects of the *Sutton* Trilogy." *Tennessee Law Review* 68: 705–23.

St. George, James R. 1995. "Unfunded Mandates: Balancing State and National Needs." *The Brookings Review* 13:12–15.

Salomone, Rosemary C. 1986. *Equal Education under Law: Legal Rights and Federal Policy*. New York: St. Martin's Press.

Savage, David G. 1999. "ADA Umbrella Starting to Close." *ABA Journal* (August): 44–46.

Schwochau, Susan, and Peter David Blanck. 2000. "The Economics of the Americans with Disabilities Act, Part III: Does the ADA Disable the Disabled?" *Berkeley Journal of Employment and Labor Law* 21:271–313.

Scotch, Richard K. 2001. *From Good Will to Civil Rights*, 2d ed. Philadelphia: Temple University Press.

Scotch, Richard K., and Kay Schriner. 1997. "Disability as Human Variation: Implications for Policy." *The Annals of the American Academy of Political and Social Science* 549:148–59.

Selmi, Michael. 2001. "A Symposium: Why Are Employment Discrimination Cases So Hard to Win?" *Louisiana Law Review* 61:555–75.

Shannon, Brian D. 2001. "A Drive to Justice: The Supreme Court's Decision in *PGA Tour, Inc. v. Martin*." *Virginia Sports and Entertainment Law Journal* 1:74–100.

Shapiro, Joseph A. 1994. *No Pity: People with Disabilities Forging a New Civil Rights Movement*. New York: Times Books.

Shuman, Grant P. H. 2000/2001. "Escaping the Purpose of the ADA: The 'Safe Harbor' Provision and Disability-Based Distinctions in Insurance Policies and Programs." *Gonzaga Law Review* 36:549–67.

Signorello, Pamela. 2001. "The Failure of the ADA: Achieving Parity with Respect to Mental and Physical Health Care Coverage in the Private Employment Realm." *Cornell Journal of Law and Public Policy* 10:349–84.

Silver, Helen D. 2003. *"Verizon Maryland, Inc. v. Public Service Commission of Maryland:* Reaffirming *ex Parte Young* and the Necessity of Finding Regulatory Hand-Back Schemes to Be a Gift or Gratuity." *Emory Law Journal* 52:1519–77.

Silverstein, Bobby. 2000. Interview with the author, August 31.

Smith, Jefferson D. E., and Steve P. Calandrillo. 2001. "Forward to Fundamental Alteration: Addressing ADA Title II Integration Lawsuits after *Olmstead v. L.C.*" *Harvard Journal of Law & Public Policy* 24:695–769.

Soifer, Aviam. 2000. "The Disability Term: Dignity, Default, and Negative Capability." *UCLA Law Review* 47:1279–1331.

———. 2003. "Disabling the ADA: Essences, Better Angels, and Unprincipled Neutrality Claims." *William and Mary Law Review* 44:1285–1340.

Stansky, Lisa J. 1996. "Opening Doors." *ABA Journal* (March): 66–69.

Stein, Michael Ashley. 2000a. "Employing People with Disabilities: Some Cautionary Thoughts for a Second-Generation Civil Rights Statute." In *Employment, Disability, and the Americans with Disabilities Act: Issues in Law, Public Policy, and Research*, edited by Peter David Blanck, 51–67. Evanston, IL: Northwestern University Press.

———. 2000b. "Labor Markets, Rationality, and Workers with Disabilities." *Berkeley Journal of Employment and Labor Law* 21:314–34.

Stowe, Matthew A. 2000. "Interpreting 'Place of Public Accommodation' under Title III of the ADA: A Technical Determination with Potentially Broad Civil Rights Implications." *Duke Law Journal* 50:297–329.

Sullivan, Paul V. 1995. "The Americans with Disabilities Act of 1990: An Analysis of Title III and Applicable Case Law." *Suffolk University Law Review* 29:1117–44.

Switzer, Jacqueline Vaughn. 2001. "Local Government Implementation of the Americans with Disabilities Act: Factors Affecting Statutory Compliance." *Policy Studies Journal* 29:654–62.

———. 2003. *Disabled Rights: American Disability Policy and the Fight for Equality.* Washington, DC: Georgetown University Press.

Tebo, Margaret Graham. 2003. "Fee-Shifting Fallout." *ABA Journal* (July): 54–59.

Thomas-Akhtar, Sheila. 2001. Interview with the author, June 25.

Troy, Daniel E. 1997. "The Unfunded Mandates Reform Act of 1995." *Administrative Law Review* 49:139–47.

Tucker, Bonnie Poitras. 2001. "The ADA's Revolving Doors: Inherent Flaws in the Civil Rights Paradigm." *Ohio State Law Journal* 62:335–89.

Ulgen, Argun M. 2003. "From Household Bathrooms to the Workplace: Bringing the Americans with Disabilities Act Back to Where It Belongs: An Analysis of *Toyota Manufacturing v. Williams*." *Fordham Urban Law Journal* 30:761–95.

U.S. Bureau of the Census. 2000. *Census 2000.* Table 1. http://www.census.gov/prod/cen2000/doc/sf3.pdf.

———. 2002. *2002 Census of Governments.* http://www.census.gov/govs/apes/02stus.txt.

U.S. House Committee on Education and Labor. 1975. *The Education for All Handi-capped Children Act of 1975.* 94th Cong., 1st sess., H. Rep. 332.

———. 1990. 101st Cong., 2d sess., H. Rep. 485, pt. 2.

U.S. House Committee on the Judiciary. 2000a. Statement of Andrew Levy. *The ADA Notification Act: Hearing on H.R. 3590 Before the Subcommittee on the Constitution.* 106th Cong., 2d sess. http://www.house.gov/judiciary/levy0518.htm (accessed June 12, 2002).

———. 2000b. Statement of Charles Canady. *The ADA Notification Act: Hearing on H.R. 3590 Before the Subcommittee on the Constitution.* 106th Cong., 2d sess. http://www.house.gov/judiciary/cana0518.htm (accessed June 12, 2002).

———. 2000c. Statement of Christine Griffin. *The ADA Notification Act: Hearing on H.R. 3590 Before the Subcommittee on the Constitution.* 106th Cong., 2d sess. http://www.house.gov/judiciary/grif0518.htm (accessed June 12, 2002).

———. 2000d. Statement of Kyle Glozier. *The ADA Notification Act: Hearing on H.R. 3590 Before the Subcommittee on the Constitution.* 106th Cong., 2d sess. http://www.house.gov/judiciary/gloz0518.htm (accessed June 12, 2002).

———. 2000e. Statement of Mark Foley. *The ADA Notification Act: Hearing on H.R. 3590 Before the Subcommittee on the Constitution.* 106th Cong., 2d sess. http://www.house.gov/judiciary/fole0518.htm (accessed June 12, 2002).

U.S. Senate Committee on Labor and Human Resources. 1989. S. Rep. 101-16.

Van Meter, Donald, and Charles Van Horn. 1975. "The Policy Implementation Process: A Conceptual Framework." *Administration and Society* 6:445–88.

Walden, Kenneth. 2001. Interview with the author, June 25.

Warden, Andrew J. 2002. "Driving the Green: The Impact of *PGA Tour, Inc. v. Martin* on Disabled Athletes and the Future of Competitive Sports." *North Carolina Law Review* 80.643-91.

Watson, Sara D. 1993. "Introduction: Disability Policy as an Emerging Field of Mainstream Public Policy Research and Pedagogy." *Policy Studies Journal* 21:720–23.

Weber, Mark C. 1990. "The Transformation of the Education of the Handicapped Act: A Study in the Interpretation of Radical Statutes." *University of California Davis Law Review* 24:349–436.

———. 1995. "Disability Discrimination by State and Local Government: The Relationship between Section 504 of the Rehabilitation Act and Title II of the Americans with Disabilities Act." *William and Mary Law Review* 36:1089-32.

———. 1998. "Beyond the Americans with Disabilities Act: A National Employment Policy for People with Disabilities." *Buffalo Law Review* 46:123–74.

Wegner, Judith Welch. 1988. "Educational Rights of Handicapped Children: Three Federal Statutes and an Evolving Jurisprudence." *Journal of Law & Education.* 17:387–457.

West, Jane. 1993. "The Evolution of Disability Rights." In *Implementing the Americans with Disabilities Act: Rights and Responsibilities of All Americans,* edited by Lawrence O. and Henry A. Beyer, 3–15. Baltimore: Paul H. Brookes.

Weston, Maureen A. 1999. "Academic Standards or Discriminatory Hoops? Learning-Disabled Student Athletes and the NCAA Initial Academic Eligibility Requirements." *Tennessee Law Review* 66:1049–1126.

Whittington, Keith E. 1999. *Constitutional Interpretation: Textual Meaning, Original Intent, and Judicial Review*. Lawrence: University of Kansas Press.

Wilkinson, Wendy, and Lex Frieden. 2000. "Glass-Ceiling Issues in Employment of People with Disabilities." In *Employment, Disability, and the Americans with Disabilities Act: Issues in Law, Public Policy, and Research,* edited by Peter David Blanck, 68–100. Evanston, IL: Northwestern University Press.

Willborn, Steven L. 2000. "The Nonevolution of Enforcement under the ADA." In *Employment, Disability, and the Americans with Disabilities Act: Issues in Law, Public Policy, and Research,* edited by Peter David Blanck, 103–17. Evanston, IL: Northwestern University Press.

Winter, Wallace. 2002. Interview with the author, March 11.

Wise, Charles R. 1998. "Judicial Federalism: The Resurgence of the Supreme Court's Role in the Protection of State Sovereignty." *Public Administration Review* 58:95–98.

Wood, Lucille D. 1998. "Costs and the Right to Community-Based Treatment." *Yale Law & Policy Review* 16:501–34.

Wright, Patrisha. 2000. Interview with the author, March 30.

Young, Jonathan. 1997. *Equal Opportunity: The Making of the Americans with Disabilities Act*. Washington, DC: National Council on Disability, July 26. http://www.ncd.gov/newsroom/publications/equality.html (accessed August 28, 2001).

Ziegler, Rachel Schneller. 2002. "Safe but Not Sound: Limiting Safe Harbor Immunity for Health and Disability Insurers and Self-Insured Employers under the Americans with Disabilities Act." *Michigan Law Review* 101:840–83.

Zucker, Kiren Dosanjh. 2003. "The Meaning of Life: Defining 'Major Life Activities' under the Americans with Disabilities Act." *Marquette Law Review* 86:957–75.

INDEX OF CASES

INDEX OF NAMES AND SUBJECTS